Library of
Davidson College

INCIPIENT FEMINISTS: WOMEN WRITERS IN THE SLOVAK NATIONAL REVIVAL

SLOVAK LANGUAGE AND LITERATURE

General Editors: Norma L. Rudinsky, Peter Petro, Gerald J. Sabo

1. *Jozef Mak* by Jozef Cíger-Hronský

2. *Valaská škola* by Hugolín Gavlovič

3. *Incipient Feminists* by Norma L. Rudinsky

INCIPIENT FEMINISTS: WOMEN WRITERS IN THE SLOVAK NATIONAL REVIVAL

Norma L. Rudinsky

With an Appendix of Slovak
Women Poets 1798-1875
by Marianna Prídavková Mináriková

Slavica Publishers, Inc.

Slavica publishes a wide variety of scholarly books and textbooks on the languages, peoples, literatures, cultures, folklore, history, etc. of the USSR and Eastern Europe. For a complete catalog of books and journals from Slavica, with prices and ordering information, write to:

> Slavica Publishers, Inc.
> PO Box 14388
> Columbus, Ohio 43214

ISBN: 0-89357-220-9.

Copyright © 1991 by Norma L. Rudinsky. Appendix copyright © 1991 by Marianna Prídavková Mináriková. All rights reserved.

All statements of fact or opinion are those of the authors and do not necessarily agree with those of the publisher, which takes no responsibility for them.

Printed in the United States of America.

CONTENTS

Preface   5

Introduction   7

Part I: Woman As Inspiration

Chapter 1: Male Apotheosis of Woman as Nation   17

Part II: Women As Help

Chapter 2: Women's Place in the Štúrist Tradition   27

Chapter 3: The Founding of Živena and Dennica   68

Chapter 4: Nationalist Heroines in Fiction   106

Part III: Women As Women

Chapter 5: Christian Equality of the Sexes   127

Chapter 6: Incipient Feminist Heroines   167

Conclusion   181

Appendix   184

Works Cited   267

Index   279

Preface

This study began with only the need to write an introduction for a translation of six stories by Božena Slančíková Timrava, but as the study grew it slowly revealed the general outlines of an imnteresting place for Slovak women writers in the national movement. Thus, two books resulted: the stories of Timrava, to be published by the University of Pittsburgh Press, and the present volume.

For stimulating discussions and a constant stream of needed photocopies, thanks are gratefully offered to Marianna Prídavková Mináriková of the Literary Institute of the Slovak Academy of Sciences in Bratislava, Czechoslovakia. So much was found that she ended up completing and editing the appendix of women's poems. I also sincerely thank Ján Števček of Comenius University in Bratislava for insights into modern Slovak literature, and to Gerald Sabo for advice and great generosity with his personal library. Numerous women have contributed by perceptive discussion of this and related subjects, especially Laura Rice. Thanks to other colleagues are given in the notes. I am very grateful to the librarians at the Matica slovenská in Martin, the Štátny ústredný archív SR in Bratislava, the Památník národního písemnictví in Prague, and the University of Illinois at Urbana-Champaign, and especially to Doris Tilles at Interlibrary Loan of Oregon State University.

The whole study was made possible by two generous grants in 1982 and 1984–1985 from the International Research and Exchanges Board (IREX), with funds provided by the National Endowment for the Humanities and the United States Information Agency. None of these organizations is responsible for the views expressed. Oregon State University furnished secretarial help to ease manuscript preparation and partially financed photo typesetting, and a fellowship from the Center for the Humanities at OSU provided an uninterrupted quarter to deepen and widen this book.

Part of this work was presented in the panel "Slovak Women Writers" at the AAASS Conference in New York City in November, 1984, and in the Seminar on Women in Russian and East European Cultures at the University of Illinois REEC Summer Research Laboratory in June, 1985.

Note on terminology--I have used the term *Magyar* to distinguish ethnic Hungarians from the political formation of the old Kingdom of Hungary as well as from the non-Magyar population. This usage has no pejorative intent.

INTRODUCTION

The history of Slovak literature illustrates very clearly the truism that in the so-called crossroads of Europe — the multinational Austro-Hungarian Empire — literature and language depended heavily upon political development and geographic position. The interplay of language and politics is so characteristic of central Europe and so uncharacteristic of the English-speaking world that the word "nationality" becomes a slippery source of confusion. The danger of confusion is doubly important in this study of women's position as a function of the national position. Thus, a few historical questions must be considered.

Slovak history seems particularly complex because the status of the Slovaks in past times cannot be defined in terms of their own political unit. They did not have a kingdom or state of their own, unless one counts the brief and cloudy period of the Great Moravian Kingdom in the ninth and tenth centuries. This kingdom centered itself in the Danube River territory of west and south Slovakia as well as along the Morava River, but was overcome by the combined forces of the German Holy Roman emperor and pagan Magyar tribes from central Asia (symbolically dated by the defeat at Bratislava in 907 A.D.). Slovakia then became an integral part of the Kingdom of Hungary, and usually was called Upper Hungary. Having been in the center of Great Moravia, the Slovaks suffered more by its loss than did the Czechs, Poles, and South Slavs, because the Slovaks had no other political center. Without a separate legal and economic system to develop an administrative language and without an aristocratic court to foster a vernacular literature, the various Slovak dialects did not coalesce into a single standard language until the mid-nineteenth century. Thus, the Slovaks could scarcely be defined even as a separate cultural group using a single literary language of their own. Yet, in spite of these disadvantages, they retained their identity sufficiently to develop into a distinct national body, and to enter under their own name into the new state of "Czecho–Slovakia" in 1918. The hyphen was dropped during the inevitable difficulties with the Czech majority, but it was de facto reinstated with the federalization law of 1969 that created the "Slovak Socialist Republic" and it caused the "hyphen war" and name change to "Czech and Slovak Federal Republic" in 1990.[1]

For these reasons, study of Slovak literature has to be construed as study of the literature of Slovakia, not of literature in the Slovak language alone, and it particularly includes literature in the Czech language as modified and used by many Slovaks as their written language for several centuries. In this larger sense, early Slovak culture existed in the conjuncture of foreign forces within Slovakia and in Slovak choices among those converging forces, not in a linear progression as occurs with a national-dynastic literature. This subtle distinction is essential to modern Slovak historians, because it underlies and supports their admittedly difficult effort to see the Slovaks as an active subject in history, not as a passive object. The very difficulty of proving Slovak nationhood has added a voluntaristic intensity to the effort, which is seen as clearly in Slovak Marxist historiography as in pre-Marxist work, and which will surely continue in post-Marxist historiography.[2]

Development into a national entity occurred in part because of the territorial compactness and continuity of Slovakia, and this obvious factor was aided by the historical importance of a central geographic area especially in the long period of Turkish occupation of lower Hungary. The millenium without the Slovaks' own political unit was not a vacuum, and research is increasingly showing that the mixture of languages and nationalities characteristic of a crossroads brought a rich multilingual culture to Upper Hungary in which Slovaks played an active though never a dominating role. Besides Magyar culture, proximity to Austria and especially its capital Vienna along with the large German colonization in the cities brought the German cultural influence that is characteristic of central Europe. Magyar and German cultures were not the only outside influences, moreover, because Czech culture traditionally played a large role through the Hussite reformation and its warriors and the large Czech emigration to Baroque Hungary after the defeat at White Mountain in 1620.

Aiding this multilingual culture in the Kingdom of Hungary was the long-continued use of Latin, since the laws by which Magyar replaced Latin as the state language were passed only after 1790. This long use of Latin hid the implicit assumption within the Magyar language that eventually collapsed the multinational concept of Hungary in the nineteenth and twentieth centuries. That is, the Magyar language did not (and still does not) have a word to distinguish the Kingdom of Hungary as a supranational geographical and political entity from the ethnic organization of Magyar tribesmen that established the Kingdom and its first dynasty of the Arpads in 1001 A.D. This lack would not have mattered if the first Magyar tribesmen had either absorbed or dissolved into the conquered and annexed ethnic groups, and if the name *Magyar* had adhered to all the people and institutions in the amalgamated Kingdom—as occurred in England, for example, where Britons, Saxons, Angles, and Normans became the undifferentiated *English* with a single language of the same name. Instead, the Magyars, Slovaks, Croatians, Rumanians, and many of the German colonists retained their separate identities and languages and kept their own names for themselves. The Magyars too used separate names for the other inhabitants of Hungary (e.g. *tót* for Slovak, *német* for German, *horvát* for Croatian, etc.), but they identified the Kingdom of Hungary as *Magyarország*, thus showing their belief that it was in some way theirs alone. In fact, the same belief originally underlay the non-Magyar names for the Kingdom of Hungary (*Uhorsko, Uhry, Ungarn*, etc.) from the Finno-Ugric root *ugor* (=*Magyar*), but these words later acquired their broader geopolitical sense as the Kingdom of Hungary.[3]

The multinational aristocratic culture of Hungary emphasized class allegiance, and the so-called feudal *natio hungarica* signified the whole nobility and gentry regardless of ethnic nationality in the modern sense.[4] This synthesis, however, collapsed following the French Revolution with its rights of the common people and especially as the new concept of a cultural nation developed with the German romantics —a cultural nation that joined the highest nobility to the lowliest serf through their common blood and common language.

This new democratic concept of an ethnic nation helped the Slovaks solve their intellectual problem in explaining themselves as a distinct people despite not having had a political state of their own. Peter Brock has summarized this solution:

> The French Revolution had equated the nation with the people; the German Romantics, led by Herder, identified the nation with the language spoken by the people. This new idea of nationality came to exercise an immense influence on the intellectual elites of all the stateless nationalities of east-central and south-eastern Europe.... Not only did Protes-

tant Slovaks eagerly seize upon it but young Catholic intellectuals ... did so too (37).

According to Herder and his disciples in eastern Europe the nation was a

> product of nature with an inborn right to develop its own language and culture, while the state was an artificial phenomenon: to deprive the nation of this right was a crime against humanity (38).

Thus, while it is an irony that the first Slovaks applying this linguistic concept of nationality to Slovakia wrote in various forms of the Czech language, this irony did not deter their more or less deliberate decision to follow their sense of separateness and declare themselves a nation in the cultural sense.

As a part of this conscious Slovak decision to become such a nation, men offered women an important role to play, and women accepted that role enthusiastically. Men's recognition of their own need coincided with women's developing recognition of their own ability and desire to help their nation. In the former political-aristocratic *natio hungarica*, only noblewomen could play a role, but in the new cultural-linguistic nation, many of the needed educative roles were close to the traditional domestic function of ordinary women. The phenomenon of men asking for women's help is by no means historically new or surprising. Often (perhaps typically) in the early, struggling period of a reform movement, women are very active and their help is valued. For instance, in earliest Christian times women were missionaries and deaconesses, and in the fifth to ninth centuries of European Christianization numerous pagan princes (and their tribes) were converted by devout princesses. Many of the major female saints came from this period.[5] The same pattern is apparent in revolutionary movements and current Third World reform efforts, e.g. the Argentine "Mothers of the Plaza de Mayo." Later, of course, when the reform movement is consolidated and successful, we typically see that women's role is diminished.[6] Slovak women were certainly co-opted by and into the national movement, which included very few feminist tenets, but one must also see the new opportunities it gave them and the way women grasped, enlarged, and internalized these opportunities.

Slovak attitudes toward women's "place" seem to show three patterns, which occurred roughly in the chronological order of the general intellectual currents they reflected. The first pattern, which I have summarized by the phrase "women as inspiration," showed women (or better expressed, showed *woman*) as the symbolic representation of the romantic Herderean nation. This pattern seems so inevitable that it needs little more than an outline. The second pattern reflected the growing women's movement by showing women as a helping hand in preserving and developing that same Herderean nation. To some extent, we can see here a special version of what Jean-Jacques Rousseau and his followers developed into the doctrine of women's place, whereby a woman should be (in Coventry Patmore's phrase) "an angel in the house." In nationalist terms she was to be an angel in the nation. The third pattern reflected the growing women's emancipation movement that brought the consciousness of women as a submerged class rather than as appendages of men, the family, or the nation. Women were not yet thought of as unisex or androgynous persons, but they began to look at and describe themselves independently. This is particularly clear with women authors.

Slovak women writers of the nationalist period were obviously not the first women writing in Slovakia, and the aristocratic period in Upper Hungary shows a mosaic of women's literature in at least the three main languages of Biblical Czech, German, and Magyar. Though the earliest female writers lie outside the range of my work, a brief comparison is instructive.

Most of the early works were devotional, which is not surprising in a time when religion was the primary intellectual sphere open to women, even women of property and power. Besides two abbesses who wrote saints' lives, at least six aristocratic women may have composed Magyar-language hymns between 1593 and 1627. The four Biblical Czech hymns attributed to Anna Czobor were written before 1636, when they were translated into Magyar. The two hymns in the same language which are attributed to Žofia Kubini and Anna Kubini at the turn of the seventeenth century, illustrate the pietist tradition of personal devotion.[7] Although several of these attributions are contested, the tradition of hymn writing continued into the eighteenth century, when it certainly included women, as will be seen.

The few political works by women followed the tradition of the aristocracy. The most political writer, i.e. the Magyar-language poet Kata-Szidónia Petrőczy, was concerned with independence of the Hungarian nobility from the hated Hapsburgs in Vienna, not with the Magyar nation as a matter of blood or race.[8] This latter interest could come only with the new democratic conception of a nation that joined the highest nobility to the lowliest serf through their common blood and common language. Such a conception gave women a new place, and it was open to all women, not just the gentry and aristocracy. Thus, not only the social position of women writers changed from aristocratic or gentry to commoner, but the number of women writers radically increased. Certain elements of continuity are apparent, for example in hymn writing, and further study may enrich and enlarge the comparison of early and later writers, as we are still very far from a complete view.

The study of women writers in Slovakia is complicated by several factors, one of which is that instead of the official history of the reigning power, we are dealing with private, unofficial, unrecognized, alternative, even underground activities of the minority nationalists. Another factor is inherent to women's studies when one has the additional disadvantage of working with numerically small nations. In a small population, the very low percentage of women that first began to write (a low percentage in any country) results in a very tiny number of women indeed. Therefore, typical research problems with lost manuscripts, pseudonymous or anonymous works, and missing biographical data become especially critical. For Slovak writers, relatively few literary texts have survived with established authorship, and one must reconstruct the circumstances (linguistic, social, and personal/family) that made it possible or impossible for a woman to become a writer. Moreover, women's literature has not yet been systematically studied in either Czechoslovakia or Hungary, inasmuch as women's studies was not an accepted discipline in the socialist theory that ruled until November 1989.

This neglect was recognized by Slovak historians at a symposium on the women's movement in 1968. The clearest statement, by the long-time Communist party member and historian Zdena Holotíková, is worth quoting in full:

> The most serious weakness ... is the several utopian beliefs about the position of women within socialism and especially the theory of the automatic solution of the women's question through the taking over of

power by the working class. This theory... is not unique to Czechoslovakia. We can find its roots in certain opinions of the great socialist thinkers of the 19th century. Bebel, that fighter for the rights of women, emphasizes markedly the opinion that all the ills of women relate closely to the capitalist order and the system of private property in general (prostitution, the financial and psychological dependence of a wife upon her husband, and so on). From this opinion it is just a step to belief in the elimination of the woman question by establishing the socialist order. This belief ... is very false and convenient. We should protest it and fight it on all sides.[9]

Similarly, in a summary article on the philosophical and economic background of the women's movement, it was admitted that the pioneering role of bourgeois women in wresting political rights from their own class had not been justly rated, and that contemporary Marxist-Leninist philosophy had not taken up deeply enough the source of its opinions on the "woman question."[10] Unfortunately, these insights were not developed or even repeated, and no complete history exists of either the Slovak or Czech women's movement.[11] Not only has there been no effort to look at literary history from the gender perspective, but materials on women have not been sought, or when found not gathered together unless they related to the history of socialism.

Therefore, to trace the ideology of nationalism as it appeared in Slovak women's literary expression required collection, translation, and comparison of the basic texts revealing the conscious decisions of women writers and those men who affected the women's movement. Since most of these texts were published in fugitive or rare journals, and a few were in unpublished letters, I have translated the most relevant documents in full, to show strategy and emotional tone as well as content. The original texts of women's verses in the nineteenth century are reprinted in the Appendix. The result is almost an anthology, though well-known and easily available documents were given only brief, illustrative treatment. Several needed sources were unavailable, and certainly other sources are as yet unknown, but hopefully the ones given here allow a preliminary analysis of women writers' part in the Slovak national movement.

NOTES

1. Obviously new histories can now be written, but until they appear the standard Slovak history remains that published by the Slovak Academy of Sciences, as *Dejiny Slovenska*, 6 vols. (Bratislava: Veda, 1985–1989). No complete history exists in English, but specialized histories are referred to later. The standard treatment of the Slovak language is by Eugen Pauliny, *Dejiny spisovnej slovenčiny* (Bratislava, 1983). For summaries in English, see Robert Auty, "Dialect, Koiné and Tradition in the Formation of Literary Slovak," *Slavonic and East European Review* (London) 39 (1961): 339–345; and Ľubomír Ďurovič, "Slovak," *The Slavic Literary Languages*, eds., Alexander M. Schenker and Edward Stankiewicz (New Haven: Yale Concilium on International and Area Studies, 1980) 211–228. The standard literary history is *Dejiny slovenskej literatúry*, 5 vols. (Bratislava: Veda, 1958–1984). Little is available in English on Slovak literature. The best short description is by Karol Strmen in *An Anthology of Slovak Literature*, comp. Andrew Cincura (Riverside: University Hardcovers, 1976) xix–liv. Longer treatments by J. M. Kirschbaum, *Slovak Language and Literature* (Winnipeg: U of Manitoba, 1975), and Július Noge, *An Outline of Slovakian Literature* (Bratislava: Tatrapress, 1966), are outdated. These references emphasize works in the Slovak language, not the literature of Slovakia in Latin, Czech, and Magyar, as will be mentioned.

2. I have briefly analyzed this tendency as it appears in Slovak Marxist literary history in *The Context of the Marxist-Leninist View of Slovak Literature 1945–1969* (No. 505 Carl Beck Papers in Russian and East European Studies, University of Pittsburgh, 1986) 34 pp. Further study of medieval, renaissance, and baroque literature will have to emphasize the conjuncture or crossroads nature of Slovakia.

3. See *Dejiny Slovenska* 1: 164, 168. See also Daniel Rapant's *K počiatkom maďarizácie*, 2 vols. (Bratislava, 1927, 1931) and

Branislav Varsik's *Otázky vzniku a vývinu slovenského zemianstva* (Bratislava: Veda, 1988) 20–21.

4. See the definition of *natio hungarica* in Peter Brock's concise intellectual history of Slovak nationalism, *The Slovak National Awakening* (Toronto: U of Toronto P, 1976) 6–7. For the slight political widening of this concept among Protestant Magyars in the early seventeenth century, see Laszlo Makkai, "Istvan Bocskai's Insurrectionary Army," *From Hunyadi to Rakoczi*, ed. Janos M. Bak and Bela K. Kiraly (New York: Brooklyn College P, 1982) 284–293.

5. See, for example, Katharina M. Wilson's Introduction to *Medieval Women Writers* (Athens: U of Georgia P, 1984) xi and notes.

6. At the end of Richard Stites' history of women's emancipation in Russia, he suggests that revolutionary and developing countries tend to show the use of women rather than their liberation, in *The Women's Liberation Movement in Russia* (Princeton U P, 1978) 419–420.

7. For the Magyar-language writers see Mariska Fáylné-Hentaller, *A Magyar írónőkről* (Budapest, 1889) 9–33, and for Ilona and Zsuzsánna Dóczy see also Jószef Szinnyei, *Magyar írók élete és munkái* (Budapest, 1891–1914) 2:953, 960. For the Biblical Czech-language works, see Jozef Minárik, *Renesančná a humanistická literatúra* (Bratislava: Slovenské pedagogické nakladateľstvo, 1985) 192, 195, and *Baroková literatúra* (Bratislava: Slovenské pedagogické nakladateľstvo, 1984) 155, 160. The earliest women writers in Austria and Hungary have not been studied intensively. My own work in progress was summarized for panel 3-03 "Baroque Writing in Slovakia" at the AAASS Conference in Chicago, 2 November 1989. Žofia Kubini is treated briefly in *Dictionary of Continental Women Writers*, ed. Katharina M. Wilson (New York: Garland, 1990).

8. Petrőczy is the most often studied Magyar woman poet; see Margit S. Sárdi, *Petrőczy Kata Szidónia költészete* (Budapest: Akadémiai Kiadó, 1976). I thank Dr. Tibor Klaniczay for this reference.

9. Zdena Holotíková, "Zástoj ženy v zápase pracujúceho človeka," *Zborník materiálov zo sympózia '100 rokov uvedomelého pohybu žien v dejinách slovenského národa,'* 27–28 November 1968, ed. Otília Chmelová (Bratislava: Živena, 1968) 23–33. The quotation is from 31–32. All translations are mine unless otherwise cited. This source is hereafter cited as *Zborník materiálov*. A little information on earlier periods is also in *Pokrokové ženské hnutie na Slovensku 1918–1980* (Bratislava: Ústredný výbor slovenského zväzu žien, 1984).

10. Blanka Svoreňová-Királyová, "Emancipačné hnutie v druhej polovici 19. storočia a na začiatku 20. storočia: (Náčrt filozofického a ekonomického zázemie)," *Zborník materiálov* 71–77.

11. In "Current Literature on the Position and Roles of Women in Czechoslovakia," *Canadian Slavonic Papers* 20 (March 1978): 78, the sociologist Jarmila L.A. Horna reports that "The well-known thesis about the relationship between the family, private property, and the state is taken for granted.... Thus, the position of women under socialism cannot be compared with their position in other social formations." The one slightly unorthodox view Horna found was in an article dated 1970 (80). For obvious reasons after 1968, Czechoslovak social theory conformed to Soviet theory, and unfortunately it has been slow even to catch up with the new social and intellectual climate under Mikhail Gorbachev. The need for and potential richness of relating the studies of feminism and of socialism is indicated by women's history elsewhere in Europe, e.g. the essays in Marilyn J. Boxer and Jean H. Quataert, eds. *Socialist Women* (New York: Elsevier, 1978).

PART I: WOMAN AS INSPIRATION

CHAPTER 1: MALE APOTHEOSIS OF WOMAN AS NATION

"Woman as inspiration for man" is a generic concept in cultural history that has appeared repeatedly from lyric poetry to the battlefield, whereas men have served as an inspiration for women only in exceptional, individual cases. Perhaps the most widespread classical tradition has related women to the Muses. A striking example of such an apotheosis in Slovak literature is the recently discovered allegorical poem by Štefan Ferdinand Selecký, *Obraz panej krásnej, perem malovaný, která má v Trnave svoje prebývání* (The Portrait of a Beautiful Lady, Painted by Pen and Ink, Who Lives in Trnava, 1701), which celebrates both the university in Trnava and the person of the poet's patroness, Lady Catherine Corbortrany (who is otherwise unknown).[1] Stereotypic invocations of the muses continued, of course, for example in dedicatory and occasional verses.

Distinct from this tradition relating women to beauty and intellectual values, the mother earth goddess directly reflected a patriarchal social structure showing women's biological function as mother, nurturer, and lover. The latter tradition was so important in the old Slavic agricultural society that male Slovak nationalists had ready-made symbols to show women in the position of national inspirers.

There was great need for such symbols. The submerged Slavic nations of Austria and Hungary wanted to establish their own identity, history, and destiny in opposition to the German power and influence which had assimilated so many Slavs in the past. They often looked for support and inspiration to Czarist Russia as to the largest independent Slav nation, but eastern elements such as the autocratic system and Orthodoxy diminished Russia's intellectual influence in Central Europe. It is no accident that much of the effort against Germanization occurred among the exposed westernmost Slavs, and it is no surprise that two Slovaks were foremost in a movement where their lack of strong national identity eased their conception of pan-Slav unity in the western Slavic lands that had been taken over by German influence. Their work is so well known that this chapter will only sketch its outlines.

Ironically, Germany provided a direct and positive influence on Slavic nationalism. The two Slovak pioneers in the Slavic movement, Pavol Jozef Šafárik and Ján Kollár, studied at Jena

University, as did their precursor Juraj Palkovič (1769–1850), who first occupied the newly established chair of the "Czechoslovak language" (actually the Czech used by Slovaks at that time) in Bratislava in 1803. While observing the German drive toward political unification, they also came under the powerful influence of Johann Gottfried Herder's concept of cultural nationalism and his praise of the Slavs as a distinct European entity. The western Slavs already had fertile ground for this concept. For example, in 1801 Palkovič published his poetic cycle *Muza ze slovenskych hor* (Muse of the Slovak Mountains), which shows his effort to create "a symbiosis of 'classical' [i.e. Greek and Latin] and 'national' elements."[2] Even before going to Jena, at age eighteen in 1814 Šafárik published a cycle of poems utilizing folk literature titled *Tatranská Múza s lyrou slovanskou* (Tatra Muse with Her Slavic Lyre). This female figure was the conventional antique muse adapted to Slavic circumstances. For example, Šafárik addressed her as *Slovanka* and said she would also be a Czech muse for a Czech poet:

> Slovanka jsi, netaj toho;
> k strunám harfy slovenské
> snaž se čisté, ač ne mnoho,
> střidat zvuky panenské.
> Kam jen přijdeš, učiň dosti:
> Češka budiz Čechovi.
> (You're a Slavic maiden, do not hide this fact;
> and on the strings of the harp
> try to alternate even a few
> pure Slovak virginal notes.
> Wherever you come, meet the need:
> a Czech [muse] for a Czech [poet].)[3]

This kind of national patriotism had scarcely been a part of Slovak literature in the beginning of the 19th century. At Jena and afterward, Šafárik turned away from literature to concentrate on his historical and philological works that stimulated and supported national movements among the other Slavs as well as in Slovakia.

It was Ján Kollár (1793–1852) who created a new female figure. In his famous epic poem *Slávy dcera* (Daughter of the Mother of Slavdom) published in 1824, Kollár celebrated Slavdom through the old mythology of the goddess mother Sláva, but he added the new character of her daughter Mína as the poet/hero's beloved. This combination of lyrical love poetry composed in 150 Petrarchan sonnets with a majestic historical, geographical sweep infused by love of the whole Slavic community made the epic unusually striking. While at Jena Kollár had fallen in love with Frederika Wilhelmina Schmidt, a German minister's young daughter who could not or would not marry him when Kollár wanted to return to Hungary in 1819 to work for the Slavic cause. She was plainly the Mína of the epic; though in a note Kollár explained the name as "a shortened form of *milena, milenka*" (beloved), she was easily recognized. Kollár and she separated and were reunited and married only in 1835, long after Kollár's epic had become famous.[4]

The first canto of Kollár's epic glorified the poet's confession of his love, Mína's beauty and innocence, and their first kisses. The lyrical hero of the epic appeared as a young lover experiencing the wonder of first love and the pain of farewell besides being the carrier of the national ideology. Despite Kollár's idealization of Mína, in sonnet 93 of Canto 2 he explicitly placed women in an inferior position:

>Ženský muž se tak jak mužská žena
>cti a štěstí svého pozbaví; ....
>Muži vůle, čin a smělost sluší,
>Ženě prosba, cit a mlčení;
>ten buď více duchem, tato duší.
>(A feminine man just like a masculine woman
>their own respect and happiness cast off; ....
>To a man will, action, and daring are
>   suitable,
>to a woman appeal, feeling, and silence;
>let him be more of spirit, her of soul.)[5]

The second and third cantos showed the poet's departure from Jena and his return through the valley of the Elbe over the Tatra Mountains to his home by the Danube. The next verses related more and more to the Slovak countryside traversed by the poet as he recollected the glorious but sorrowful history of the Slavs which he had begun in the Prologue with the famous opening epigram on the lost and assimilated Slavs:

>Aj zde leží zem ta, před okem mým smutně slzícím,
>   někdy kolébka, nyní národu mého rakev.
>(Before my weeping eyes, here lies the land,

which, once my people's cradle, is now their grave.)(142)

Literary historian Milan Pišút summarized the epic as a poetically excellent political statement. It was an

> appeal to post-Napoleonic Europe which was still illumined by the idea of the natural rights of nations and greater civil liberty, and an appeal to the Europe of the Holy Alliance united for the first time from the Atlantic to the Urals by a sense of cultural community. The elegiac tone ... changed into joy and the resolute tones of faith and hope.... The Enlightenment dawn of national feeling, the cult of the native language and tribe, faith in the spiritual and moral progress of the world, and the free-minded but disciplined attitude of an intellectual toward reality—all this would lead to the dawn of national sentiment which would overcome the dark and fulfill all hope.... The epic was a lament but also a program.[6]

Slávy dcera was very popular among most of the Slavs, and was followed by imitations such as *Múzy dcera* and *Matka Slávie*.[7] An exception was Kollár's lack of effect among the Poles and Ukrainians, who were at that time occupied by Czarist Russia and who feared the idea of Slavdom as a means of further Russian control. Among other Slavs, however, the epic did much to foster linguistic and cultural nationalism in individual nations as well as a sort of international Slavism.[8]

Kollár greatly enlarged the three later editions (1832, 1845, and 1852) by detailed treatment of Slavic history and geography, and he increased the exhortative, didactic parts of the epic. For example, he added a Dantesque descent into Hell and ascent into Heaven in which Sláva showed to the epic hero the enemies and friends of Slavdom, and she described the great services the Slavs had rendered to humanity for which they received almost no reward. These changes diminished the importance of the beloved Mína and also destroyed the high poetic quality of the epic, as critics pointed out. It was also the enlarged version of *Slávy dcera* which influenced the national movement, but only the first version remains poetically effective today. It is still being translated, e.g. into Russian in 1973 and modern Slovak in 1979, although only parts have been translated into English.[9]

Kollár's combination of a real woman with the feminine symbol for Slavdom had no immediate major successors. The next great Slovak epic poet, Ján Hollý (1785–1849), used the classical models of Homer and Virgil with the recently published histories of Great Moravia to create an epic on King Svätopluk's battle with the Germanic Franks (1833), as well as a spiritual epic on the missionaries to the Slavs in *Cirillo-Metodiada* (1835). Hollý based his third epic, *Slav* (1839), on an imaginary war in which the Slovaks, personified by their warrior king Slav, battled against pagan enemies. Although he de-emphasized Kollár's female Sláva, he used Živena, the old Slavic goddess of life, among the divine beings that helped the Slovaks.[10]

In his occasional poems (1835–1840), Hollý sometimes used the classical female muse, for example in his eclogues or pastorals (*selanky*). He also used mother nature as the good force threatened by evil city life, a Rousseauesque theme placing him in the Herderean tradition of emphasis upon the rural folk, but also showing realistically his personal knowledge of the Slovak peasantry.[11] More important, in *Plač matky Slávy* (The Lament of Mother Sláva) in 1837–1838, Hollý used the common image of the mother of Slavdom weeping over her denationalized sons. While in his epics Hollý had mainly written of the Slovaks themselves, in these poems he like Kollár made Sláva represent all of Slavdom, and the composition and meter were also similar to Kollár's. Hollý (a Catholic priest) used the Sláva symbol as a political term with no apotheosis of a real woman.

In this same period, other symbols for the nation were used besides female ones. Historical interest in heroic Slavic warriors increased with the addition of folk heroes from ballads and tales, particularly the Robin Hood-like brigand Juraj Jánošík. This is seen in Ján Botto's *Piesne Jánošíkovej* (Songs of Jánošík) in 1846, and especially in the poems and ballads of Samo Chalupka and Janko Kraľ, who were affected by their participation in the Slavic revolutions of 1830 and 1848–1849. Janko Kraľ also introduced a Byronic condemnation of women that exceeded the standard folk figures of sirens, unfaithful wives, or malevolent mothers-in-law, for example among his earliest works in *Zakliata panna vo Váhu a divný Janko* (The Bewitched Maid in the Váh River and Strange Janko) in 1844.[12]

Notwithstanding this contemporary emphasis upon warrior heroes, Kollár's apotheosis of his beloved was repeated a generation later by young Andrej Braxatoris Sládkovič (1820– 1872). Unable to marry his first love, Mária Pischl, Sládkovič symbolically immortalized her in his first long poem *Marína* (published 1846), aptly called "the daughter of *Slávy dcera*."[13] For example, strophe 73 begins, "Chcel bych vás objat', kraje rodiny!" (I should love to embrace you, my native land!) and ends with the desire

Vlast' drahú ľúbit' v peknej Maríne,
Marínu drahú v peknej otčine,
A obe v jednom objímat'!
(To love my dear land in fair Marína,
And love dear Marína in my fair land,
And embrace both together in one!)[14]

The poem has a motto from Alexander Pushkin's *Eugene Onegin* and obviously shows some similarity in the treatment of Marína. Besides realistic description of the countryside where he lived, Sládkovič utilized folk and classical mythology, mixing river spirits and sirens with abstract beauty and love. He also used Biblical parallels; e.g. strophes 103–105 show Mary and Jesus in danger of Herod's evil wrath. Like the symbolism of *Slávy dcera*, Sládkovič's use of general symbols was extensive. As Pišút said,

The woman Marína is fused into one with his native country, equally enthusiastically, so that the celebration of love turns into a celebration of his home and native land, until at the end she is entirely spiritualized and becomes the very celebration of life, eternal desire, and love that ennobles the poet.(263)

In Sládkovič's next long poem, *Detvan* (Man from Detva) in 1853, he transformed his love for Marína into love for the peasant pair Martin and Elena and for the Slovak land represented by the mountain village Detva, whose peasants Sládkovič saw as preserving the nation. This poem exchanged the symbol of woman for that of folk hero and fighter for justice.

Despite the striking similarities between the works of Kollár and Sládkovič, Sládkovič showed a greater tendency toward realism than Kollár had shown. As Cyril Kraus noted, "To Kollár the ethereal being [Mína] was only an idol, a guide to a bigger-than-life country or to the weaving of dreams of the past and the future of Slavdom. Sládkovič used his ethereal being to confront visions with the real world, in favor of the real world."[15] This difference, though not large, was real. Victor Kochol's textual analysis of *Marína* led him to find the chief difference in Sládkovič's sensuousness in contrast to Kollár's rationalism.[16] Both characteristics, of course, reflected changes in Slovak (and other) literature of the period. Perhaps this literary realism also indicated a slightly increased awareness of women as real beings that unconsciously presaged but did not yet illustrate the changed role for women that lay in the future.

Although other examples of apotheosized women occurred in Slovak literature, these two are by far the most striking. They serve to show that the poets were thinking of their own relation to the women, not the women's personal relation to the nation they symbolized.

There is little evidence of how Kollár's beloved felt about her public apotheosis, although her acceptance of his second marriage proposal suggests that she found it flattering. A century later, in a similar situation such fame was perceived to be a mixed blessing, as one sees in the memoirs of the Russian woman Liubov' Blok, whose poetic idealization by her husband Alexander Blok clearly caused her to feel a conflict between this etherealized public image and her real self.[17] Kollár's marriage was apparently happy, although not only was Mína of German nationality but their household language was German, and this fact was scandalous for Kollár's Slavic friends in Budapest.[18] In her widowhood Mína's letters to an old friend show considerable sympathy for the Slavic cause against German domination in Austria-Hungary:

> Poor Slovaks and Czechs, who have to turn into either Magyars or Germans! What are Rieger and Palacký doing? I often feel angry at the Germans, who always want to rise higher and who think it's possible to erase a nation with the stroke of a pen. If only Nemesis would pay them back, and while I'm still alive to see it. But at my advanced age, I always have such desires that won't be fulfilled.[19]

Apparently Mína had partly adopted the position attributed to her. Nonetheless, though the Kollárs' only child Ľudmila learned both Slovak and Magyar, she married a nationalistic German, and Kollár's descendents ended denationalized.

The situation with Sládkovič's Mária Pischl was comparable. She was the daughter of a prosperous dyer, and they became acquainted in the Slovak city of Banská Štiavnica in 1840. Their love continued through his university studies in Halle, and under his influence she became a Slovak nationalist and subscribed to a Štúrist magazine. In 1845, however, she married a successful baker, Georg Gerzso. Whether she was compelled by her mother or whether she herself tired of waiting for Sládkovič is disputed.[20] Sládkovič soon married someone else and dedicated the later edition of *Marína* (1861) to his wife in a verse that asks her to accept Marína as her spiritual and national partner. The poor state of research on Mária Pischl, however, is shown by the fact that literary historian Štefan Krčméry denied she was the real inspiration for Sládkovič since he soon married someone else, but literary historian Pavol Vongrej thinks she was also the inspiration for the peasant girl Elena in *Detvan*.[21]

It is clear that the national images of both women were imposed upon them. These apotheosized women were only means of inspiring males to work for the nation. The idea of real women who would themselves be useful in the national movement may have occasionally occurred in this period, but it developed into real activity only later, as is shown in the next chapter.

NOTES

1. Štefan Ferdinand Selecký, *Obraz panej krásnej, perem malovaný, ktorá má v Trnave svoje prebývání*, in *Z klenotnice staršieho slovenského písomníctva. 3. Antológia barokových literárnych textov*, ed. Jozef Minárik (Bratislava: Tatran, 1989) 265–275. See also Minárik, *Baroková literatúra* 178–180.

2. Cyril Kraus, ed., *Na lutnu: Výber zo slovenskej klasicistickej poézie* (Bratislava: Tatran, 1986) 360.

3. Pavel Jozef Šafárik, *Basnické spisy*, ed. Jan Vilikovský (Bratislava: Učené Společnosti Šafaříkovy, 1938) 7. Little of early Slovak literature has been translated into English; lists have been compiled by George J. Kovtun, *Czech and Slovak Literature in*

English (Washington, D.C.: Library of Congress, 1984). Kovtun found only two translations from Šafárik 117 – 118.

4. Kollár's biography is summarized by Michal Eliaš in "Problémy Kollárovej biografie," *Biografické štúdie,* 6 (1976): 103–139. Biographers disagree on why Mína refused Kollár, perhaps because her mother believed faraway Hungary was too wild; Michal Bodický summarized this view in *Životopis Jána Kollára* (Ružomberok, 1893) 14–16, 31. The opposite and more likely view is that she loved someone else, who disappointed her; see Ján Kabelík, *Rodina pěvce Slávy dcera* (Prague, 1928) 8–10. The best English source is Robert Auty, "Jan Kollár, 1793–1852," *Slavonic and East European Review,* 31 (December 1952): 74–91.

5. Ján Kollár, *Slávy dcera,* in *Na lutnu,* ed Cyril Kraus (Bratislava: Tatran, 1986) 207.

6. Milan Pišút, "Klasicizmus (roky dvadsiate a tridsiate)," *Dejiny slovenskej literatúry* (Bratislava: Obzor, 1984) 217.

7. Ján Tibenský, "Uloha Jána Kollára v slovenskom národnom obrodení a hnutí," *Biografické štúdie,* 6 (1976): 42–43.

8. For English accounts of the effect of Kollár's *Slávy dcera,* see Auty 74 and 83–89, Brock 22 and 65, n.8, and Kirschbaum 140–144. For Kollár's effect on Ljudevit Gaj, see Elinor Murray Despalatovic, *Ljudevit Gaj and the Illyrian Movement* (Boulder: East European Monographs, 1975) 51–55.

9. Kovtun shows numerous translations of individual sonnets and three translations of the Prologue, 75.

10. The substantial body of research on Ján Hollý was summarized in the large four-language volume published when the 200th anniversary of his birth was included in the UNESCO calendar for 1985, Juraj Chovan, ed. *Pamätnica z osláv dvojstého výročia narodenia Jána Hollého* (Martin: Matica slovenská, 1985). Kovtun found only two short poems in English, 110.

11. Kraus, ed., *Na lutnu* 426-427.

12. See, for example, Štefan Krčméry's discussion in his *Dejiny literatúry slovenskej*, ed. Ján Števček and Emília Nemsilová (Bratislava: Tatran, 1976) 2: 88, 130–133.

13. Pišút 262.

14. Andrej Sládkovič, *Marína*, in *Sobrané básne* (Martin: Matica slovenská, 1939) 73. Kovtun found only two poems in English, 118.

15. Cyril Kraus, "Kollár a štúrovci," *Biografické štúdie*, 6 (1976): 68.

16. Victor Kochol, *Problémy a postavy* (Bratislava: SAV, 1965) 274–275.

17. See the discussion of Liubov' Blok by Barbara Heldt in *Terrible Perfection* (Bloomington: Indiana University Press, 1987) 93–98.

18. See Lászlo Sziklay, "Maďarské vstahy Jána Kollára v Pešti," *Dějiny a národy: Literarněhistorické studie o československo-maďarských vztazích* (Prague: ČSAV, 1965) 92; also, Kabelík 13–14, 22–26.

19. Her letters have not been published, but Kabelík selected a few and translated them from German into Czech. The quotation is from a letter dated 10 October 1869 (111).

20. See Pavol Vongrej, *Diamant v hrude* (Martin: Matica slovenská, 1970) 7–8.

21. See Krčméry 2: 94–95 and Vongrej 10.

PART II: WOMEN AS HELP
CHAPTER 2: WOMEN'S PLACE IN THE ŠTÚRIST TRADITION 1835–1875

It is certain that even while Slovak women were being apotheosized by male nationalists, they also had begun to think of doing something themselves, not simply passively standing as inspiration for their men. In much of Europe, women's ambitions had been aroused in part by the French political revolution (as with Mary Wollstonecraft) and in part by Jean-Jacques Rousseau's new ideology of women's place. This latter influence was greater than the former among the stateless nations struggling to keep their cultural identity. Women's inherent virtue as nurturer was supposed to give them a special mission in life, not only to bear and raise children, but to soften men's roughness and add feeling to men's cold reason. They were the guardians of civilization.[1]

This doctrine was naturally attractive to the stateless nations that relied upon domestic and private culture to combat what they regarded as the foreign public culture imposed upon them. Moreover, it was only a short step from Mother Sláva as nature goddess to the inspirational, supportive wife and mother in a nationalistic household. Part of the change from "women as inspiration" to "women as help" consisted of domesticating Sláva's daughter Mína by decreasing her halo and increasing her realism. To some extent, this had occurred with Sládkovič's Marína, who was created to be more concretely "Slovak" and less abstractly "Slavic." She was also closer to the common people in keeping with the Štúrist emphasis upon folk language and literature. Yet Marína was still only a created female, whereas the new women would help the national cause by themselves becoming creators.

No comparative study is yet possible, but it is clear that Slovak developments were similar to those happening elsewhere, though often events occurred earlier among the nations in Austria and Hungary which had a clearer identity than the Slovaks had. Surprisingly, however, the earliest reference to women nationalist writers which I have found occurs in a Slovak source in 1803 in a poem "Plésáné (Rejoicing) praising the establishment of Juraj Palkovič's chair of "Czechoslovak language and literature" (see Chapter 1).[2] Samuel Rožnay (1787–1815) summarized the past darkness for the Slavs, then greeted the new dawn in which literary inspiration would come also to women, not just from women:

> I plésej vděčně, národe Slovanský!
> že tě i zem tvou jasný den osloní:
>> Jen za dne půjde rolník orat;
>> za dne jen bude teď' mudřec učit.
> I vy též, dcery šlechetné Slovanů,
> den tento slavte! z srdce se veselte!
>> Neb již se blíží čas, v němž Muzy
>> a Milostenkami k vám zavítají.
> (And rejoice gladly, Slavic nation!
> that upon you and your land a bright day shines.
>> Only in the daylight the farmer goes to plow;
>> so in the daylight only will the wiseman study.
> And you also, daughters of the noble Slavs,
> celebrate this day! from your hearts rejoice!
>> Because the time is nearing when the Muses
>> with the Graces will also visit you.)(86)

Further search of Palkovič's group will likely reveal other such early references. In fact, a more comprehensive, thorough search of enlightenment and neoclassical writings among all the central European nations from the late eighteenth century on, will probably provide other references like those shown below. Even the enlightenment salons apparently had a certain influence in central Europe, and the idea of women's activity was increasingly present as an idea whose time had come.

In 1822 a Magyar literary yearbook for women was founded in Pest; named *Aurora*, it became also the leading publication of Magyar romantic nationalism. The paternalistic mixture is illustrated in an exclamation from 1826: "At the same altar where the virgin swears eternal love to her beloved, she will also promise faithfulness to the fatherland."[3] In Croatia Count Janko Drašković (1770–1856) called for feminine help in the national movement in his *Ein Wort an Iliriens hochherzige Tochter* in 1838, which also appeared in Czech in 1845. This book apparently gave part of Drašković's program for the Croatian delegates at the joint parliament in Bratislava in the 1830's.[4] Dedicated to the "noble-minded Illyrian daughters," the book's foreword gives Drašković's goal:

> When you shall have read these pages, I know you will be drawn to the national cause with that holy warmth which is the exclusive property of your

compassionate hearts. You certainly will feel no less of the most exalted emotion — love of country — than the great-souled ladies of other cultured nations, and by your deeds you will show the world you are worthy daughters of the oldest nation [*kmene*] of that race [*národu*] which has its name from Slavdom [*Slàwy*]. (8)

Draškovič's program had few specifics, but he showed the general pattern of criticism and praise common among Slavic men who exhorted women to join the national cause.

Also in 1838, the Czech magazine *Kwěty* carried a one-page exhortation to nationalist women as a New Year wish, "Wlastenkynym k Nowému Roku," by the nationalist poet Baron Karel Ignac Villani (1818-1883).[5] He expressed the need to justify such an article addressed to women, which apparently was a new idea. The first two paragraphs speak of the need to cultivate the Czech language and end with the general wish that Czech women would become nationalists. After summarizing the fact that both sexes speak one tongue, live in one land, and worship one God, and after urging women not to be ashamed of their nationality, the article ends, "At' žigi wlastenkyně — at' žigi sestry naše!" (Long live nationalist women — long live our sisters!). By this time, Slovak nationalists were also thinking of engaging female help, and Villani's piece was doubtless read in Slovakia too.

I have so far treated Slovak writers without regard for the language they used, although in this period Slovak became formally established as the only language of the Slovaks. This development passed through three stages that are easily illustrated by Kollár, Hollý, and Sládkovič. *Slávy dcera* was written in Kollár's somewhat Slovakized Biblical Czech, while Hollý used the cultivated west Slovak that had been codified in 1787–1790 by Anton Bernolák and his colleagues, and Sládkovič used the central Slovak codified by Ľudovít Štúr and his followers in 1843, which eventually became standard modern Slovak. Fierce linguistic battles continued for two decades among Slovaks themselves and even longer with Czechs who felt betrayed by the Slovak decision to develop their own language. These battles are outside our scope, but it seems likely that the immediate need to justify and establish the newly codified Slovak may have helped Štúr and his followers recognize the value of women's help. As we shall see, women writers played at least a small role in explaining to Czechs the Slovak desire for their own language, and in establishing that language by its use.

This Štúrist period has been studied in detail by Slovak historians, but almost without reference to any part women played in it. A summary treatment by Jarmila Tkadlečková-Vantuchová gives a general view of men's desire for women's help in the national movement.[6] In 1968 a historical symposium was held on the Slovak women's movement, but it emphasized the organization Živena.[7] Only an unpublished dissertation by Anna Mikušťáková has specifically treated women's activities in literature and the other arts.[8] Thus, my treatment of women's literature in the national movement has elements of a pioneering effort.

Women's literary activity showed itself first in poetry, or at least imitative versifying, so it was necessary to search for all of the women poets before the 1870s, at which time women writers began to multiply. The difficulty of finding these scattered materials and the unexpected number of poems found (123) suggested the value of reprinting all the collected texts in the Appendix. Known biographical information on these women (ca 39) is given there, so references here in the text are kept to a minimum. Though uneven in poetic quality and without major status, these verses deserve stylistic treatment in relation to Slovak prosodic development, as well as in their own right as women's literary expression, but I am not qualified and that is not my interest here. Even roughly translated and summarized, they show much that is new about women's relation to the national cause since over two-thirds have nationalist themes. As with the minor male poets, these themes are repetitious, monotonous, and even claustrophobic in that they express more hope than expectation, more frustration than activity. In that way, however, they characterize those elements of this period of Slovak history. Before taking up the poems in detail, I should like to give their context from 1836 to 1867.

A Conscious Deliberate Role for Women

By at least 1839, the leading writer and nationalist Jozef Miloslav Hurban (1817–1888) had become very interested in nationalist women, as his diary of a trip through Moravia and Bohemia shows.[9] He praised the beauty of Moravian women and hoped for their future interior beauty as they came to love their nation. He stated that the Slovaks too had nationalist women (54), but Polish women were more constant nationalists than Slovak, Moravian, or Czech women (70). After visiting the Czech publisher Jaroslav Pospíšil, Hurban published in Pospíšil's journal *Kwěty* the first of many poems titled "Slowenka" (Slovak Woman), praising Slovak maidens for their musicality and beauty, then urging them to be proud of their native tongue.[10] This magazine was already carrying articles on women's help in the Czech national movement (e.g. Villani above), and Pospíšil's daughter Maria (1821–1876) is presumably the author of two poems "Sen" (Dream) and "Ginocha žel" (A Young Lad's Despair) signed only "Maria." With another poem signed by the feminine name "Lidmila Tichá," they had appeared in *Kwěty* a year earlier,[11] and are among the earliest writings by Czech women. They likely were known to nationalist Slovak women as well as men.

In this period the seven earlier Slovak women poets who were not nationalists (see below) apparently attracted no attention from the Štúrists, and were perhaps forgotten or unknown. For the Štúrists the idea of women writers seems to have been a novelty. By the publication of *Nitra* in 1842, Hurban rejoiced that he had collected eight poems by Slovak women, which he called the "valuable pearls of the young, comely imagination of our Slovak women." He saw them as evidence that "the fair sex, despite cruel denationalization by others, is contributing to the nation. This situation is even more important to us, since that sex is the one which will rear our coming generations." He hoped they would continue "with the objectives they had set for themselves."[12]

Hurban prepared a second volume of *Nitra* in 1843, with at least five poems by women, but it was not passed by the censor.[13] In the next decade he and Ľudovít Štúr published at least five more poems by women, most of them with pseudonyms that are still undecifered, as will be seen.

One of these women, however, became very well known. Johana Vyšná Lehocká seemed to embody the ideal which Hurban and the others envisioned for Slovak women. The modern editors of her letters regard her as "the greatest nationally conscious Slovak woman of the time"[14] and "probably the first Slovak woman who claimed her right to be evaluated also for her intellectual abilities."[15] Štúr wrote of her: "She is a lady not only full of noble feelings, cultured, and of an exemplary life, but also, to tell the truth, with a man's heart."[16] Ján Francisci-Rimavský in 1846 dedicated his publication of a play to "Miloslava [lover/beloved of the Slavs], the most worthy daughter and ornament of the Tatras," and in the dedicatory poem addressed her (with a pun): "You were the first to rejoice in our Slavdom-glory [sláva] / And to feel joy at our burst of light." In his autobiography Francisci called her "among Slovak women the most excellent nationalist."[17] Hurban contrasted her to the "countless mass of her sisters, who know nothing but fashion, the ladle, house slippers, pomades, and a 'sharp tongue.'"[18]

Daughter of a small town official but essentially without formal education, Lehocká was childless and the pastor's wife in a supportive community, so she had leisure to read, think, and develop a sort of salon for Slovak nationalists. Her husband, Ján Lehocký, was a friend of Štúr and was himself imprisoned by Magyar authorities in the revolution of 1848–1849.[19] Their household also welcomed Czech Slovakophiles trying to develop closer ties between the two national movements. Plentiful evidence of this activity appears in Lehocká's extant correspondence.

An important part of our information about Lehocká comes from her letters to the Czech nationalist and Slovakophile Antonia Reisová, who took the name Bohuslava Rajská (1817–1852). Under the guidance of Karel Slavoj Amerling (1807–1884), founder of a Czech teachers' school that educated women too, Rajská in 1843 founded an institute in Prague to educate Czech girls in the national spirit. Acquainted with Štúr and his group, she began writing to Lehocká to encourage her to found a similar school for Slovak girls, but the plan was not realized.[20]

During the period of this correspondence, the Štúrists' decision to use Slovak as their standard language caused consternation among Slovakophile Czechs such as Rajská. Lehocká's letter of 12 November 1843 shows her feeling of personal responsibility and unity with the codifiers:

> Don't think that by this act of publishing our newspaper in the Slovak language we wish in some way to turn away from the Czech nation. Oh, never! One reason for our action is that the other Slavic nations don't yet recognize us as independent with

our own political rights in Hungary. Another reason is that this act, instead of splitting us off, actually integrates Slavic relations, since our language is most easily understood by all the Slavs. But especially the reason is that our nation [*národ*] itself requires it. Only in this way can we awaken our neglected peasantry from its present state of somnolence to a life of spiritual elevation and national pride. (151)

Some of Lehocká's letters show depression, as in the following one of May, 1844:

> You despair over your struggle with Germanizing elements. Our situation too is bad. The aristocracy is entirely Magyarized, city people are given over to German and Magyar, and the miserable peasants don't even know what nationality [*národnosť*] means. You're trying to increase industry and improve education, but here we can only wring our hands over the miserable state of schools and commerce....
>
> In the whole of Hungary there's not one well-run school, and whoever will not study by himself or doesn't have the capacity for it, remains a dunce despite all his teachers. (152-153)

The next letter shows Lehocká bitter over continued refusal by Vienna to approve a newspaper in the new Slovak language which Štúr had petitioned for:

> They keep putting him off, from one period to another. Before parliament met, they said it was absolutely impossible because it might cause a stir, but we were assured of permission after the session. Parliament is dissolved, and we're right back where we started. Nine times our worthy Štúr has submitted his request to the throne, and twice he went there in person, but nothing helps. They treat us worse than serfs—we're like slaves. (157)[21]

Lehocká's obituary in 1850 in the first issue of the *Slovenské noviny* (Slovak News) published in Vienna called her one of the "most noble-minded daughters of Slovakia" and ended with the belief that her "memory will awaken other daughters."[22] Such elaborate praise allows us to infer how most of Lehocká's female contemporaries were regarded, but, of course, this low opinion of women and the desire to awaken them to participate in the national movement were salutary in bringing efforts to improve women's education. These efforts deserve detailed treatment despite their lack of concrete success.

Need for Women's Education

An article calling for education "in the national spirit" appeared in Štúr's new *Slovenskje národňje novini* (Slovak National News) on 31 March 1846. Written by Štefan Homola, a Lutheran pastor (1811–1881), it argues the need for women in the national cause:

> Where a father looks upon the world as a Slovak, but the mother plays a German tune and the daughter sings still another song, ... national upbringing will be lacking. In this way our nation is losing out, and our ideal of a national spirit is just a dream.... A mother should bring up her children to love their nation and mother tongue along with all the other virtues. The school should confirm and refine this love, and life itself should complete it. But how can a Slovak mother fulfill her duty when she herself lacks education, or was educated only in a foreign institute?[23]

Homola listed the various excellent schools that Slovaks had established for men, but none for women, and he contrasted this situation with the German effort to establish excellent schools for women—which then attracted Slovak girls. He attributed many of the losses Slovaks had suffered to this deficiency, and blamed Slovaks themselves for it. As a result, Slovak women became ashamed of their native tongue and in the end acquired no real education in any language.

A long editorial note by Štúr continued Homola's argument:

> As the highest and best characteristic of young ladies and women whenever we are on the subject of choosing one for marriage, we praise her above all as "a good housekeeper." That is, she knows how to keep a budget and save money. Of course, this is a good quality, but certainly at present it is too little and too low. A wife should be a good housekeeper, and a stimulating, pleasant companion and

careful, serious, cultured mother. In general, a wife should make her way among the higher things, not actively (which we are not in favor of) but at least passively.... Already, even among our women, the female sex has begun to talk of the nation, fatherland, and so on, pretending to understand these terms. But with few exceptions, these words in our women's mouths are only empty sounds, without meaning. Our women lack enough education to understand and appreciate them, and they only mouth them from others, usually a few months before and a few months after their wedding. (278)

Not unexpectedly, Lehocká herself reacted to this article with a long letter that Štúr published. For its interest and apparent uniqueness in this period (though it must have reflected the unpublished thoughts of other women), I am giving it in full.

From Liptov. It was certainly with unutterable joy that every Slovak woman read the first article in the 70th issue of our *Národňje novini* on the need for a school for young women. Overwhelmed by deep emotion, I read it and thanked God that one man of our nation feels the need for such a school, and that one voice is courageously speaking out in favor of elevating the neglected and—let me say it—humiliated souls of our Slovak sisters. At least one man has the courage to say publicly that, for the accomplishment of great national works and endeavors, women are responsible to help men. This idea is clearly expressed: "Like a person with only one hand, so our enthusiastic work to enlighten our nation is, without women—I won't say destroyed—but certainly it is only half as effective as it could be." Who would not joyfully take part in your holy works and high endeavors—not an active part, to which you say you are an enemy, but at least a passive part—when you yourselves want us at your side? Just show us the right path, teach us and cultivate our spirit yourselves since we do not have our own school. Praise God, you already have permission for revival in our dear Slovak language, so now turn its dear sounds for once to us women, who are still asleep, and you shall see how we shall awaken and gratefully follow in your footsteps.

Righteous indeed is the charge our highly respected Slovak brother Š.H. [Štefan Homola] makes against our forefathers, who established Slovak churches but did not take care to keep them, and who established schools but did not think of the flowering of their language. Indeed, they had the same right as the other nationalities in the Kingdom. The fact that they did not establish women's schools for our nation resulted also from the belief current then, and in some places even now, that women should care only about household matters, and could learn to weave and cook without an education.

Regretfuly, I must admit that often an educated man choosing his life's companion is moved, not by higher feeling, but by the lower emotion of need. He does not consider the fact that his wife should be his children's first teacher and the "implanter" of love for God and nation, of all the good virtues, in the tender breasts of his own dear children. What kind of children can come from a marriage where the father deems the mother unworthy to bring them up?

The poor little creatures scarcely become aware they are on earth with their own mother, before they are passed into the hands of a foreign, merciless nursemaid. Already their soul lives on foreign nourishment in an unnatural life. After such a miserable, sunless upbringing, these greenhorns often go off to a foreign school, so that when the young lady returns home, she does not even want to speak her own language, saying she "no longer understands it." Don't be surprised, you Slovaks, while traveling around our country, that you find this perversity everywhere, as referred to in the article on educating girls. It is understandable, because people will always turn to wherever they hope to receive greater recognition and respect, and I think this is the motive of our sex for neglecting our own language and craving foreignness. You, our Slovak brothers, are also guilty that we are what we are. God has fated you for action and given you brains and strong shoulders, but you have not acted on our behalf. You left us in contemptible blindness while you went after your own education. In a word, you sinned against us, and we are now paying you back by our incapacity for anything higher.

Thus, I will not dispute the fact that a noble-minded young Slovak man looks vainly for a young Slovak woman equal to him in feeling. But let us try to to understand why.

Dear Slovak women, forgive your sister for daring to admit our common fault, since admission of guilt is already one half of its cure. And, again, forgive my overflowing heart which cannot control itself when I read of our Polish and Czech sisters who put all their effort into becoming worthy daughters of their nations.

The editor in his note to the article also spoke a vital truth, regardless of his sex or ours, when he showed us where we could become educated Slovak women and worthy, capable teachers for our national girls' school. I have no doubt that several qualified women will be found to dedicate themselves completely to this goal. I myself would take the road with these worthy Slovak women to glorious "hundred-towered" Prague to learn her wisdom from Libuše. But bonds keep me at home, and I fear that obstacles may keep other women from realizing their desire.

Of all the relevant obstacles, I shall consider only the following: a woman wanting to educate herself in Prague must go there not just for a year, but for three to four years, because in a shorter time she cannot comprehend all the subjects taught there. (I have at hand the private outline of sciences in Dr. Amerling's lectures to girls and women, which were sent me by A.B.R. [Rajská], the foundress of the

Czech school for young girls. Therefore, I can confidently say that we Slovaks are not yet so capable as the Czech women who from infancy can move gradually through their education.) Moreover, to go to Prague for such a long time takes money, and which father or brother recognizes this need enough to sacrifice his fortune for it? Few respect the greatness of this calling, and even if such noble-minded nationalists were found, who could guarantee that such a woman returning adorned with all the capabilities of a teacher would receive her due? Don't we ourselves know many examples where, although the parents are Slovaks (and good Slovaks who are recognized as such), they nevertheless happily stuff their children's little mouths with foreign words? No matter how badly their children speak, they are still delighted, because this is the fashion now in our country. Would such a family turn its child over to a teacher who is known to teach in the Slovak spirit?

One could go on in this way, but the question is whether Slovak women are not the heirs of that sister in our fairy tale who went out all alone into the wide world to endure muteness, ridicule, and the terror of the gallows, just to free her brothers from their curse? In this case, it is a matter of the neglect and scorn of our own sister!

Well, I hope that my letter will not be held against me, nor my words considered a call for, as it is contemptuously termed, *Emancipation der Frauen*. This phrase is empty to my ears, and the Slovak heart does not respond to it because we do not even have our own words for it.

Besides, I know our vocation, I know what our nature destined us for, and I know how to esteem it. Kollár sang beautifully of this destiny in one of his sonnets: "What are stars among the creatures" and so on.[24]

Lehocká's dissociation from "emancipation" and her favorable reference to the female domestic vocation became typical of the women's movement, with both men and women. Štúr replied to Lehocká's reference to his "enmity" against the idea of an active role for women by correcting her confusion of the word *ňeprjateľja* (=enemy) with his words *ňje prjateľja* (=not favorable). Štúr's distinction, however, typified the limits on women's activity which were set by even fervent nationalists, and such limits remained a touchy point for a long time, as will be seen.

The examples of good Slovak schools given by Homola were mainly Protestant schools, but in this period Slovak Catholics were also thinking of the need for women's education. This interest occurred primarily under the influence of Štefan Moyses (1796–1869), Slovak nationalist and bishop in Banská Bystrica. He had earlier had a distinguished career helping Croation nationalists such as Janko Drašković in Zagreb and Vienna. During Moyses's time in Banská Bystrica, the Catholic gymnázium adopted the Slovak language, and his cooperation with the Slovak nationalist and Lutheran superintendent Karol Kuzmány (1806–1866) became a rare example of Slovak nonconfessionalism.

On 18 September 1852 the weekly *Cyrill a Method: Katolický časopis pre cirkev a školu* (Cyril and Method: Catholic Magazine for Church and School) carried an article on the need for Slovak education "especially for the female sex." Apparently by the editor, Michal Chrástek (1825–1900), priest and gymnázium professor, the article emphasized education to continue and deepen the Christian faith and criticized money spent on national exhibits and entertainments. But it also argued for the good effect of educated and nationally conscious mothers and said education should be both religious and national (*nábožensko-národnie*). As the best place for educating girls, Chrástek praised the convent schools taught by nuns who had chosen female education as their special vocation. Convent schools should also be a remedy against the materialism, shallowness, and frivolity of secular schools. He defended convent schools against the charge that they "taught young girls only how to say their prayers" by emphasizing the high academic quality in languages, sciences, and arts, as shown by pupils' performance on the state examinations. As an example to be followed, he cited a successful school recently founded by private donations and given to the "English Ladies" of Mary Ward, but also recommended other religious orders that were less expensive and performed nursing duties as well as teaching.[25]

A second article on education for females appeared in the same Catholic newspaper in April 1853, but primarily it complained against education that concerned only worldly fashions and manners, or that was anti-Christian and anti-Catholic. The human need for education to bring the body's physical passions under the soul's control was said to be especially great for daughters, because of their "emotionality," which must be governed for them to become good wives.[26]

A year later, *Cyrill a Method* carried an article on the great improvement over pagan societies, past and present, which Christianity had brought to women, and historically traced it to Jesus Christ having surrounded himself with good women, who alone were faithful to him at the crucifixion. Arguing that women are stronger and more constant in their faith than men, the author Ján Bílý took up the question of women as teachers, and concluded conventionally that they must teach privately at home, not in public. Nevertheless, in a strikingly modern spirit, he cited Thomas Aquinas' argument that special grace ("charisma, which had no relation to gender") might be given to women too. He drew no practical conclusions, however.[27]

The end result of these efforts to found educational institutes for girls and women was modest at best. Increasing Magyarization and the generally difficult conditions for Slovak cultural growth in the mid-nineteenth century took an especially heavy toll of potential women's activities. Men's formal education in the Slovak language was very insecure, and in this situation, what could be expected for women?

Nevertheless, private classes and self-study groups, those mainstays for oppressed groups, were continued by a few exceptional talents. For example, the minor poet Ján Capko (1846–1867) organized a women's group called *Ženská beseda* in the small town Kláštor pod Zvievom in northern Slovakia where a new Catholic gymnázium for boys had been established. After Capko's death, in gratitude the townswomen dedicated a monument to him in 1871.[28]

The women's study group about which we now know the most was the "Beseda dievčenská," founded in the northern Slovak city of Liptovský Svätý Mikuláš in 1860. It had 50–60 regular members, and besides reading literature and history the women organized fund drives for Slovak schools. Its young founder,

Marína Hodžová (1842–1921), illustrates its relation to the Štúr movement as she was the daughter of Michal Miloslav Hodža, one of the leaders of the movement and a participant in the 1848–1849 revolution. Hodžová became famous (and several poems were published in her honor) after her spirited defiance of county officials in demanding punishment of Magyarone hoodlums who had attacked her father, for which she herself was sentenced to a day of house arrest in May 1861.[29] She was a highly praised dramatic actress in the Slovak community theater movement, and she contributed news articles to magazines as well as a romantically sad poem published in 1865 and an earlier one which remained in manuscript (Appendix, Nos.68–69). According to private correspondence recently published, she experienced in 1861–1865 a hopeless, repressed love for the (married) national leader Viliam Pauliny-Tóth (1826–1877). She went to Germany for a year's study to become an accredited teacher, and on her return founded a small girls' school, but closed it in 1867 to accompany her father to his forced retirement in Silesia. After his death and Hodžová's return to Slovakia in 1870, embittered by perceived national failures she apparently stopped all nationalist activity, married, and lived quietly in Trnava and Bratislava. The suggestion by Peter Liba, editor of her correspondence, that she identified too closely with her father to be able to find a separate role for herself, seems plausible.[30]

Other study groups and private schools were as ephemeral as Hodžová's short-lived effort, including the girls' school founded by Samuel Ormis (1824–1875) as a complement to the boys' gymnázium in Revúca.[31] Most women were educated in Slovak literature and language only at home and by their own efforts. Yet the results were not totally depressing, as indicated by the cheerful praise of nationalist women by gymnázium professor A. H. Škultéty in 1862.[32] In these circumstances, the private activity of poetry writing and the easy circulation of verses among friends and extended family were probably inevitable for Štúrist women.

Women Poets: "Brides of the Nation"

For historical reasons dating from the Reformation, the Slovak literary intelligentsia in the nineteenth century was Protestant in numbers disproportionate to the general population, according to social analysis by Ján Hučko.[33] Therefore, it is not surprising that almost all of the women writers we know of were daughters or wives (or both) of nationalist Lutheran pastors and teachers. Following Martin Luther's happy marriage, Protestant theology tended to glorify marriage as a partnership in raising a good Christian family, and the pastor's wife had an honored position serving to compensate for the loss of female independence in the closed convents.[34] This "holy" family easily became construed as also a nationalist family. Steeped in the Protestant tradition of vernacular literature, many of these Slovak pastors were also inveterate scribblers, and there is anecdotal evidence of a family custom of versifying together. In this period when so few Slovak men were both educated and nationalist, their families assumed a critical role in the nation, especially for women whose education occurred primarily at home. Nationalist but celibate Catholic priests had very different households from those of Lutheran pastors and their wives. Moreover, much less research has been done on Slovak Catholic families, with almost none on the lives of nuns who may have been the counterparts of Protestant literary women, as happened in numerous Catholic countries. This gap remains to be filled.[35]

All but the earliest of the known women poets accepted and pictured the nationalist ideal, though with varying degrees of imitation of the standard symbols. About two thirds of the known poems are nationalistic, and most of the rest are more or less conventional love poems, with a few folk genres and a few religious hymns. The categories overlap, of course, and the most interesting poems are those that integrate the nationalist and love poetry. All the poems found are given in the Appendix in the original language and with available bio-bibliographical data.

The earliest known poem by a Slovak woman (after the contested attributions of baroque hymns to women of the aristocratic Czobor and Kubini families) was a long verse published in Prague in 1798. Rebeka Lešková (1773–1856) was the daughter of the Lutheran pastor and writer Martin Lauček (1732–1802) and the wife of pastor, writer, and publisher Štefan Leška (1757–1818), who was influenced by enlightenment ideas of education. Born in southeastern Slovakia, Lešková attended the Latin school in Skalica and married in 1793. Her husband had been editor of one of the first Slovak newspapers in Bratislava, where he was also an organist and choir director, but from 1784 he was a pastor among

Czech Lutherans and from 1786 the superintendent in Prague. There he worked with Czech linguists and provided a meeting place for the poetic circle of the Czech priest and nationalist Antonín Jaromír Puchmajer (1769–1820). As hostess for this circle, Lešková was known for her love of poetry at the readings and discussions of the circle, and in 1798 Puchmajer published her "Wýstraha předswůdcy wssem pannám" (A Warning to All Young Ladies against Seducers) in his *Nowé básně*. It was the only poem by a woman, and Rebeka Lešková, writing in the Czech language used by Lutherans as their liturgical and literary language, is considered the "first woman poet of the restored Czech language."[36] However, her husband returned to Hungary that same year and she no longer enjoyed such a supportive literary circle. They lived in Slovak colonies near Pest and then in Kiskőrös, where Lešková died. She collected folk songs for Šafárik and Kollár, and perhaps continued to write, but nothing is certainly known of any later work.[37]

Lešková's poem of 1798 was signed by her initials and identified as hers in 1812, erroneously attributed to a male poet in 1896, then identified as hers again in 1927, but it has scarcely been noticed by current historians though it was also set to music by the popular composer Jakub Jan Ryba.[38] Heavily moralistic but otherwise skillful, it is in places charmingly ironic even in this simple translation of several stanzas:

A Warning to All Young Ladies against Seducers
1. Beware the attentions,
Young ladies, of deceitful seducers!
Govern by your modesty,
Guard yourself against those unworthy
2. Who will skillfully tempt
Your innocent hearts to sin,
Speaking words so convincing;
Though they really ridicule you.
5. They will attract your pure eyes
From purity and light
To rancid abomination,
To darkness.
6. On a spring evening they enjoy
A walk with a young lady;
Her innocence they cleverly deceive,

To their damnable ways.

      7.In the summer when it is very hot
Together somewhere they take a nap,
And at dusk like beasts of prey
Go out on their hunt.

      10.Damned and accursed
May you be, you despoilers of virtue!
Prepare for them their condemnation,
O, you earthly judges!

      13.And those words of the Creator
Which say: Be fruitful and multiply!
They boldly twist against respectable girls,
To their misery, to their ruin.

      14.For with the dress of true love
They cloak their lechery.
Since in them, as in beasts of prey,
Lechery roars, and pretends this love.

      15.Therefore, young ladies, flee these
Seducers while you can,
And to true love give your hand:
Thus will you be happy!

      (Appendix, No.1)

With the next woman, authorship is established by contemporary statement though little else is known of her. "Mária Kubini, a young unmarried woman of Dechtáre in Liptov county," is listed by Ján Kollár among the authors known to himself in his *Národnie zpiewanky* (National Songbook, 1834–1835). Described as a "Pjseň Insurgentská," a song on the mobilization of the aristocracy, and dated 1798, Kubini's song is a facile exhortation to the young men of the author's acquaintance to ride gallantly away to war and smite the "Frenchman," following the example of their ancestors with the Hungarian kings ("králowé uherský"). If one of them should be killed, the author promises him a tombstone engraved *Hic miles quiescit*, and she will hold a ball for those who return.[39] Obviously the song is in the aristocratic military tradition (Appendix, No.2).

One other woman was identified by Kollár as an author. Little is known of Estera Šuleková's own life, but in her family were literarily active Lutheran pastors and minor gentry. Her father, the pastor Matej Šulek (1748–1815), was also a minor poet and historian, her mother Juliana Zmeškalová a member of the gentry, and her brother Gašpar (1788–1827) a professor of theology. We can see here a certain continuity with the tradition of literary activity by the gentry in the eighteenth century, because Juliana was the second cousin of Orava governor Job Zmeškal, who wrote *Sskola Jobowa* (1770), and her father Václav may have translated a German operetta.[40] Also Matej Šulek's patrons were Lorinc Kubini (?–1761), whom the genealogist Iván Nagy shows as a nephew of the attributed poet Anna Kubini,[41] and Juliana Platthy, for whose funeral Matej Šulek preached a funeral sermon in 1790. Estera Šuleková's immediate family were not strikingly nationalist, but her uncle Ján (1774–1857) wrote a Latin-Slovak grammar, his son Viliam was hanged as a Slovak revolutionary in 1848, and another son Ľudovít was a follower and friend of Štúr.[42]

Šuleková's poem is in the section of Kollár's *Národnie zpiewanky* called "city and gentry songs." Titled "Skrytý pohled lásky" (The Secret Glance of Love), it addresses a lover who has turned cold and urges him to remember her faithfulness (Appendix, No.3). A conventional love song, it is similar to other poems in the same section with male personae grieving over their lost loves. No other work by Šuleková is known, and this poem apparently attracted little attention, presumably because it did not fit the coming nationalist model.

The tradition of literary gentry was apparently carried on in 1800–1830 by four gentlewomen in central Slovakia whose manuscripts were published by Rehor Uram (1846–1924) only in 1894–1895. These poems are imitation folk songs, in the so-called *ponáška* tradition that was popular from the late eighteenth century through the nineteenth century, when it was especially cultivated by nationalists. Judita Kisely Ruttkay and Judita Ruttkay Mayer (presumably a sister-in-law or daughter) wrote seventeen verses on a variety of folk motifs (Appendix, Nos.4–21). Katarína Kisely wrote two satiric verses against lazy, spendthrift, shrewish wives (Appendix, Nos.22–23), and Terézia Vitališ wrote six verses including a longish "dialogue of two lovers" (Appendix, Nos. 24–29).[43]

All of the preceding works followed traditional poetic forms, but during the 1830's the new nationalistic model developed. Confessional, exhortative, didactic verses celebrated specifically Slovak virtues and beauties, or mourned Slovak faults and losses.

This new pattern scarcely appeared in the love poems of the young Czech women, Maria Pospíšilová and "Lidmila Tichá" in 1838, but it was explicit in J. M. Hurban's "Slowenka" in 1839 (see notes 10-11). The same new themes appeared in both male and female poetry. For example, such titles as "Dcérka a mat'" (Mother and Daughter), "Opustená" (Abandoned [female]), and "Na hrobe materi" (At One's Mother's Grave) are found in Andrej Sládkovič's collections in 1846 and 1861.

As already said, Hurban deliberately collected verses by women for his first *Nitra*, which was still in the Czech language in 1842. There he published two poems by young women named "Rosália" and "Amália," who wrote jointly "as is a custom of our dear Slovak girls" and requested anonymity. Though Hurban says he knew them, they are not identified today. The first of these simple poems is similar to the nationalistic, didactic verse written by many men of the time, as shown in the following excerpt:

> Below the Tatra Mountains blows
> A fresh and healthy breeze,
> And a Slovak song
> Angelically rings. ....
> Slovak students,
> Keep your heart true,
> And everywhere guard
> Your love for the nation. (Appendix, No.30)

The second verse is romantic and equates an unreachable white tulip in the garden to a lover who does not come to visit (Appendix, No.31). Yet perhaps one can see the lover as an implicit nationalist figure. The words *šuhag/šuhaj* (lad, which is used here) and *ginoch/junák* (young man or warrior, which are used elsewhere) are laden with Slavic connotations. This suggestion, perhaps farfetched here, becomes certain in later poems.

An explicitly nationalistic poem in the same issue of *Nitra* was signed by "Slowenka Rymawská" and titled "Slowenka" (Slovak Woman). It gives a woman's sad song comparing the state of her nation with its fate in Turkish times and regretting that women can do so little. Only recently identified, the author Zuzana Reguli Moravčíková lived in Klenovec and died on 21 March 1861 (Appendix, No.32). A second poem, "Potěšenj" (Consolation), possibly by the same woman but signed "Wlastimila Rymawská," exhorts young women to make wreaths and pray for men fighting for the nation, then if they fall, to decorate their graves and rejoice at their glorious death for their country (Appendix, No.33). A third poem by "Wlastimila" was not published until much later (see below).

The only woman to sign her work in *Nitra* was Anna Zuzana Šoltýsová, wife of the Lutheran pastor in Važec, a small town at the foot of the High Tatra mountains. As early as 1848 she was publicly known from an article in *Kwěty* about the temperance union she founded.[44] Her first poem "Žárliwost" (Jealousy) is a long (86 lines) drama about a good man's death as a result of his wife's obsessive jealousy. Though it shows sympathy for the peasantry, it has no explicit nationalism (Appendix, No.35). Her second poem "Chwála Tater" (Praise of the Tatra Mountains) is a paean to the Tatras for their obstructive wildness that keeps out foreigners and protects the Slovaks—again a theme that was common among the Štúrists (Appendix, No.36). Šoltýsová published two other short verses, "Zradná straka" (The Traitor Raven) and "Ňespravedlivá hana" (Unjust Pursuit), in a popularizing calendar with primarily an educational purpose in 1849. They are close to folk literature and may have been offered as collected verses, not originals (Appendix, Nos.37–38).

The other two poems of a woman author in the first *Nitra* were by "Miloslawa," who was quickly identified as Johana Lehocká. Her first poem, "Podkřiwánský wlastenec" (Patriot near Mount Kriváň), describes a young man with a lyre sitting in romantic despair, "His dark eyes tearful" and "His heart bleeding." As he prays that his death may be recompensed by honor to his nation, the black clouds suddenly part, and from Mount Kriváň comes a maiden/muse to place a wreath upon his brow (Appendix, No.39). Lehocká's second poem, "Slowenka," is a sonnet that asks

> How could I not be a Slovak woman?
> Why, I was born under a linden tree,
> A Slovak mother nursed me,
> And taught me to be a true patriot.

It ends with her promise: "I would instead tear my heart from my body,/ If I had to separate from you,/ Or betray you, my nation!" (Appendix, No.40)

Three poems by Lehocká were prepared in 1843 for the planned second volume of *Nitra* that was not passed by the censor.

The first, "Hrob" (Grave), a romantic meditation at her mother's grave, was rewritten by Hurban into the newly codified Slovak language and published in the *Nitra* of 1844, which became the first book published in the newly codified Slovak (Appendix, No.41a,41b). Though "Hrob" may have been a real elegy, it resonates with the symbolism of Mother Sláva, and an orphan separated from its mother became a common trope in many later poems about the Slovaks' plight.

Lehocká's other two poems, "Sen" (Dream), and "Ljpa" (Linden Tree), remained in manuscript until 1965 (Appendix, Nos.42–43), because they could not meet the conditions of the censor, which were more severe than with the first *Nitra*. As Brtáň summarizes these rules,

> It was not allowed to refer to Slovakia as a separate homeland because there existed only one united homeland (Hungary); Slovak nationality could not be referred to in opposition to Magyar nationality; there could be no reference to "renegades"; and generally there could be nothing that would arouse bad feeling.[45]

Lehocká's "Sen" pictured a flag for "King and Slavic Rights," and her "Ljpa" spoke of oppression and sorrow, so they obviously could be suppressed. Another short melancholy love poem, "Peseň labutia" (Swan Song), which appeared with the pseudonym "Želmíra" in Hurban's *Slovenské pohľady* after Lehocká's death, has been attributed to her (Appendix, No.44).

Two other poems written by women for the planned second *Nitra* remained unpublished. "Hlas Nitranky" (The Voice of a Nitra Woman) by "Wlastimila" (presumably the same woman in the first *Nitra*) emphasizes the duty of Slovak girls to love the nation in general and brave young Slovak nationalists in particular:

> Handsome are the young men
> Who love Sláva,
> And these nationalists
> Deserve love.
>
> Our pure love,
> And their just actions,
> Will surely raise
> Nitra to its golden glory. (Appendix, No.34)

The word "Nitra" probably means both the historic city, which was for the Štúrists a symbol of former Slovak glory that must be regained, and Hurban's magazine *Nitra*. "Žalost a potěcha Nitranky" (Despair and Comfort of a Nitra Woman) by "Ľudmila K" also exhorts Slovak girls to love only men who stand by their nation," not "unworthy, shameless renegades" (Appendix, No.45).

Hurban and Štúr published at least four more poems in this period, but the pseudonyms are undecifered. "Pjeseň" by "Slovenka Sitňjanska" in Štúr's *Orol tatránski* in 1846 praises the valley she lives in, urges her sisters to sing Slovak songs, and promises their love to a "junák" (Appendix, No.46). "Smútok" (Sorrow) by "Sofia z Oravi" expresses romantic yearning for an absent lover with the folk elements typical of the Štúrists:

> The lilac blooms below our house,
> What's lilac to me, when I've no one to give it to?
> The red rose smells so sweet,
> What's a rose to me, when I feel no peace?
> I pick a sprig of rosemary to put in a jar,
> What's rosemary to me, when I have no Janko?
> (Appendix, No.47)

Presumably the same woman, now signed only "Žofia," published two nationalist poems in Hurban's *Nitra*, 3 (1846). "Slávnosť jara" (Spring Celebration) has six stanzas calling Slovak sisters to make wreaths for the nature goddess Vesna, their countrymen, and their "dear mother," i.e. Mother Sláva (Appendix, No.48). The second poem, "Slovenkám" (To Slovak Women), makes the allusion explicit by a call to Slovak women to awaken from their long sleep and join their mother, who has fainted from despair over abandonment by her children (Appendix, No.49).

In the same period numerous poems were written for and about women by men using a female persona. Hurban's "Slowenka" published by Pospíšil in 1839 had used "we" (e.g. "Slowenky gsme krásné") and his "Slowenka" for *Nitra* in 1842 begins "My homeland is Slavia, I am a Slovak woman."[46] The minor Štúrist writer Bohuslav Nosák (1818–1877) also had a "Slowenka" in *Nitra* in 1842 with the poetic persona "we Slovak women, endearing sisters" who exhort each other to cheer the grieving Mother Sláva, love only their brother Slovaks, and adore their great family of Slavs.[47] Although both men signed their full names to these poems, certain later critics suspected Hurban of "mystification," i.e.

deception, in the belief that women could not have written the poems he published with feminine pseudonyms.[48] This doubt seems to rest more on the rarity of women's writing than on any known evidence against their authorship.

Besides these poetic female figures, another kind of Slovak heroine was shown in the play *Dobrovol'níci* (Volunteers, 1854) by Ján Chalupka (1791–1871), a lyceum professor and Lutheran pastor in central Slovakia. Of two young women patriots, one is a quiet girl determined to keep her Slovak name despite her father's change to a Magyar form, and the other is an energetic heroine who succeeds in rescuing her lover and other revolutionaries from prison and defending them with a bayonetted rifle.[49] Although such a masculine heroine had counterparts in real life, e.g. Jana Bóriková Hrebendová (1812–1880), authors usually pictured women only in their domestic roles.

An exception was the story "Ani to čert nevymyslí, Čo žena má v svojej mysli!" (Even the Devil Can't Figure Out What Goes on in a Woman's Mind!), by the prolific writer Daniel Bachát (1840–1906). Published in 1862, it is a conventional story of lovers' misfortune, but interestingly the heroine "Miloslava" writes and publishes love poetry in Slovak. Clearly she is offered as an example for Slovak girls.[50]

One of the most interesting writers was Karolina Puliny (? –1888), whose eight known verses reflect her unfortunate life and her strong national feeling. As an adolescent suffering the loss of both parents at once, she "became dumb" and from then on used her writing as her main outlet. During the period of her known poems—1861 to 1868—she lived with her sister, wife of Štefan Homola, the Lutheran pastor whose advocacy of education for women in 1846 was summarized above. Puliny's earliest published poems are two hymns in the Biblical Czech language which follow the long tradition of hymn writing seen with the attributed Baroque authors Anna Czobor and Žofia and Anna Kubini. The first stanza of each of her two hymns show this nature:

> Harsh are the paths of earthly life,
> Along which Divine power leads us,
> Weeping and laments resound everywhere,
> Wherever I turn sadness awaits me....
>
> (Appendix, No.50)
> Jesus, dear Lord,

> In You I place my hopes,
> In Your almighty protection alone
> Can I find help;
> [To me] fatigued by suffering,
> Depressed by battling illness,
> Under the weight of swooning,
> You thus give refreshment. (Appendix, No.51)

This religious feeling was easily transferred to Puliny's poems about the sickness of her nation, as in this one printed in 1861 and titled from the first line "Žalostne sa dívam":

> Despairingly I watch in the wide world
> The oppression of my dear nation.
> Wherever a dear Slavic voice resounds,
> A tyrannical enemy torments it;
> Angry envy sows discord,
> Dear peace turns into ceaseless fights....
> You shall have help from God, dearest Slávia!
> You too shall sometime bloom like a lovely rose.
> Your son will not boast of dead treasures,
> But heroically achieve a spiritual foundation....
> Fervent prayer from honest hearts
> Is always heard by the Almighty.
> So I too fall on my knees before Him
> And evening and morning ask only this:
> May mighty God dwell with you, my dear nation,
> And crown with success your great efforts.
> (Appendix, No.54)

Unlike most women's verses of this time, Puliny has more specific detail than general laments, as in "Milá bola i mne", which is given here in full.

Dear to Me Too

> Dear to me too was the Magyar tongue,
> As long as our Slovak tongue suffered not,
> As long as pressures and wild brutalities
> And cruelties were not falling upon it;
>
> But as the show of contempt began,
> The repression of other nationalities,
> The agitation of enemies against it:
> Innocent blood just had to rebel.

Thousands of voices arose:
"I want nothing to do with that Slovak herd,
The Slavic language is a laboring tongue,
Not for masters, only for servants."

Born into the Slavic family,
Grown up in Slavic country,
The turncoat now conceitedly claims
He can't understand the Slavic tongue.

This heretic son will only say:
"Let the Slovak herd die out,
No need to give it freedom's rights,
We must glorify the Magyar tongue."

What must the heart of a Slovak feel
At the speech of this wiseacre?
Bitter regrets for such falseness,
Fervent love for one's own tongue.
                    (Appendix, No.53)

In 1868 Puliny wrote a longer (22 octameter lines) allegorical poem, "Pravda" (Truth), that showed a sense of the classical tradition of allegorical irony and satire (Appendix, No.56), and an aphoristic verse "'Čas vše mení'" (Time Changes All):

    Time Changes All
The dedication of a true Slavic man,
    No time or terror will change;
The loyalty to her nation of a true Slovak woman,
    No time or tempest will change;
The character and purity of the Slovak nation,
    No oppressor will change. (Appendix, No.57)

A spinster invalid like a minor Elizabeth Barrett, Puliny used no pseudonyms, and often the editors praised her literary accomplishments in notes to her poems. Yet little else is known of her.

Poems by men about women also continued. A satiric verse "Moderná Slovenka" (A Modern Slovak Woman, 1860) by Janko Čajak (1830–1867) ridiculed women's national fickleness:

    A Modern Slovak Woman
She is a Slovak during the week,
    But a German on Sunday;
She wears a bodice during the week,
    But a crinoline on holidays.

In Slovak she orders flour,
In that tongue she knows the weights,
But with guests from higher society,
"Mit wos kan i dínen!"[51]

Numerous women seem to have published only one or two poems, then ceased writing; those we can trace wrote mainly while young. Their verses are usually nationalistic with romantic elements, and many were published in the journals edited by Viliam Pauliny-Tóth.

Amália Launer, as a sixteen-year old girl in Krupina, corresponded with Pauliny-Tóth, who published her "Potecha" (Consolation) in 1861 and "Sokol" (Falcon) in 1862 (Appendix, Nos.58–59). A. Emília Rumanová signed her name to two poems in 1861 before marrying the nationalist writer Daniel Bachát, who later became the Lutheran superintendent in Budapest (Appendix, No.60–61). Four other poems by "Milina" are also tentatively attributed to her (Appendix, Nos.62–65), and the last one, if hers, would mean Rumanová Bachátová returned to poetry in 1879 after a long pause. In this poem, "Šuhajovi" (To a Young Man), the author first praises him, then finds him weak in national matters, and scorns him (Appendix, No.65). Marína Hodžová's two known poems were mentioned earlier (Appendix, Nos.66–67). Pauliny-Tóth also published a romantically sad poem "Moja láska" (My Love) by "Zlatina," and a balladic treatment of the folk motif of the snake as a threat to virginity in "Rada matkyná" (A Mother's Advice) by "Anička" (Appendix, Nos. 68–69) in 1862. The latter ballad conceivably shows nationalist symbolism in the mother's advice to her daughter to prefer the Slavic "sokolík" over the snake. "Mína Kováč" is unknown other than for "Na Sylvestra" (On New Year's Eve) in 1862 (Appendix, No.70). "Sirota na hrobe matkinom" (An Orphan at Her Mother's Grave) in 1862 was signed by "Opustená" (Deserted) (Appendix, No.72).

The most surprising poem is the harshly satiric "Milá – milému" (Lover [female] to Lover [male]), which uses all the classic animal comparisons to sarcastically describe a Magyarone lover: "a mouth like a gate, as bent as a drum, teeth like shovels, ears like a donkey, eyes like a tomcat, cheeks like an old rag" (Appendix, No.71). The name "Tomónia Haff," otherwise unknown, is likely a pseudonym, and quite possibly the author was a male.

In 1866 a new but short-lived magazine for youth, *Junoš*, published in Budapest by Ján Nepomuk Bobula (1844–1905), who was apparently a Catholic, printed two short poems by "Milina Lohinský," who has not been identified (Appendix, Nos.73–74). A similarly melancholy poem was signed "Hronka" but had a female persona (Appendix, No. 75).

Otherwise unidentified, Emília Vadászfy wrote an amateurish poem about rude treatment of Slovaks, "Ohlas zo Spyša" (A Voice from the Spis Region) in 1866 (Appendix, No.76). A woman known only as "Eva z pod Baby" responded in 1866 with sisterly encouragement to Vadászfy (Appendix, No.77). In another poem by "Eva," "Národní veniec" (National Wreath), the metaphor of lilies of the valley, violets, and red "smrkalôčky" [spruce buds?] woven together into a wreath of the national colors, turns into a symbol of Slovak sisterhood:

> You [flowers] are three dear sisters,
> I'll weave you into one wreath.
> Mother Nature gave you life,
> Gave you sweet odors to drink,
> You live together as one sapling,
> You get along so well together.
> Dear daughters of Mother Sláva!
> Let us take this as our model:
> From these pure, dear flowers,
> Learn how to live sister with sister.
> One mother gave us life,
> And nursed us with Slavic milk,
> Let us love one another, be true to ourselves,
> Let us not be divided.... (Appendix, No.78)

Despite the conventionality of references to the Slavic family, one can read the poet's emphasis upon sisterhood as a feminist element encouraged by nationalism. Her other two poems showed a similar emphasis upon sisterhood (Appendix, Nos.79–80). One of them, "Naša vd'aka" (Our Thanks), welcomed the formation of the women's organization Živena in 1869, which is treated in the next chapter.

A different extension of traditional nationalist symbols occurred in several poems. In "Dumka" (Meditation) by "Marína z pod Kohúta" in 1867, the last lines create an explicit parallel between nation (*národ*, masculine gender) and lover. Such a parallel had probably been implicit in all of the poems which identified a heroic young man as Slavic, e.g. from the Czech Maria Pospíšilová's "Sen" and "Ginocha žel" in 1838 and Johana Lehocká's "Podkřiwánský wlastenec" in 1842, right up to the poems treated here. This parallel, of course, is simply the obverse of Kollár's equation of Mína to the Slavic race and Sládkovič's equation of Marína to the Slovaks. Yet it represents a startling, even daring, change from the passively inspirational woman to one who actively creates a symbol of the man she desires.

This "Marína" has apparently not been identified but was presumably associated with the town of Revúca. The poem is given in full:

   Meditation
Blow little breeze, evening breeze,
Blow away my deep despair,
Take away on your wings
The sighs of my yearning soul.
The rose bush is turning green,
Its lovely bud is partly opened,
When will you blossom
Into a full-blown rose, covered by love? —
   In Revúca town
   The dawn is coming
   And the Slovak companions
   Merrily sing.
   A lad and lassie,
   Merrily sing
   Like merry birds
   Below Muráň Castle.
Ah, in our country too
Souls are coming of age
As now merrily
They sing Slovak songs.
The merry lads
Sing and leap,
Because they are ringing out
The nation's hangman;
But the yearning maiden
Asks for doubled [joy]:
Her nation glorified

And paradise with her lover. (Appendix, No.81) "Marína" is asking for paradise for herself—she is neither an inspiration to her lover/spouse à la Kollár, nor a domestic "helpmeet" for him.

This fact differentiates the poem from the male voices constantly exhorting Slovak women to help the nation as wives and mothers. Such exhortations were even dropped into prose fiction, e.g. by Daniel Bachát, whose story "Ľudmilka" in 1868 began on the following sermonizing note:

> Our *Národní hlásnik* is calling the hour at dawn for the nation, the hour of resurrection. It calls the hour not to men alone but also women, not to our young warriors alone but also our young virgins. For if our nation does not reach a higher level as a whole, the hour of our resurrection will not sound. Dear virgins, our daughters of the Tatras, give your hands to our young warriors, and we shall become more than we have ever been. For your entertainment and instruction, let me tell you the story of pretty Ľudmilka.[52]

Bachát intended a real Slovak hero for his heroine, and most women's love poems also seem directed to real males, or at least imagined ones. The symbolism of nation and male lover, however, was evoked in at least two later poems, as seen below.

Conventional imagery continued too. "Radosť Slovenky" (Joy of a Slovak Woman) by "K—š" appeared in 1867 (Appendix, No.82). Oľga "Sládkovičová," actually Braxatorisová, published three nationalistic poems in 1868–1871 (Appendix, Nos.95–97). The eldest daughter of the poet Andrej Braxatoris Sládkovič, she married Ján Mocko (1843–1911), a Lutheran pastor who was himself literarily very active, and she continued to write occasional journalistic pieces. In 1868–1869 seven verses were published by Ľudmila Kulišková. Printed in a section of *Sokol* called "Literary Beginnings," they include a melancholy description of a village funeral called "Všetko sa minie" (All Things Pass Away) (Appendix, No.98), and four poems named for the seasons to sketch an unsuccessful love affair (Appendix, Nos.101–104). Her other two verses have typical nationalist themes: the Tatra eagle as protector of the Slavs in "Na orla" (On the Eagle) and pride in being a Slovak girl in "Slovenka" (Appendix, Nos.99–100). These were apparently her only verses, though she also translated two pieces from Russian.

More consistent and sustained than any one else in this period was Zuzína Ružena Zajacová Lojková (1848–1886), who usually signed her full name and who continued publishing after her marriage to G. Hostivít Lojko (1843–1871), a nationalist professor of history and languages at the Slovak gymnázium in Revúca. He apparently was especially supportive to women, perhaps in part because his mother, Zuzanna Marčeková, was a "well-known nationalistic woman" according to his obituary.[53]

Lojková started with two short comic poems about village lovers in 1867 (Appendix, Nos.83–84). Her first serious poem, "Dumka" (Meditation), extends the nation/lover parallel seen in the earlier anonymous "Dumka," and correlates this love to physical nature in a much more complex way than we have yet seen. To indicate this interplay, which depends upon an inflected language, I have used the archaic familiar second person singular pronoun "thou" to distinguish the lover from the nation and from the several personifications of physical nature:

> Meditation
> I love the nation, I love thee,
> What else do I need?
> It's an honor to love the nation,
> To love thee, darling — the same!
> Musings [*dumky*] of mine, do not betray me,
> Don't betray who entertains you;
> Musings, love the nation openly,
> But love my darling — love him secretly.
> You slender, lovely blossoms,
> Why do you look so sad?
> By chance, is it the evening breeze
> That you are longing for?
> The sun is slipping behind the peak,
> The quiet breeze begins to stir:
> Blossoms, you're at once already gay?
> No longer are you wilted,
> Your delight has come,
> For which you yearned so long!
> Here already is your sister,
> The silent — the cool dew;

And wafting to you through the valley,
Is your longed-for one, your darling one!
Here with you I gladly spend my time,
When I'm brooding in despair:
For you — my dear nation,
Secondly for thee — my darling!
Musings of mine, fly grandly,
Glorify the nation resoundingly,
Magnify its beauty,
While still there's time enough!
Nature is asleep — refreshing itself.
Of me, I wonder, does my darling dream?
It's better for thee to sweetly dream sweet dreams,
Than for me to live in this desert foreign!
(Appendix, No.85)

This poem was followed (now with her married name) by an aphoristic quatrain advising a daughter that the rose's beauty fades, in "Zmena" (Changes) (Appendix, No.89), and four long poems. One of the four is a love poem, "Pierko kvetov" (A Nosegay, i.e. a trophy for a lover's hat) (Appendix, No.86); one is a conventional lament over a mother's grave, "Sirota" (Orphan) (Appendix, No.88); and one is a balladlike account of a poor family killed by lightning, "Hrom" (Thunder) (Appendix, No.90). Only "Vzdych" (Sigh) has an explicitly nationalist theme, ending "Good night to you, my nation!/ Lord, protect — save your people!" (Appendix, No.87). In 1872 Lojková published four poems, three of them nationalistic laments (Appendix, Nos.91–93), and one, "Lúčenie" (Farewell), an elegy for her late husband which is kept personal without nationalist symbolism (Appendix, No.94).

In 1868–1869 three long works by "Slovenka zpod Choča" were published in two new organs of the liberal democratic group that was usually called the New School. Edited by Ján Nepomuk Bobula, these periodicals are generally considered progressive, but the poems are not noticeably different from other nationalistic poems by women (Appendix, Nos.105–111). The first is a series of five poems with the same refrain about finding one's happiness in the Slavic lands by the Tatras (Appendix, Nos.105–109), and the rest on the Slavic family theme. In 1869 Bobula's almanach *Minerva* published an interesting philosophical poem "Try žitia hodiny" (Three Hours [= Stages] of Life) by Anna Philadelphi, the wife of a Lutheran pastor and minor writer, Moric Philadelphi (1834–1905). The stages of life are compared to the budding, blossoming, and fading of a rose (Appendix, No.112). A second poem by Philadelphi is a nationalistic exhortation "K sestrám slovenským" (To Slovak Sisters) which celebrates the founding of Živena and the Matica (Appendix, No.113).

There are puzzling biographical questions about Mária Praisinger, whose one known poem "Slovenkám" (To Slovak Women) in 1869 welcomed the women's organization Živena, which was then being formed (see Chapter 3). Like two of the preceding poems, this poem changed the standard Slavic family symbolism of mothers, sisters, and brothers, into a lover/nation symbol. But Praisinger, apparently a Catholic unlike most if not all the other women poets found, goes further and suggests a "national bride" who should marry the nation itself, not a nationalist Slovak man. She is no longer thinking of a male at all, but a mystical spouse. The poem is given in full.

To Slovak Women
Oh, Slovak women, sisters, let us listen to *Hlásnik*
When it calls us to work, to join the men at the steam engine,
Though not to pound rocks, or build gables:
But to love our nation and support his rights.
Slovak women, Slovak women, dear darling sisters,
Become the noble-minded young brides of the nation!
Why don't you want him as your bridegroom
Who sighs so painfully for your love?
Let us eagerly nestle close to him,
And there we'll find our honorable brother warriors!
In him we find everything, except that vanity
Which is adored by nations out in the wide world.
So let us daughters become vain only of this,
That we be worthy of his love and trust,
That we desire him, that we love him,
That we be mindful of working for his glory.
Let us go then, all, to where our *Hlásnik* calls us:
And follow him to Martin, into the women's circle dance
(Appendix, No.114)

It does not seem too extreme to compare this idea of the "bride of the nation" to the Catholic concept of the nun as the bride of

Christ. Despite the very strong Protestant presence in Slovak nationalism, the idea of celibacy as a sacrifice for the nation has a noticeable historical basis, because several members of the Štúrist movement, including Štúr himself, refused marriage in favor of "fuller freedom to serve the nation."[54] This ideal periodically resurfaced among other Protestants, as will be seen in Chapters 4 and 6 when we consider the spinster nationalist heroine in prose fiction.

Not all love poems carried nationalist tones, however, even among strongly nationalist women. Klema Augustiny Ruppeldtová (1850–1926) wrote two conventional love poems in 1872 and a third in 1886 (Appendix, Nos.115–117). She remained an active nationalist but with no further literary work.

Of all these women writers, only Zuzína Lojková continued to write during most of her life. Though apparently no longer writing poetry, in the early 1880s she wrote moralistic children's stories before her early death as still a young woman of thirty-nine in 1886.[55] She too must have felt the stress of household duties and Magyar pressure against the gymnázium in Revúca where her husband was a professor, and his early death in 1871 must have brought financial and family problems. Why did she persist in her writing when other women did not? Was it because her husband had been especially supportive to women writers? Besides apparently encouraging his wife, he had sent poems by Karolina Puliny to *Sokol* with a sympathetic note about her difficult life (see Appendix, Nos.50–57). As was said with "Marína z pod Kohúta," Revúca was a center of literary activity at this time, and a group of women and girls may well have been writing together and supporting each other. Detailed biographical study can perhaps answer such questions and contribute to our understanding of why one woman persisted as a writer while another did not.

At any rate, in the next generation numerous women appeared who continued to write throughout their lives. One was Terézia Medvecká Vansová (1857–1942), whose career began with six conventional poems in 1872 (Appendix, Nos.118–123) before she turned to prose fiction, as did all of the major women writers.[56] The poetic tradition was carried on primarily by Ľudmila Riznerová Podjavorinská (1872–1951), whose higher literary quality was apparent in her first poems in 1887, but she too wrote much prose fiction. The trend from poetry to prose reflected the general trend from romanticism to realism occurring everywhere at this time. Moreover, women's opportunities were increasing, and in Slovakia new opportunities arose from organizational changes in public life. These changes are the subject of the next chapter.

NOTES

1. Barbara Corrado Pope, "The Influence of Rousseau's Ideology of Domesticity," *Connecting Spheres*, ed. Marilyn J. Boxer and Jean H. Quataert (New York: Oxford U P, 1987) 136–145.

2. Samuel Rožnay, "Plésáné, in *Na lutnu,* 85–56. Rožnay was a very young student when he wrote these verses, which are among his little original work in a life devoted to highly praised translation from the classics and several Slavic languages. He studied at Tubingen University, became a gymnázium teacher and Lutheran pastor, but died young; see *Encyklopédia slovenských spisovateľov*, 1: 84–85. It seems likely that he would know of Rebeka Lešková's work published in 1798 and perhaps also the gentrywomen's verses of that same time (see below).

3. Laszlo Deme, "Writers and Essayists and the Rise of Magyar Nationalism in the 1820s and 1830s," *Slavic Review*, 43 (Winter 1984): 638–639.

4. The book is now very rare. The original German version (which I have not seen) is listed in the Bibliothèque Nationale in Paris as *Ein Wort an Iliriens hochherzige Tochter, uber die ältere Geschichte und neueste literarische Regeneration ihres Vaterlandes, vom Grafen Janko Drašković*. Agram, E. Hirschfeld, 1838. I have used the Czech version lent by Yale University Library: *Staršī dějepis a nejnowějšī literarní obnowa národu ilirského* (Prague: Jar. Pospíšil, 1845) 72 pp. Neither this book nor other forms of interest in women's part in the national movement are mentioned in treatments of Drašković and the Croatian national movement. See Francis H. Eterovich, ed., *Croatia: Land, People, Culture*, 2 vols. (Toronto: U of Toronto P, 1970) 1: 274, 2: 276, and Despala-

tovic's much more detailed treatment, 71–75, 94, 104, 115. This fact exemplifies the extent to which historians, even female ones, have not considered women's activities as national activities.

5. Karel Ignac Villani, "Wlastenkynym k Nowému Roku," *Kwěty*, 5 (January 1838): 5. Though a baron of an old Italian family which had settled in Rudolf Hapsburg's court in Prague, Villani became a fervent Czech nationalist who participated in the 1848 revolution and was elected to the Czech parliament. *Kwěty* published his first verse in 1836.

6. Jarmila Tkadlečková-Vantuchová, *Živena--spolok slovenských žien* (Bratislava: Epocha, 1969) 15–17.

7. *Zborník materiálov*; see also Introduction, n.9, 10.

8. This "diplomová práca," which was found by Marianna Mináriková during final review of Chapter 2 and the Appendix, is useful on the other arts but on literature is much less detailed than our study: Anna Mikušťáková, "Žena v slovenskej literatúre (Literárne a kultúrno-umelecké počiatky ženského hnutia na Slovensku)," Education Faculty in Nitra, Czechoslovakia, 1987, 148 pp.

9. Jozef Miloslav Hurban, *Cesta Slováka k slovanským bratom na Moravu a v Čechách, 1839* (Pest 1841; Bratislava: Slovenské vydavateľstvo krásnej literatúry, 1960) 22.

10. Hurban, "Slowenka," *Kwěty* 6.32 (5 May 1839): 181.

11. The two poems by Maria appeared in *Kwěty* 5 (1838): 65, 351. On their identification, see Hurban's *Cesta Slováka*, 195 n. The poem "Zdálená" (Distant) by Lidmila Tichá, who is otherwise unknown to me, appeared in *Kwěty*, 5.11 (15 March 1838): 81. It is primarily a love poem but uses the nationalist word *otčina*.

12. Hurban, ed., *Nitra: Dar dcerám a synům Slovenska, Moravy, Čech a Slezska* 1 (1842): 295. See poems Nos.30–33, 35–36, and 39–40 in the Appendix.

13. Extant manuscripts for the planned volume in 1843 were published with radically modernized texts by Rudo Brtáň, "Torzo Hurbanovej Nitry 1843," *Slovenská literatúra* 12.5 (1965): 597–530. See poems Nos.34, 41a, 42, 43, and 45 in the Appendix.

14. Eugen Klementis, ed., "Listy Johany Miloslavy Lehockej Bohuslave Rajskej a Samoslavovi Bohdanovi Hroboňovi," *Literárny archív* 7 (1970): 143. Lehocká is the only early woman poet treated in this chapter who is listed in the *Encyklopédia slovenských spisovateľov* (Bratislava: Obzor, 1984) 2: 381–382.

15. Flóra Kleinschnitzová, "O Johane Miloslave Lehockej," *Živena* 23 (1933): 137. Kleinschnitzová's various publications on Lehocká were collected as *Z našej romantiky* and republished in Bratislava in 1958, but I have cited the original version here.

16. Letter by Ľudovít Štúr of 11 September 1842, in Kleinschnitzová, *Z našej romantiky* 131.

17. Cited by Kleinschnitzová, *Živena* 136–137.

18. Hurban, "Opis Liptova," *Nitra* 4 (1847): 38–39.

19. As an exception among the Štúrists, Lehocký came from a gentry family; see Jozef Novák, *Rodové erby na Slovensku II* (Bratislava: Osveta, 1986) 88–89.

20. See Klementis 149-150. Rajská's Czech-language school was short-lived and became a German school shortly after she left it to be married.

21. The newspaper was approved and begun on 1 August 1845, but continued only to the revolution, ending on 15 June 1848.

22. Obituary, *Slovenské noviny* 1 (1 January 1850): 4.

23. Štefan Homola, "Ústavi pre vichovávaňja ďjevčat," *Slovenskje národňje novini* 70 (31 March 1846): 277.

24. Lehocká, "Z Liptova," *Slovenskje národňje novini* 83 (1846): 330–331. Her reference to having at hand the outline for Amerling's lectures in Prague is explained by her fourth letter in Klementis, where it is clear that Rajská sent her the outline as part of the effort (unsuccessful) to help her set up a similar girls' school in Slovakia.

25. Michal Chrástek, "Nekoľko slóv o vychovávaní vúbec, a zvlášte pohlavia ženského," *Cyrill a Method* 1.37 (18 September 1852): 299–300, and 1.38 (25 September 1852): 309–311. The article is unsigned, but Rizner (2: 210) lists it for the editor.

26. Ján Mallý, "Vzdělanosť se zvláštním ohledem na ženské pohlaví," *Cyrill a Method* 2.18 (30 April 1853): 136–139. The author was identified by Rizner (3: 143) as Mallý (1829–1902).

27. Jan Ev. Bílý, "Osud ženy v pohanstvu a ve křesťanstvu," *Cyrill a Method* 3.5 (1854): 34–36.

28. See Jaroslav Zniovský [pseud.?], "Z Kláštore pod Znievom," *Orol*, 2.11 (30 November 1871): 352.

29. See Zora Jesenská, "O Maríne Hodžovej," *Živena* 31 (1941): 142–144, and Tkadlečková-Vantuchová 18. Andrej Sládkovič, Ján Botto, Daniel Bachát, and others wrote poems in honor of Hodžová.

30. Peter Liba's introduction and notes to Hodžová's letters give the most detailed treatment of her peculiar life, *Listy Maríny M. Hodžovej Viliamovi Paulinymu-Tóthovi* (Martin, 1965). See also Liba's *Listy Viliama Pauliny-Tótha Maríne Hodžovej* (Bratislava, 1961). Hodžová's obituary by Klementina Augustiny Ruppeldtová suggests that the persecution witnessed and shared by Marína as her father's secretary finally shattered her optimism, in "Marína Hodžová," *Zivena* 11.3 (1921): 57–58.

31. See Tomáš Srogoň, *Samuel Ormis: Život a dielo* (Bratislava: Slovenské pedagogické nakladateľstvo, 1976).

32. A. H. Krčméry, "Hlas k dcerám Slovenska," *Sokol*, 1.10 (1862): 390–392.

Women in the Štúrist Tradition 65

33. See Ján Hučko, *Sociálne zloženie a pôvod slovenskej obrodenskej inteligencie* (Bratislava: Veda, 1974) 24, 48, passim.

34. See Roland H. Bainton, *Women of the Reformation in Germany and Italy* (Minneapolis: Augsberg Publishing House, 1971) 7–14.

35. Bio-bibliographical sources have few or no data on most women writers, though the *Slovenský biografický slovník* now being published is improving this situation. Ľudovít V. Rizner lists most of the works treated here in his *Bibliografia písomníctva slovenského*, 6 vols. (Martin: Matica slovenská, 1929). Corrections and additions were prepared by Ján Mišianik, *Bibliografia slovenského písomníctva do konca XIX. stor. (Doplnky k Riznerovej bibliografii)*, 2nd ed. (Martin: Matica slovenská, 1971) and by Ján Ormis, *Doplnky a opravy k Riznerovej bibliografii* (Martin: Matica slovenská, 1972). Anna Mikušťáková's lists of girls who sent riddles and puzzles to Pauliny-Tóth's *Sokol* (40–52) and of women who were active in the community theater movement (114–123) probably provide clues to those women writers who signed only pseudonyms.

36. Václav Jílek, "R – a L – ová v Puchmajerových 'Nových básnich' z r. 1798 je Rebeka Lešková," *Listy filologické*, 54 (1927): 267-270. See also *Slovenský biografický slovník*, 3: 393. Lešková's sister Zuzana Laučeková (married to Ján Šafárik) collected folk songs for Kollár.

37. Jan B. Čapek suggests that Lešková wrote or at least inspired an anonymous poem with the same theme and rhyme scheme, "Napomenutí mladému diewczeti" (Admonition to a Young Girl) in *Vídeňské noviny* in 1816; see Čapek's *Československá literatura toleranční 1781–1861*, Vol. 1 (Prague, 1933) 221–223.

38. Bohuslav Tablic identified it as Lešková's in his *Poezye*, Vol. 4, but Jaroslav Vlček arbitrarily or carelessly identified it as Tablic's; see Jílek, 268.

39. Ján Kollár, *Národnje zpiewanky*, 2 vols. (Budapest, 1834–1835) 1: 55. The name Mária is relatively rare in the Kubini family, and the author is probably not directly descended from Žofia's and Anna Kubini's brothers, although these families lived near each other in the central Liptov valley, according to the genealogical

tables of Iván Nagy, *Magyarország családai*. Vol. 6 (Budapest, 1859): 478–496 and other sources (work in progress). Kollár's list of the song collectors who helped him gather over two thousand songs shows 88 men and 21 women — a not inconsiderable number of women in 1835. Most of the songs were anonymous folk songs, but of the four authors Kollár listed, two were women: i.e. Mária Kubini and Estera Šuleková.

40. See Rudo Brtáň, "Z kultúrnej a literárnej činnosti Mikulášťanov a Liptákov v 16.–18. storočia," *Liptovský Mikuláš* (Liptovský Mikuláš, 1968) 108–109.

41. See Nagy, 6: 481.

42. See the references on the Šulek family in Rizner (2: 264–267) and on Ľudovít and Matej in *Encyklopédia slovenských spisovateľov*, 2: 175.

43. Rehor Uram, ed., "Zemianskí veršovníci slovenskí," *Slovenské pohľady*, 14–15 (1894–1895): exact pages in the Appendix. Several male gentry of the same families composed similar songs that Uram also published.

44. *Kwěty*, 5.16 (1838); cited by Rizner (5:235) and Liba, *Listy Hodžovej* 13, but we could not find this information.

45. The censor's conditions are cited in Brtáň, "Torzo Nitry" 513.

46. J. M. Hurban, "Slowenka," *Nitra*, 1 (1842): 168–169.

47. Bohuslav Nosák, "Slowenka," *Nitra*, 1 (1842): 162–165.

48. See, for example, Štefan Krčméry 2: 83, and Brtáň, "Torzo Nitry" 512.

49. The play was published in Vienna after the 1848 revolution. A modern edition is in Ján Chalupka, *Vyber z diela v dvoch zväzkoch* (Bratislava, 1950) 2: 287–339.

50. Daniel Bachát, "Ani to čert nevymyslí, čo žena má v svojej mysli!" *Černokňažník*, 2 (1862): 45–46, 60–62, 65–65, 74–75, 81–83.

51. Janko Čajak, "Moderná Slovenka," *Sokol* 1.2 (1860): 9–10.

52. Daniel Bachát, "Ľudmilka," *Národní hlásnik* 1.6 (30 June 1868): 138–142. Exhortations were also addressed to men, of course, e.g. Bachát's "Naša nová pieseň" (Our New Poem) in *Sokol* 1.11 (1860), which ends, "The circle dance of true brothers defies disaster/ Everyone shake hands in brotherly union/ And we shall become what we should be."

53. Ivan Br. Zoch, "Hostivít Gustáv Lojko," *Orol*, 2.10 (30 October 1871): 292.

54. Typical statements on how an unmarried man with no family responsibilities can better devote himself to public affairs appear in Ľudovít Štúr, "Život domáci a pospolitý" and "Pospolitosť a jednotlivosť," *Dielo*, 5 vols. (Bratislava, 1954) 1: 112–127, 128–145. I thank Dr. Jozef Ambruš and Marianna Mináriková for these references.

55. See the list by Rizner (3: 106). I have read only two stories, "Dobré dieťa poklad rodičov" (A Good Child Is Its Parents' Treasure) and "Kto do teba kameňom, ty do neho chlebom" (If Someone Throws a Stone at You, Return Him a Piece of Bread), which were reprinted under the title of the first story by J. Gašparík in Martin in 1907 and 1924.

56. Romantic nationalist poems were still written for some time, e.g. "Slovenkám" with the usual exhortation to remain faithful sisters and daughters, by Luiza Rigellová, *Dennica* 2.6 (June 1899): 18–19. This poem was found accidentally by Marianna Mináriková, and systematic search would probably reveal many such poems outside the time period of my study.

CHAPTER 3: FOUNDING OF ŽIVENA AND *DENNICA*

After the failure of the 1848 revolution, Slovak expectations were again disappointed when the Memorandum of 1861 for the emperor failed to bring greater political freedom. However, the Hungarian government itself was relatively liberal in the so-called constitutional period of 1861–1867 and allowed the Slovaks to establish three Slovak-language gymnázia in 1862–1869. One of these schools in the southern Slovak town of Revúca has been mentioned as a possible center for women's poetry, but the ones in Martin and Kláštor pod Znievom also encouraged women in various ways.[1]

The largest action of this liberal period was the establishment in 1863 of the Slovaks' first national cultural institute, the *Matica slovenská*. The various Slavic maticas inspired great devotion among the nations that had few other cultural institutions in the Austro-Hungarian empire. A specifically Slavic and central European concept, it was a national library, publishing house, academy of scholars, and nationalistic missionary society all in one.[2] The Slovak Matica was also an ecumenical action, with Catholic bishop Štefan Moyses as president and Lutheran superintendent Karol Kuzmány as vice president. Although it lasted less than a decade, it provided activities for women and more importantly supplied a model and stimulus to the establishment of a women's organization.

An Organization for Slovak Women

This relatively optimistic period re-emphasized the idea of women's activity as a further means of national development. In the background, of course, was belief in women's special domestic sphere. To foster women's activity, an organization named *Živena* after the old Slavic goddess of life was founded in 1869 for all Slovak women without distinction of class, religion, or education. The general goals of Živena paralleled the goals of the Matica. Slovak historian Jarmila Tkadlečková-Vantuchová relates these goals to contemporary conditions in Slovakia:

> The history of Živena is the touchstone of our national history, because the internal rhythm and the proportion between what was accomplished and what was stifled in both cases are the same.... After all, our national history is the account of vain

struggles, unfilled desires, and efforts that were always undermined — more "the history of what should have happened and did not" than the history of actual events.³

The founding of Živena in 1869 represented the congruence of male and female perception of the immediate need for women's help in the national movement. The extent to which it was a male activity cannot be determined without studying all the correspondence among those who formed the planning committee of Živena, as well as other available records. Male nationalists were certainly among the instigators and enthusiasts, and their primary motive was certainly to strengthen the national movement.

The first specific call for women as national workers came in a new feature called "Slovenkám" (To Slovak Women) in the May 1869 issue of the Slovak-language monthly magazine *Národní hlásnik* (National Crier). This magazine, founded by Mikuláš Štefan Feriencik (1825–1881) in 1868, showed in its subtitle *Noviny pre slovenský ľud* (Newspaper for the Slovak Commoner) its aim to reach the literate rural population. The new column was written by Ambro Pietor (1843–1906), whose law studies in Pest, Vienna, and Prague had enlarged his acquaintance with women's movements abroad. Pietor showed exceptional sensitivity to women's new desires, and he accepted male responsibility for women's condition more than did most Slovak men of the period. His column is given in full to show this tone.

> To Slovak Women
>
> We hereby dedicate a new section of our *Národní hlásnik* to our Slovak sisters, and warmly recommend it to them.
>
> Let us speak to our Slovak women.
> Culture already stands at a high level,
> Though man works alone in isolation;
> The help of a woman would double his results,
> And humanity would build a temple of glory.
>
> In speaking now, we are undertaking an enormous task — enormous because everything we see before us is lying useless. We see a desert barring an effective and worthy start. Above all, the task will be hard because, inexperienced as we are, we do

not know the right path to our goals of penetrating the hiding place of a great national treasure, then plucking the rich emotional strings of our Slovak daughters and stirring to national work this sex oppressed by various disadvantages and sentenced to the silence of the grave.

Yet, this is where we must start. We absolutely must, fathers and brothers in the nation, because as long as the daughters of our nation do not stand beside us in the national work, by so long our work will be ineffective and bitter—much less effective than when the powerful words of Slovak daughters will accompany us, and much bitterer than when their sweet tears will bless us and we shall see at our shoulders multitudinous platoons of future national warriors grown up in the care of Slovak mothers!

I am convinced that even the so-called national education movement, to which we rightfully give great weight in our national life, will always be one-sided and incomplete until it penetrates every level of our nation and spreads from the palaces of wealthy Slovaks to the most poverty-stricken hovel of Slovak peasants. Our national education movement will remain just a half measure until women fight along with men in at least a few fields. Without women's cooperation, we cannot build the complete temple of national enlightenment.

Yes, dear Slovak sisters and mothers, I am convinced that also your hour for action has struck! Now you must leave your domestic retreats for public fields of action suitable to your sex. Now—on every occasion when time permits— you must turn your mind far from your domestic fires, and use your strength to build that great national temple which we call national enlightenment. Slovak daughters must start to work if we would navigate to our exalted goal of true freedom for the whole Slovak nation. You are part of our nation just as we men are, and you too must place your talent on the altar of the nation. After all, you too care for our national freedom, which will become your own freedom. Finally, you too care that the position of women in our social life should be basically changed.

The opinion inherited from your forebearers that women belong only to the ladle and distaff is false. Your human status is much more honorable. Your own vocation is to fulfill in every respect the vocation of all humanity!

Other nations already enjoy marked support from the female sex. The Slovak nation unfortunately has so far lacked this help. Our women have so far lived only a menial life. On the one hand, we see indolence and neglect of our national concerns, and on the other hand, slavish dependence upon fathers and husbands. Admittedly, honorable exceptions exist, as at the last parliamentary elections where our Slovak women showed a truly exemplary awakening. But, as a whole, they have not lived as is proper for daughters of the Tatra Mountains.

Who, however, is to blame?

Regretfully, since I wish to be open and sincere, I must state that we men are mainly responsible. Let us admit the truth that we really did very little, actually nothing, for our female sex. Concerned only with ourselves, i.e. with the male sex, we prepared only men, we opened the doors to national education only for men, and we founded schools only for men. The female sex was on very few minds, as if it weighed nothing in the national balance. We did not even speak to it publicly. In a word, we were egotists. Yet the female sex is a great factor in our national life, without which our national history can only show a gap.

Now, dear contemporaries! We have before us a wide field of activity—let us not hesitate but go into manly action! Despite the above difficulties, our national task will be much easier than we expected. Our Slovak women can be proud of their good, generous hearts which are not yet weighed down by the benumbing fashions of the West. Exactly this circumstance, that foreign culture has not yet gained access to the sanctuary of our Slovak daughters' hearts, which are thus still virgin, lays upon us the responsibility to understand this situation and benefit from it. Let each of us bring what we can to the altar of learning for our Slovak daughters! Our own consciousness that we did not leave this important branch of our national life lying useless, and our dear nation's appreciation, will be our generous reward.

Now, still a few words to you, our dear Slovak mothers and sisters. So far, you have heard our speeches addressed only to our "brothers," and seen only the male sex excelling. There was no concern for you. Here is our hand, and here is our Slovak word that we shall no longer leave you out. Our words must and will in the future speak also to Slovak daughters. From now on we will speak to you too, and speak openly and sincerely. Do not take it badly, please, when we speak the truth. Our words shall be those of true sons of the Slovak nation to their dear mothers or sisters, and therefore please accept these words in the way we mean to offer them to you.

We will speak to you of the patriotism of the female sex, of your education, responsibilities, etc, etc. We will offer you nourishment worthy of Slovak daughters.

Morever, our words shall thunder against anyone who scoffs at the female sex. We will sternly chastize anyone who begrudges women's growth and does not want women to escape from that spiritual slavery in which their lives till now were wasted.

So, as you see, dear Slovak mothers and sisters, we are going into spiritual battle for you. We hope you will not leave us standing alone, but your voices will ring out in our *Hlásnik* to give us your helpful advice. You can be certain our camp will grow and grow, and on our day of national victory not a single man will dare attribute it only to the male sex.

So, then, come join us, all who are friends of women's progress, and we shall become what we have never yet been!

Till then, farewell![4]

Essential to the success of Pietor's appeal for women to participate in the national movement was the language of family and church. Religious emphasis was basic to Slavic nationalism, as seen already, but here it had a new use. Concepts of brotherhood, sisterhood, motherhood, sanctuary, and temple added theological weight to Pietor's moral emphasis on women's national duty. This weight was doubtless necessary to overcome male resistance as well as encourage hesitant females.

The concrete proposal for a separate women's organization appeared in the June 2 issue of *Pešťbudínske vedomosti* (roughly, Budapest News), the Slovak-language, twice-weekly newspaper published by the same group of Slovak nationalists who published *Národní hlásnik*. As its subtitle *Noviny pre politiku a literatúru* indicates, it was intended for a more educated and intellectual readership than the *Hlásnik*. Pietor's article is given in full.

A Slovak Women's Association

Recently during my seven-month stay in the glorious old city of Prague, I had the chance to know better that youthful life of the Czech nation which has so many admirers in the world. I also got to know those means helping the Czech nation to resurrect and strengthen its life.[5]

Often my thoughts flew to my native Tatra country, and I would look around to see whether we too had this or that, and whether we too were providing at least the majority of needed means. Alas, I found great lacks everywhere, and in many respects a complete desert. The cause of this situation appeared to be everywhere and always *only* our lack of organization.

However, I do not want to write now about these faults and our likelihood of getting rid of them, nor do I intend to point to the final victory of our nation. My purpose here is to turn our dear nation's attention to a major subject not yet mentioned in our public life. This is the question of how to help the spiritually backward female sex.

The female sex lacks that education basic to the moral life of nations. If I were tracing the cause of this lack, I would ascribe it less to the female sex itself than to the partisan world of the ruling male. He certainly bears the greatest guilt for the fact that half of humanity remains unenlightened, and thus social life and the family have taken such a turn for the worse. But of this elsewhere.

The Slovak nation, praise God, has not yet wandered far astray on that dangerous sea. However, we must build a strong barrier against that sickness before it comes to our nation. Let everyone work according to his strength. For my part, I have become firmly convinced that, just as with everything else in our nation, nothing can help us better than working together, i.e. forming an association based on self-help, according to the proverb "God helps those who help themselves."

This conviction brings me to our urgent need to found a general "Association of Slovak Women."

I scarcely must emphasize the importance of such an association. Besides the above, I point only to the universal spread of Magyarization as a situation bidding us to take heed.

I will not here enter into the question whether the female sex is capable, and to what extent capable, of education and progress. I refer instead to the May issue and the coming issue of the Národní hlásnik, where this matter and many others will be discussed.

An "Association of Slovak Women" will become for now our Slovak slogan. As much as our young but valiant strength allows, we will not abandon this slogan even if half the world conspires against us, until we see our goal accomplished, until the Slovak female sex is gathered together in a single central organization suitable to its role in life.

In the meantime, we shall not be frightened by great obstacles, because this matter has already gained many friends, and we are sure that you, our beloved fathers and you our contemporaries in the nation, will also contribute your help and advice. We are sure that especially you, dear Slovak mothers and sisters, will engage yourselves in a *manly* way (since that expression is necessary) in this means of escaping from the slavery in which you have groaned for centuries. We are sure you will try to reach that level of humanity Divine Wisdom has honored you with—that level you will have to reach if you wish our nation to free itself from the spiritual and material slavery into which it was thrown by our adversaries, and in part by our own neglect.

As far as this whole effort to found a woman's organization is concerned, I can say that we are almost prepared to publish the proposed charter, which has been reviewed by several leading nationalists. In the second half of June we shall invite every Slovak daughter, as well as all friends of learning for women, to the general assembly to be held on the same day as the general assembly of the Matica slovenská in Turčiansky Svätý Martin. I firmly hope this day will be crowned with positive results.

This much I considered it my duty to announce to the worthy Slovak public.

Thus, with God's will and heroic good fortune, in the month of August we shall lay the foundation for our second edifice of national learning and welfare.

Nation, we will not let you die out!
Till then, farewell![6]

The next week's issue of *Pešťbudínske vedomosti* published the proposed charter for Živena. The ad hoc founding committee consisted of the publisher Mikuláš Ferienčík and two other prominent nationalists, Viliam Pauliny-Tóth and Martin Čulen, besides Ambro Pietor, who served as secretary. As with the Matica, it was deliberately ecumenical, with two Lutherans and two Catholics.

The June issue of the *Hlásnik* printed several responses to Pietor's new column for Slovak women. Of special interest was a letter from a woman identified only as a "highly respected nationalist." It is given in full.

> Our *Hlásnik* was always dear, very dear, but from now on it will be a hundred times dearer. Like every Slovak daughter who nurtures in her heart at least a spark of respect and love for our wounded nation, I have long felt, painfully, that women's social position in general and our national position in particular were not and so far never have been what they should and could be. Women of other nations have taken a respected place in public life, distinguished themselves as writers, stood up for national rights honestly and fearlessly at the shoulders of their men, and even competed with them for honors. We Slovak women alone are without means, we alone are tied to our kitchen and household, and no one is concerned about our national development. No wonder then that we have so few nationalist women, and especially so few educated nationalist women.
>
> Therefore, I welcome with unutterable joy the sincere, warm voice of the *Hlásnik* speaking out in favor of the female sex in Slovakia, in favor of raising Slovak daughters to their proper vocation, and especially in favor of their national education. Educate us, instill in us a warm love for our nation, and permit us with our modest strength to turn aside the poisoned arrows which our enemies shoot at us. You shall see that your battle too will be fought more easily, and the results for our nation will be more excellent. We shall rear up effective new generations. From the cradle to adulthood we shall care for our children, guard over every movement of

their hearts, every word, every act, to preserve our sons and daughters for the nation. They shall grow into worthy, willing, self-sacrificing nationalist men and women, for the glory and good of our beloved nation. May God help us!

As a result of that article in the *Hlásnik* a beautiful scene occurred in our house. Whenever a new issue arrives, several dear neighbors gather with me, and we read the issue together. So it was this time. The news that our dear *Hlásnik* carried an article specially for us Slovak daughters flashed through the city like lightning. The issue passed from hand to hand, and the joyous result of this national wave was that seventeen women (some of them already awakened and some only now proclaiming themselves daughters of their nation) paid for subscriptions to the *Hlásnik*. Their names are enclosed here.[7]

Like Pietor's articles this letter used religious language, but both writers are also talking about a phenomenon very close to the modern sociological concept of consciousness-raising. Women must have their "national consciousness" awakened so that they in turn can awaken those around them and rear new generations of nationally conscious youth.

Another interesting response to Pietor's first article was a congratulatory letter from a group of nationalist Czech women (not otherwise identified but presumably including the leading writers Karolina Světlá and Eliška Krasnohorská). Significantly, the Czech women mentioned "our responsibility to ourselves" only after their national responsibility, and they included a disclaimer of "so-called emancipation" that imitated men. Such a disclaimer had appeared in Lehocká's letter of 1846, and was often invoked in the Slovak women's movement. The letter is given in full.

Czech Sisters to Their Slovak Sisters
Prague, June 17 [1869]

We joyfully welcome your movement, and consider it our sacred duty to send you these sincere, sisterly words.

You well know what kind of battle you face against intellectual prejudices. You also know what kind of weapons can be turned against you in such a conflict. It is a very hard fight. We speak from experience because we too must combat enemy elements. But nothing frightens us, and we manfully hold firm on the designated battlefield, boldly hoping for the victory of our sacred rights.

Your interests being the same as ours and your purpose identical, we find in you, dear sisters, our ally and joyfully welcome you to our ranks.

Our ranks are becoming more powerful, which is a good sign.

Among the many motives urging us on, foremost is doubtless our responsibility as nationalists.

If we are to gain the desired result of our national yearning, we too must contribute our talent.

In what way?

We are all educators, and not only history but also our own experience teaches us how education increases national enlightenment.

Therefore, may our chief aim be the rearing of youth in a noble, national, humane, and self-sacrificing direction.

In second place lies our responsibility to ourselves. We shall not expand upon our situation, because we all know what it is, what it should be, and, God willing, what it shall be.

We can attain this goal only by the right kind of women's education, without the appendage of that destructive so-called emancipation which merely copies men.

Our only criteria must be the noble principles flowing from worthy learning. We must make the effort to attain such learning, and no longer allow ourselves to passively watch the exemplary fervor of our brothers. Let us endeavor to make our valiant nation boast of its successful daughters and conscious nationalists. This is the effort of us all!

So, honorably to battle, dear sisters!

> Accept our hearty, sisterly greetings, and our sincere good luck!⁸

Besides these two letters, the male nationalist Daniel Bachát wrote to welcome the new organization. His letter illustrates, however, how closely the idea of women as inspiration still adhered to the newer idea of women as help. He suggested that the women's organization should have its own magazine with a section to "foster the memory of glorious women," and he promised to supply an "interesting novella" about one of these women.⁹ Numerous poems and other letters greeted the new organization.

In addition to Živena as the central organization for women, local branches were planned to fill the need for smaller groups in a single town or region.[10] Government permission was required, but in the meantime local groups formed. Most striking for my purposes, at least, was *Vesna*, founded in August 1869 in the central Slovak town of Liptovský Trnovec. The organization and purpose of Vesna were announced in the *Hlásnik*,[11] and the opening speech at the first assembly in October was also published.[12] In several ways this speech by Juraj Kello (1844–1898) contrasts Pietor's call for women's help in the national movement. Kello's metaphorical explanation of the names of both organizations shows how easily the idea of women as help slid back into the idea of woman as inspiration. This section of Kello's speech is given:

> I proposed that our organization take the unfamiliar name *Vesna* for an important reason. It is the pagan Slavic name our ancestors used for the goddess of growth. Similarly, our leaders and valiant women in Martin founding the women's organization have named it for the old Slavic goddess of life, Živa or Živena. Just as the goal of that organization is to infuse life where it is lacking and resurrect the spark of national life that has gone out—not only in the pillars of the organization nor only in the female sex, but in every son and daughter of our extended nation—so also the goal of our Vesna is to do the same in our town. The goddess Živa gives life, and the goddess Vesna helps this life to grow and blossom. The organization Živena is to give life,

> and Vesna is to help, cultivate, and extend that life, at least in our town. Živena is to light the fire, and Vesna to fan it. Živena resurrected it, and Vesna should nurse it. Živena began it, and Vesna should spread it.
>
> Just as Vesna was the goddess of spring and flowers, so may also this organization become the impulse, the wellspring, the hearth of national flowering among the youth and aged alike of both sexes in our town. The goddess Vesna was the prime of life, so may this organization Vesna become the prime of our domestic and national life. (340)

Unlike Pietor, Kello does not blame men for women's state of backwardness, nor does he seem aware of women's personal suffering from their status. His speech is purely exhortative, and he places more responsibility upon women than upon men for saving the nation. He builds up women's place as the peak effort for the nation in a clear form of the "feminization of virtue." This appears in the following part of his last paragraph:

> I again maintain that the fate of the nation rests in the hands of women more than of men. Men are fervent nationalists, but nationalist women, our national mothers, pass on the spirit of their child rearing from generation to generation. If a mother is cultured, her descendants will be cultured. At any critical moment in times of danger, a woman of vigorous resoluteness and energy often achieves more than the most learned man. Women affect their husbands, the rearing of their children, and thereby the growth of national strength. Without education, this national strength is only raw, and outsiders use it for their own ends. Therefore, the special goal of our organization is women's education. I do not mean education as pure learning, but as the popular training we need most strongly. I mean education fitting both the household and our higher organizations—because it seems to me that

a reasonable and cultivated housekeeper will always
be better than just a housekeeper. (342)

The good effect to be accomplished by local branches of Živena did not occur, because the government refused permission for them although Živena itself was approved in 1870. In fact, the optimistic period that saw the founding of the Matica slovenská and three Slovak-language gymnázia as well as of Živena, lasted only until Magyar efforts to make multinational Hungary into a monolithic Magyar state brought the closing of both the Matica and the schools. In 1875 the Matica's assets, building, and museum collections were confiscated, while its membership was disbanded and its publishing activity forbidden. The three gymnázia were closed and later reopened as Magyar-language schools. In the ensuing vacuum, the national movement was able to keep little more than a few newspapers, the monthly magazine *Slovenské pohl'ady* (Slovak Views, founded in 1881), and a museum society (founded in 1893).

Živena was spared, however, presumably because of its unimportance in official eyes as only a women's group.[13] It was usually able to hold its annual convention which, being scheduled to occur at the same time as the Matica convention, served to replace the forbidden annual meeting of the closed Matica. For over four decades, Živena was able to hold various manifestations with entertainment and exhibits, and to accomplish other activities such as in 1895 supplying Czech women's organizations with Slovak embroideries, woven textiles, and folk costumes for exhibit and sale. These handicrafts were always identified as Slovak in Prague, whereas they were misidentified as Magyar elsewhere.[14] The Czech women also made a Slovak exhibit at the Paris *Exposition de l'art dès femmes* in 1903, where identical items in the Hungarian and Austrian pavilions were labelled as Magyar handicrafts. Such international exhibits were a much-used device for publicity by those nations which had no state of their own.[15]

Interestingly, a sister organization to Živena was founded in the United States in 1891, which had 138 small branches by 1905. Its goals and activities were similar to those in Slovakia, and it sent financial contributions back to the homeland.[16]

Despite Živena's relative successes, its mixed status as unofficial national organization and official woman's organization had been apparent from the beginning in its officers. Though the temporary founding committee was composed of four men, the first officers were women except for Ambro Pietor, who was secretary until 1897, when the Slovak novelist Svetozár Hurban Vajanský replaced him and remained secretary of Živena until World War I. The first president, Anna Pivková, worked energetically to establish domestic-training programs for girls and women, but it was the next president who gave the greatest impetus to the Slovak women's movement.

Elena Maróthy Šoltésová (1855–1939) became the women's intellectual leader for over a quarter of a century. She was elected vice-president in 1883 and president in 1894, then re-elected until she retired in 1927. Daughter of Daniel Maróthy, a minor Štúrist poet and Lutheran minister, she was influenced more by her father than her mother and stepmother according to her autobiography.[17] She married young and moved to the northern town of Turčiansky Svätý Martin, which though small was the center of Slovak nationalism. Equally as important as her position in Živena were her editorial work on the annual publications *Národní almanach Živeny* (1885) and *Letopis Živeny* (1896, 1898, 1902, 1906), and her editorship of the monthly magazine *Živena* from 1910 to 1922. Her fiction will be taken up in Chapter 4, and her philosophical essay on women's rights in Chapter 5.

With Šoltésová, Slovak women gained a strong voice in the arguments with male nationalists which occurred whenever women nationalists attempted separate activities for women.

Efforts to Found a Girls' School

One of the earliest disagreements stemmed from Magyar officials' repeated refusal to allow the establishment of a Slovak-language school for girls and women, though such a school was a major goal of Živena in the charter approved by the government in 1870. For a decade permission was expected and a plan prepared, but Pietor and the other men closely involved with Živena apparently gave up hope that the school would ever be approved. In 1882 they changed the Živena constitution by adding an objective to publish "entertaining and instructive" books in the Slovak language. This change allowed Živena to replace the forbidden publishing activity of the closed Matica, but it de-emphasized women's education.[18]

The young Šoltésová, who had just been elected a member of the executive committee, responded with a moving justification of women's desire for their own school, *Dozvuky k poslednému valnému zhromaždeniu Živeny* (Reverberations from the Past General Assembly of Živena, 1882).[19] Besides the usual eagerness to help the national cause, Šoltésová's article emphasized the psychological burden of foreign languages that Slovak women carried. Students from all of the small nations had to learn the major languages of science, art, or diplomacy, and women of other nations too complained of this burden. The Slovak girl, however, had to learn both Magyar and German (the former being not only a difficult language but of no earthly use outside of Hungary) while trying to study general subjects. Nothing was taught in her native language, so that for girls science and other serious courses "served only as a means of teaching languages" (75). Women felt this burden more than men because of their other disadvantages:

> Many of our problems come from the hostile conditions in which we live; women of other countries and other ethnic groups have no idea at all of what it means to allow one's whole education to be swallowed by foreign languages. (76)

This necessity to learn foreign languages well enough to receive a genuine education, moreover, involved also the risk of denationalization and defection of the educated Slovak woman to the Magyar or German nations. Such a risk added to the psychological burden for herself and her family.

A separate problem from Magyar and German educational pressure, whether direct or indirect and psychological, was the linguistic pressure of the Czech language, particularly because Czech had been used voluntarily by many Slovaks as their standard language in preceding centuries. Biblical Czech was still the Protestant liturgical language, and many needed books were available to Slovaks only in Czech. Yet this relation too had become thorny, and even the most ardent Slovakophiles in Bohemia and Moravia condemned the Štúrists' decision to use Slovak as the standard language of the Slovaks. This whole linguistic problem was not gender-determined, of course, but women showed especially great fervor in defending Štúr's recognition that an existing native language could not be uprooted but instead must be stimulated to blossom. As women feeling all the other disadvantages facing them, they wanted at least schooling in their natural language.

In 1843 Johana Lehocká had justified use of the Slovak language in a letter to Bohuslava Rajská (cited in Chapter 2), and almost identical arguments were given in 1888 by Izabela Textorisová in a letter to the Czech nationalist and Slovakophile Vilma Sokolová.[20] Textorisová's first reasons were political and social:

> There is much condemnation of our turning away from the Czech language, and Czechs feel themselves weakened by the loss of three million people. But this is false. I don't know—not to overstate the figures—whether scarcely 30 or 40 thousand Slovaks have a somewhat clear idea of who they are, others live in the dark, and a million certainly couldn't even tell you what language they speak. While we could agree that you were decreased in pure numbers, you were not decreased in substance: *such* a million would never conquer anyone, never exalt anyone, and never assimilate with anyone—so leave our poverty to us! Even if the barriers set up by the government didn't exist, a half century would scarcely be enough to turn these millions of pollywogs into conscious humans.

Textorisová's second reasons for use of the Slovak language were personal and psychological:

> Setting aside the fact that we're politically divided, I myself could not imagine how we could get along without our standard Slovak if Czech were still in its place. I love the Czech language, take pleasure in reading it, and by means of it have come to know so many excellent books. But if we had to write it, use it to express our own thoughts—I don't know if anything would result. It's a general truth experienced by so many of us that whenever our common people have the opportunity, they joyously take up reading in Slovak, whereas the Czech language is difficult to understand even for the most educated of them. For that reason, we strongly hope and expect that the voice of history will assign our warriors and

their supporters not only honor but also the true number of those they affected, accurate to the last digit, even where they could not foresee so many Satanic obstacles to their work.[21]

One of the most compelling public statements of the Slovak need for their own language appeared in Šoltésová's letter to Tereza Nováková, the editor of the new Czech women's magazine *Ženský svět*, who published it there in 1897. It is given in full.

Martin, 16 January 1897

As I promised, and also from my own desire, I again send a Slovak message to this our dear Czech magazine. It might be most fitting if I wrote of our national life, especially of ourselves and our share in that national life. But this subject is just now being taken up by our well-known friend and expert on Slovakia, Vilma Sokolová, in a much more detailed way than I could do in a short letter. I shall not abandon the matter without sometime in the future giving a glimpse of how we look to ourselves. For now, however, another matter urges me to take up my pen, a less substantive one, but it needs discussion in the interests of mutual understanding between Czechs and Slovaks.

This is the question of Slovak as our standard language, and I was led to it by a remark of the respected editor of this magazine in her recent, and most appreciated, letter to me. After considering our very difficult position in Hungary, she wrote:

> Despite everything, I believe in your final victory, and I also believe, forgive me if I am wrong, that you shall reach this victory sooner the closer you draw to us Czechs. I still have not forgiven Štúr and Bernolák for what they did to wreck the work of Kollár, which seemed to be so solidly built. It can no longer be completely rebuilt, and as far as I know Slovaks would not accept its total rebuilding—but a new, dif-

ferent relation between us could achieve much good.

These frank words come from a sincere heart that above all else desires the success of our Czechoslovak affairs. Her words reveal love for us Slovaks, but also anxious concern that we may be taking the wrong path to our goal. The good will behind her words must be evident to everyone, and I take her opinion as universal among all those in Bohemia who consider themselves our brothers and sisters. Exactly because of this fact, I cannot help answering as our side of the matter requires.

While recognizing and appreciating all your good thoughts, to promote mutually sincere understanding we must stand up for Bernolák and Štúr in raising Slovak to the status of our literary language. Thereby, you too will finally see the matter correctly, which means favorably. Whoever truly knows our internal and external conditions will correctly guess our viewpoint, and will have to admit that raising our rooted domestic language to a higher function was essential. If Štúr and Bernolák had not done so, there is no doubt whatsoever that someone else would have. Moreover, if the Slovak language had found no one to give it life, doubtless we should no longer be using the Czech language either, and the Slovak intelligentsia would no longer exist. The Slovak language would have stagnated among the common people, and Czech as a non-native language would have been forced out of the lands of Hungary. The Slovak language, rooted in the soil and growing from it, is holding out against the wild current of Magyarization, but the Czech language, artificially implanted, would have been flooded away.

The Slovak intelligentsia, despite its extraordinarily constricted position deprived of all external conditions of existence, is determinedly holding onto its origin and to its moral strength, despite powerful denationalizing forces. It draws chiefly upon its living language growing from the common people. This statement is not exaggerated, and it becomes easily believable when we consider the fact that language is nature's outlet for the whole character of the common people, and nature's means of maintaining and maturing the internal being of the nation. To be born and come into its own are possible for a nation through its language — and we Slovaks are still only a nation that is just being born. Therefore, from both external and internal viewpoints, we absolutely must hold fast to our own language above all else. Those who raised Slovak to the status of our literary language did so less as a deliberate act than from the instinct of self-preservation. No one who desires the Slovak nation to survive for itself and for Slavdom can condemn their work. We have made a great effort with only miserable results, but we are still holding on as a nation through the power of our language. If we had kept the Czech language as standard and left the Slovak language for only the everyday needs of the common people, then we would probably have supplied Czech literature with a few writers, but in our difficult conditions the Czech language could not have maintained us as a nation. Moreover, it was not in your power to give us any other, more actual help, and even if we had kept Czech as our literary language, you had no power to do more for us.

Recognizing so well our own situation, we can look at this matter only in this way, and if you want to be fair, you also must look at it *from our point of view*. By doing so, you will show us true brotherliness and sisterliness, and you will free our mutual relations from that suffocating, bitter antagonism which cannot die out as long as you, admittedly well-intended but looking at it solely from your own viewpoint, construe this question coldly and unemotionally, whereas it is for us a matter of life or death. Only when you honestly see the truth of our position can we have a new, unforced, and beneficial relationship, and only then can we make a united effort with our common interests.

If future conditions should become ripe for a change and the two languages should be united as a single literary language (which already now many people foresee with no opposition on either side), i.e. neither Czech nor Slovak but a single branch of Slavdom, then at that time a fresh and *mature* Slovak language would certainly contribute to the change. Actually one could say that Providence itself destined the Slovak language to flower, because it is close to almost every other Slavic language, despite its being the tongue of a tiny nation that is unable even to create and maintain a literature to serve its own needs. The Slovak language is like a late-born child, the thirteenth sister with twelve brothers in the folk tale, who by the grace of her simplicity and her unfrightened sisterly love overcomes the hatred of her brothers, frees her family from its old curse, and leads it to love and happiness. Apparently the Slovak language has a similar role to play. She too is the daughter of the great Slavic family, she too enters the service of her brothers, and in the bewitched castle she would for their sake live on a crust of bread and a little soup. I am convinced that, in time, you too in Bohemia will cease considering the Slovak language an unwanted guest, and your hearts too will be conquered by her. Of everyone on your side, I think my conviction would not be rejected by dear Adolf Heyduk, who so tenderly loved the Slovak language and expressed his feeling with such moving words.[22]

This is what I have to say on the matter which clouded, and still in part clouds, our relations, and which requires clarification if we are ever to stop floundering around in disagreement. I sincerely beg all of you who read this letter to accept my honest, candid words as sincerely and unreservedly as they are intended and written. If they bring even a little more understanding between us, I shall be happy.

I end this letter with a heartfelt prayer: Oh Lord, give us strength and unity, love, and blessed success in all our joint activities![23]

In an almost casual manner Šoltésová introduced the great providential destiny of the Slovak language in supporting Slavdom, which was probably a reference to the theory, not accepted in modern linguistics but popular among the Štúrists as well as some of the Baroque historians, that the Tatra mountains were the cradle of all the Slavs. This theory increased the moral intensity of Slovak nationalism as a cause benefitting not only the relatively few Slovaks, but the whole family of Slavs. It must also have increased the idealistic sense of mission that characterized the Slovak women's movement in general, and the desire for women's education in the Slovak language in particular.

For these reasons, Šoltésová refused to abandon the idea of a Slovak school. The men's pessimism, however, was well founded, and in fact Živena was not allowed to sponsor a girls' school until Czechoslovakia was established in 1918. Women turned to educational publications as a substitute for the school that could not be established. Besides Šoltésová, the other enterprising woman editor was Terézia Medvecká Vansová (1857–1942). The daughter of a nationalist Lutheran pastor, she also married a Lutheran pastor and lived most of her life in a small town in southern Slovakia. Her brief period as a poet was treated in Chapter 2 (Appendix, Nos.118–123), and her fiction will be considered in Chapter 4. Her editorial and journalistic work showed less intellectual rigor than Šoltésová's essays, but she performed much valuable service.

In 1885–1886, after the second *Národní almanach Živeny*, edited by Ambro Pietor, had carried a preponderance of male authors, Vansová proposed a "domestic calender" for women to be published by Živena. She sent the proposal to Šoltésová, who agreed heartily. However, Pietor (who as secretary had been given the deciding voice by president Pivková) refused the calendar on financial grounds. Šoltésová ironically summarized the situation in a letter to Vansová:

> You know, in a parliamentary and constitutional monarchy the king doesn't count for much, and

> that's how it is with us, the presidency of Živena. We have little enough influence, and even less of a deciding voice in our own organization. The guilt lies not with personalities but in our circumstances …. But please don't be disgusted…. If you can still gather the material, we'll find some other format if not a calendar, as soon as we shall feel strong enough.[24]

The women did not, however, feel strong enough to produce an independent publication for another decade.

A Magazine for Women, Dennica

Just as the public impulse for founding Živena had come from a man, Ambro Pietor, so also the effective public appeal to found a woman's magazine came from a man. Earlier ideas of starting such a magazine in 1869 had not been realized. Therefore, in 1896 the magazine *Dom a škola* (Home and School) carried an article "Ženská otázka" (The Woman Question) by its editor Karel Kálal advocating a Slovak woman's magazine as a means of attracting women and girls to the national movement and morally and physically improving society.[25] Kálal (1860–1930) was a Czech pedagogue working in Moravia and eventually in Slovakia, who as a Slovakophile supported nationalist efforts against Magyarization. His article shows considerable understanding of women's desire for intellectual advancement in their own right: "A man does not have the right to smother the talents given a woman by the Creator" (313). He also shows the usual nationalist desire to enlarge the ranks of men by women's help: "Small nations should most of all be concerned with women's education" (314).

An interesting response to Kálal's article from a Slovak woman, Klementina Augustiny Ruppeldtová, was published in the January, 1897 issue of *Dom a škola*. Given below in its entirety, it shows less nationalism as well as more feminism than Kálal's article.

> —From Liptovský Svätý Mikuláš ("The Woman Question")
> Welcome among us, thou dawn of a better future! Let no one think it a better future only for us women, because it is our common, general future,

better for society itself and particularly better for our Slovak nation.

Welcome thou again, and all the more because it comes from a masculine pen for the first time in our dear *Dom a škola*. After all, everyone knows that our gentlemen fear this future as the Devil fears holy water! They will not hear a word on this subject, closing their eyes and gritting their teeth against it. But still it is here, and will remain, and its natural current throughout the world will overtake us too and accomplish a great deal for us Slovak women, even without our participation. Therefore, let us learn of it, so that we shall not be found lacking.

We women certainly have our own special claims on the future which we must already be considering. When we have analyzed these claims, we must propose them as one woman to another, discuss them, and by this means reach our goal.

Behold the clear need for our Slovak women's magazine, just as our friend—the author—offers it to us. Let us undertake it, dear Slovak sisters, let's awake from our sleep! Let's think for ourselves! Let's once and for all rid ourselves of that supposedly sweet sloth, which is actually indifference—or should I call it numbness?

Let us read and learn how in other nations women are proceeding and advancing because they are more educated. Thus blessed, they work with their minds, not only their hands. Our nearest sisters are the Czech women, to whom I point as an example for their excellent magazine *Ženské listy*, which is even more interesting and more worthwhile in its second year than its first. But this magazine only whets our appetites, since obviously we need our own, our own pure spring from the Tatra Mountains. We hope that in time others will also understand our need.

It is always true that the beginning is difficult, especially in work like this—which those who come later usually do not see. We shall not think of those later people but rather of the difficult beginning, even if it is feeble. We shall cheer ourselves with the thought that from tiny acorns grow great oak trees.

Listen, Slovak sisters, to what the so-called feeble voice of Živena is saying! It wants to live! It will not, cannot, live without us! Only our good will is needed! If each woman pours in the strength of pennies, and if many women add in the power of words, then Živena will operate, alive and fearless! "The organization Živena, our own women's magazine, and a Slovak school for girls"—this trinity will be the slogan of every true Slovak woman! More education for women! I mean the right kind of women's education that brings employment! More decent employment for women! More honorable self-support for women! Workplaces, not bawdy-houses, for women! Let us prepare for the future, let us save the great female half of humanity, which was created by God for honorable work equal to that of the male half. After all, the favorable result is not just ours but also yours, my dear brothers, and everyone's.

Think it over, talk it over, write about it, you who carry the responsibility for such matters, whether man or woman. Let us exchange our opinions and views. Let us start out prepared for the coming jeers and ridicule! Oh, how much there will be!

Conscious of our weakness, we shall nevertheless be unafraid. Good works take time and effort.[26]

Although the public appeal came first from a man, Kálal later published a chronology indicating the part Šoltésová and Vansová had played in founding the first Slovak women's magazine, *Dennica*. After he advocated such a magazine in the summer of 1896, he spoke of it with both women, who "had long entertained the thought of such a magazine."[27] In August, 1897, their plans were made, Vansová became editor, and the first issue of *Dennica*

Founding of Živena and *Dennica*

appeared in January, 1898 Before *Dennica* is taken up, however, we must consider its context.

In the background of the founding of *Dennica* lay the fact that the Czech nationalist women had established a new magazine, *Ženský svět* (Women's World), and published the first issue in January, 1897. Vilma Sokolová wrote a long article called "Slovenky—naše nejbližší sestry" (Slovak Women—Our Nearest Sisters), which described for Czech readers the organization Živena, the work of several Slovak women writers, and the difficult national life of Slovak women.[28]

Terézia Vansová wrote an enthusiastic review of the new Czech magazine and sent it to Šoltésová for revision if needed and submission to *Národnie noviny*, which was edited by Vajanský and Pietor. Šoltésová described its reception in a long letter to Vansová:

> Hurban [Vajanský] did not promise for sure they would publish it, but they would read it and decide. Then at once they took the opportunity, he and [the editor Jozef] Škultéty (Pietor was not there), to express their dislike of separate women's magazines in general and especially of that *Ženský svět* in particular. They said it was just a forced division, and magazines should not be specifically feminine or masculine. What was the point, and what would we say if they began to publish *Chlapský svet* (Men's World)? (That really does sound funny.) They said it's just idle talk about women's "equality," because women are equal to men in everything relevant to them. These women's magazines smell of socialism, and anyway the propagation of women's equality with men is antireligious, because the Holy Bible says a woman must be governed by her husband, and all natural order says the same, etc. etc....
>
> Such a skirmish I had with those editors, but still I thought they would publish the article after they read it! At least I see nothing dangerous in Slovak women reading *Ženský svět*, which in my opinion is entirely well conceived. But our nice little review just didn't appear, issue after issue. Hurban sent a message he would come to explain it personally, but

in that well-known punctuality of his he never came. I was anxious because you would be wondering what to think, and I hated to write until I found out from them what they were doing with it. So today coming home from church I stopped in at the editorial office—and there they declared they could not recommend *Ženský svět* and similar things, because it would be against the platform of the newspaper.... What do you say to that? I stood there flabbergasted, because I must admit I haven't had occasion to think so highly of their strict adherence to the platform. Then I asked for the manuscript back, expressing my wish that the editors would hold to the platform as strictly in everything else as they had in this matter. A little wounded, they answered that in small matters they could make errors or exceptions, but this they considered a serious matter. Actually only Hurban said it because by chance he was alone, but he claimed Pietor didn't want the article either. I am sending the manuscript back, so you can see what I added. You could give it to *Dom a škola*, but shorten it a little, and don't mention emancipation and equality so it won't cause a panic. It bothers me that I can't keep my promise (to publicly recommend *Ženský svět*), but anyway the recommendation would not have helped much. There's no interest here in such serious magazines, as our women are still just looking for entertainment. For that reason too our editors' fears were groundless.... Honestly I'd never have thought our exceedingly fearful gentlemen would pay us off like that.[29]

As this incident shows, Pietor had become more conservative than when he first supported the women's movement in 1869. Vajanský's view of women was actually more complicated than appears from Šoltésová's letter; it will be taken up in Chapter 4 on the nationalist heroine, since it appears not only in his editorial positions but also in his fiction.

Vansová published her review of *Ženský svět* in *Dom a škola*. She praised the magazine for its useful information, much of which was not available to Slovak women in their relatively more isolated situation. She described the magazine's spirit and goal in terms of the emancipation that is

> pure and strictly moral in a healthy direction. Its goal is not that emancipation which, according to its detractors, makes a woman into some kind of doubtful being grasping for men's responsibilities and forgetting her own duties. Instead, it is the healthy, desirable emancipation which wants to free women from stupefying prejudices that keep them in darkness, sloth, and spiritual emptiness. Such emancipation wants to raise up a woman from backwardness and widen her spiritual horizon and develop her capabilities to make her become an adult creature, useful to herself and her husband, so that in case of need she can independently and honorably support herself, and be not only a wife but also her husband's worthy helper in life's trials.[30]

Probably Vansová was referring to Vajanský's behavior when she rhetorically asked if Slovak women should not show their appreciation of the Czech articles on Slovak literature, and answered that to ignore them would look very shabby (128). Then she concluded that Slovak women also needed their own journal.

Perhaps for these reasons Vansová's opening article in the first issue of *Dennica* in January 1898, which she titled "Nový rok, nový krok" (A New Year, A New Step), established the strong nationalism characteristic of the magazine. It is given in full.

> A New Year, A New Step
>
> With desires in our heart, with fears, but also hope for a better future, we begin each year anew. What will it bring us, what will it fulfill for us, and how will it disappoint us? Who of our dear ones will leave us, going on to eternity? Will we ourselves even be here among the living a year from now? Such questions involuntarily occur to a thinking creature when the old year draws to its end.
>
> Everything is in the hands of God.

> The recent past years were bad for us. We saw more than one of our hopes and joys fall into an early grave. We did not reach our desired goals, nor even better times. Our dear language, given us by God, is like Cinderella in having no place in public life, society, or school. It has no other refuge than our domestic household, our hearts, and the hearth of our ardent love. Only there is it still uncondemned and safe to unfold its beauty, its capability, and the richness of its vigorous independence. We have the power to preserve its original purity and beauty, so that our more fortunate descendants may someday appreciate its bright form.
>
> "Not from a jaded eye, but from a diligent hand does hope grow," sings our glorious Kollár. We should follow the example of our forefathers and study, so they shall not lament their "dumb children." Within the framework available to us, let us look for noble entertainment and instruction, leaving empty, stupefying pastimes and revels to people with no higher impulse or sacred responsibility.
>
> Every beginning is difficult. Fears are building about the outcome of our action, but such fears are too anxious. Our responsibility is to work sincerely, put our hand to the common task, and leave the result to Him with Whom even the impossible is possible.[31]

The Christian fatalism implicit in the article was characteristic of Vansová's view of women's struggle. In the same first issue her article "O nás" (About Us Women) summarized the history of Christian treatment of women and cited Biblical evidence of the worth of women by their service to Jesus Christ.[32] More declarative than argumentive, Vansová's essays often carried lamentations, and often gave only general directives for the women's movement — directives which can be summarized as simply to work and pray.

Despite this quality of Vansová's work, the first issue of *Dennica* did not satisfy the conservative men grouped around the Slovak newspaper *Národnie noviny* in Martin. Their opinion appeared in an unfavorable review by Ján A. Wagner, which also

Founding of Živena and *Dennica* 97

reflected two background issues: Slovak fear of Czech influence on social policies as well as on language use, and the Svätý Martin group's advocacy of passive resistance against Magyar political repression rather than the active campaign for popular education advocated by the Hlasist group.[33] These issues doubtless limited the intellectual role in the national movement which Wagner allowed women to play, but he was also condescending and paternalistic. Pertinent parts of the review are given:

> In the first place I want to say that the contents of the magazine indicate it is supposed to be a new Slovak literary magazine. Of course, the articles are written by women and concern women's matters, but permit me to say that from a woman's magazine I would expect something other than just fiction, meditations, and verses. I do not know if the greatly respected editor would agree with me when I say that the highest calling of a woman is in domesticity! To lead and support women in that calling is the most beautiful and most important function of a woman's magazine! What great subjects and how much material are available! What lively contents the first issue of *Dennica* would have had if we could read here of the kitchen (for example several good recipes and menus), of bringing up children, of women's employment, of how to entertain guests in a specifically Slovak way, of the biography of outstanding Slovak women, and so on. A single novella might be there too—but how many better subjects could be found!
>
> We see none of this in *Dennica*, and instead among these ten articles are three Czech ones and a letter from Moravia! Now, wasn't there enough Slovak material for these modest sixteen pages? We do not need a new magazine to train Slovak women writers, who can always find an honored place in our special literary magazines. We need a "women's newsletter" [*ženský list*] but in Slovak, a women's *magazine [časopis]*, which by training our women would take the place of the schools we lack, and which would help the activity of our only women's

organization Živena! Behold, even this found no place in the issue!

I also have a remark for the publisher himself! The format and appearance of *Dennica* are not worthy of our women. They deserve something better! I am not thinking here of a lavish edition like the Berlin *Basar* or similar magazines, but *Dennica* almost looks more like a children's magazine than one for Slovak women! They are supposed to be proud of it and display it on a parlor table! Of course, the price of one goldpiece is truly low, but if the magazine presented our women well, they would gladly save two or three goldpieces from the grocery budget! After all, it is in our interest to supplant the foreign press! If our fashionable women really need a woman's magazine, they will not be satisfied with *Dennica* and will continue to turn to foreign magazines.

This is my opinion of the Slovak woman's magazine. I have imparted it *sine ira et studio*! After all, the magazine is just beginning—it can be corrected, but we would be better off with nothing than with a magazine lacking the right goal![34]

In the second issue of *Dennica*, an article by Šoltésová titled "Načo sú tie ženské časopisy?" (What Good Are These Women's Magazines?) responded to criticism of the magazine without referring directly to the review in *Národnie noviny*, which she was doubtless generally aware of even if the review had not yet appeared. Šoltésová posed the question whether separate magazines were good for women themselves. She answered that she herself would prefer to see all but the most specialized journals published for both sexes alike. However, in women's current state of ignorance and anti-intellectualism, many women tended to dismiss as "men's affairs" all but their own immediate domestic concerns. Therefore, such publications as *Dennica* served a valuable function in raising women's intellectual standards.[35]

Besides such defensive articles, *Dennica* carried fiction and poetry treating women's position in the national movement. Doubtless one of its greatest values was the news it gave of

Founding of Živena and *Dennica*

women's activities elsewhere. For example, in the second year, it reported on the International Congress of Women in London in July 1899, and it often carried the names of women who first gained entrance to various European universities or first practiced in a "male" profession. These items alternated with such standard "women's items" as gossip about royalty, legends from exotic lands, recipes, household hints, and advice on cosmetics and clothes, including a piquant appeal (signed by Vansová) against wearing feathers on women's hats because they induced a bloodthirsty trade in helpless tiny birds.[36]

In 1902 *Dennica* carried an article by a Czech nationalist, Hynek Štěpánek, which he had earlier given as a speech to a women's group in southern Bohemia.[37] By no means a radical article, it said nothing not already said by Šoltésová in her long essay on women's education published in 1898 (see Chapter 5). However, it strongly criticized men's egotism and selfishness in the double standard of sexual morality, and condemned women's lack of economic independence. Štěpánek also expressed sympathy and understanding for women's suffering. This latter idea of women's suffering, especially with its implication of male guilt, was a sensitive point for the moralistic, conservative Slovaks around *Národnie noviny*. Štěpánek's article caused so much opposition that Vansová had to defend its publication in an editorial note preceding the second and last installment. Vansová's defense is given in full.

> The Women's Movement: Editorial Note
>
> We accepted Mr. Štěpánek's manuscript as a reference on the women's movement, so that we could learn how the movement arose and what it consists of. We were even happier to accept the article since it came from the pen of a man, who would not likely be biased. After all, we are not narrow-minded, and want to see it clearly and judge it — we do not want to draw a circle around ourselves from which we cannot get out, or get back in again. To clarify a question, one must always grant a place to diverse opinions, without passion or blind emotion.
>
> By publishing this article we did not in any way abandon our own principles. Fears that such an article could bring any "infection" into our society

are premature. Since we want to speak judiciously and objectively, however, we must add that the direction now taken by the emancipation movement is greatly in error. It has diverged from Christ's teaching, from Christianity — it puts the human being above God. After all, who freed women from bondage and vassalage and set them at the level of men? Jesus Christ. "There is no man nor woman, but you are all one in Jesus Christ." Supported by this position, we are convinced that possible progress toward the happiness and elevation of humanity can come only on purely Christian ethical principles. Wherever these principles rule, the "slavery of women" cannot exist. But where do they rule? Where is love? I mean Christlike love. It is not found in the struggle for survival. There lies the rule of force.

In a bazaar fire in Paris, 120 women burned to death, but only five men!

So much, then, as explanation and reassurance for those who were surprised at our publication of the article by Mr. Štěpánek.[38]

Vansová continued as actual editor of *Dennica* until 1907, and her name remained on the title page until the magazine stopped because of the war in 1914. In 1907, however, for personal concerns with her ill husband, she gave the editorship to the young literary critic František Votruba (1880–1953), whose aesthetic interests turned the magazine into primarily a literary journal from 1907 to 1910. The subtitle *Ženský list pre poučenie a zábavu* (Women's Magazine for Instruction and Entertainment) was changed to *Illustrovaný časopis rodinný pre literatúre a otázky spoločenské* (Family Magazine of Literature and Social Questions). To some extent, this change co-opted a women's resource to the service of the national movement and literature as such. The fact that the new editor raised the magazine's quality scarcely balanced women's loss of their forum as a means of enlarging their intellectual horizon.

The direct forum of journalism, however, was not the only one available to these women. Women could find their voice in the indirect forum of fiction and the nationalist heroine. We turn now to that voice.

NOTES

1. Typically women collected money for the privately financed schools and organized benefits for scholarships. See Tkadlečková-Vantuchová 22-23. Marína Hodžová refers to activities of the "Kláštorčianky" in a letter, *Listy Hodžovej* 274, 278.

2. See R. W. Seton-Watson, *A History of the Czechs and Slovaks* (London: Hutchinson and Co. Ltd., 1943) 265–266, and S. B. Kimball, "The Austro-Slav Revival: A Study of Nineteenth-century Literary Foundations," *Trans. Amer. Phil. Soc.* NS 63 (1973): 3–83. My brief article "The Matica slovenská and Its Relation to the Development of Slovak Literature," *Slovakia* 31 (1984): 47–57, outlines the Slovak tendency to identify nationhood with language and literature.

3. Tkadlečková-Vantuchová 11. The early period of Živena is covered by Štefánia Votrubová, *Živena: jej osudy a práca* (Martin: Živena, 1931).

4. Ambro Pietor, "Slovenkám," *Národní hlásnik* 2.5 (May 1869): 143–146.

5. The Czech women's movement, while basically a branch of the national revival, had also indirectly received an impulse from the American women's emancipation movement through Josef Náprstek, a Czech scientist who moved to the United States then returned to Prague and in 1861 (with Karolina Světlá and others) founded an American-style women's club (Americký klub dám). See Svoreňová-Királyová 65 and Tkadlečková-Vantuchová 18.

6. Ambro Pietor, "Spolok slovenských žien," *Peštbudínske vedomosti* 9 (June 2, 1869): [2].

7. *Národní hlásnik* 2.6 (June 1869): 176–177. The letter was untitled and the woman who wrote it is unidentified. Hodžová comes to mind, but she was then living in Silesia.

8. "Sestrám slovenkám sestry Češky," *Národní hlásnik* 24 2 (June 1869): 175–177.

9. Daniel Bachát, "Ozwena z Liptowa," *Národní hlásnik* 2 (June 1869): 173–175. This idea of a magazine for women was picked up by Pietor in the November issue of *Národní hlásnik*, but nothing came of it for twenty years.

10. Ambro Pietor, "Slovenkám: Zakladajme miestne spolky ženské," *Národní hlásnik* 2.11 (November 1869): 337–339.

11. Juraj Kello, *Národní hlásnik* 2.9 (September 1869): 275. This brief article in the news section had no title. Liptovský Trnovec was the town where Johana Lehocká had lived until her death in 1849, and the president of the new organization was her widower's second wife, Žofia Lániová.

12. Juraj Kello, "Reč," *Národní hlásnik* 2.11 (November 1869): 340–342.

13. Votrubová 21–22; however, for some of the Magyar opposition to Živena, see Tkadlečková-Vantuchová 36–41.

14. Votrubová 22–27. See also the account by the Czech woman writer Vilma Sokolová-Seidlová of her visit to the Živena meeting in 1887, *Slovenské pohľady* 45 (1929): 464–465, 474–475.

15. Votrubová 28–33, 37–39, 43–44; Tkadlečková-Vantuchová 51.

16. See Ľubica Bartalská, "K začiatkom organizovania sa slovenských žien v Spojených Štátoch amerických," *Slováci v zahraničí* 11 (1985): 135– 147.

17. Šoltésová's autobiography was published in *Slovenské pohľady* in 1925; I have used its reprint in *Pohľady na literatúre*, ed. Ivan Kusý (Bratislava: Slovenské vydavateľstvo krásnej literatúry,1958) 23, 28, 30. Many of her writings on women were also reprinted by Lea Mrázová, ed. *Začatá cesta* (Martin: Živena, 1934).

18. For these organizational changes, see Tkadlečková-Vantuchová 23–25, 53–54, 61–64.

19. Šoltésová, "Dozvuky k poslednému valnému zhromaždeniu Živeny," *Pohľady na literatúre* 73–80.

20. For Izabela Textorisová's life, see Chapter 4. Her correspondence is in the Památník národního písemnictví in Prague in Fond Vilma Sokolová-Seidlová 34/40. This letter, numbered 3–16 and dated 20 February 1888, was published in part by Sokolová-Seidlová in *Slovenské pohľady* 45 (1929): 461–462.

21. Textorisová had taken up the language question as early as 1884 and returned to it repeatedly. For example, see her letters for 12 April 1886, 8 August 1889, 6 December 1889, 8 December 1895, and 23 March 1927. Her correspondence is extremely interesting and should be published in its entirety, not only for her comments on women and feminism but for her opinions on leading male figures such as Vajanský.

22. Adolf Heyduk (1835–1923) was a Czech nationalist gymnázium teacher, poet, and prose writer who described Slovakia with great sympathy from his travels there. Živena had given him a laurel wreath in 1874 for his poems *Cimbál a husle*; see Tkadlečková-Vantuchová 35.

23. Šoltésová's letter was first published in the letters column of *Ženský svět* 1.5 (1897): 78–79, but I have used the text in *Pohľady na literatúru* 88–91.

24. Šoltésová's letters of 7 March and 11 April 1886 in *Pohľady na literatúru* 224–229.

25. Karel Kálal, "Ženská otázka," *Dom a škola* 12.10 (1896): 311–315. A woman's magazine had been advocated twenty years earlier but without result; see note 9.

26. *Dom a škola*, 13.1 (1897): 20 21. The pseudonym "Slovenka" was identified as "Pani Ruppeldtová z Lipt. Sv. Mikuláša" by Kálal in his chronology (see the following note). According to Tkadlečková-Vantuchová 45–46, this was Klementina Augustiny Ruppeldtová.

27. Kálal, "Dopisy," *Dennica* 1.1 (1898): 14–15.

28. Vilma Sokolová, "Slovenky--naše nejbližší sestry," *Ženský svět* 1.2, 6, 10 (1897): 24–25, 9–10, 146–147.

29. Šoltésová's letter of 14 February 1897, *Pohľady na literatúru* 229–230.

30. Terézia Vansová, "Pila v Gemeri. (Sestrám slovenským)," *Dom a škola* 13.4 (1897): 127.

31. Vansová, "Nový rok, nový krok," *Dennica* 1.1 (January 1898): 2–3.

32. Vansová, "O nás," *Dennica* 1.1 (January 1898): 11–12.

33. For a good English source on the split between Slovak liberals and conservatives, see the work of Edita Bosak, "Czech-Slovak Relations and the Student Organisation Detvan, 1882-1914," *Slovak Politics* (Cleveland: Slovak Institute, 1983) 6–36, and "The Slovak National Movement, 1848-1914," *Reflections on Slovak History* (Toronto: Slovak World Congress, 1987) 59–72. The newspaper *Hlas* lasted only from 1898 to 1904, but its name became a synonym for the movement, which was greatly influenced by the "realist" philosophy of Thomas G. Masaryk. The Hlasists protested against Vajanský's program of passive resistance, criticized his romantic waiting for liberation by the Russian czar, advocated close cooperation with Czech political efforts, and approved of radical social and economic changes.

34. Ján A. Wagner, "Umenie, veda a literatúra," *Národnie noviny* 26 (February 3, 1898).

35. Šoltésová, "Načo sú tie ženské časopisy?" *Dennica* 1.2 (February 1898): 17–19.

36. Vansová, "Prosba k našim dámam," *Dennica* 1.4 (April 1898): 52–55.

37. Hynek Štěpánek, "Ženská otázka a ženské hnutí," *Dennica* 5.1 (January 1902): 14–19, and 5.2 (February 1902): 35–38.

38. Vansová, "Ženské hnutí. Poznámka redakcie," *Dennica* 5.2 (February 1902): 34–35.

CHAPTER 4: NATIONALIST HEROINES IN FICTION

In the last two decades of the nineteenth century, Slovak women writers showed a surprising burst of creativity different from their preceding activity. It undoubtedly was fostered by their more organized role in the national movement shown in the preceding chapter, but, in addition, such female creativity seems to occur in historically flux situations where women see men losing their dominant position. Mary Beth Rose has argued from her work with seventeenth-century English women who wrote biographies and autobiographies in and after the English Civil Wars, that "loss of the social superiority and political hegemony of the men who dominate their world" fosters women's assumption of a new role.[1] The English Civil Wars of 1642–1651 were a more discrete and focussed event than the long process of increasing Magyarization which deprived most Slovak men of normal public roles, yet the comparison seems valid. In the vacuum of Slovak national life after the closing of the Matica and during the "passive resistance" of the Martin nationalists, women writers apparently felt free to write stories and novels embodying their observations and desires in heroic roles for female characters whom we can now see as a new type of heroine.

These Slovak heroines were analogous to the reform heroines of the nineteenth-century English novel. This is not surprising because the various English reform movements, like the Slavic nationalist movements, encouraged women to take up new roles that were otherwise unthinkable in their patriarchal society. Working conditions of the industrial revolution horrified both Christian and socialist reformers whose ranks included women that became simultaneously models for and imitators of the reformist heroines of such novels as Elizabeth Gaskell's *Mary Barton* in 1848, Charlotte Brontë's *Shirley* in 1849, and George Eliot's *Middlemarch* in 1872. Besides such novels ending with marriages, certain fiction shows striking single women, as in Charlotte Yonge's *The Daisy Chain* (1865), whose heroine Ethel May founds a village school and builds a church in a rural area. Similar American heroines appear in Elizabeth Stuart Phelps's *The Silent Partner* (1870), where both a woman factory owner and a mill girl refuse suitable marriages to dedicate themselves to Lady Bountiful–like charity and street preaching respectively. Ellen Moers has named this the "epic age" phenomenon, because it showed the "submersion of private, brooding, female resentment ... in the Christian humanitarianism which, for women and men both, was the major current of Victorian thought."[2] It was not just "stifled feminism that inspired women's literature of social action.... It was also women's craving for a share" in current social movements (21).

To some extent, as said in Chapter 2, these social movements showed a special form of Rousseau's doctrine of women's place, of domesticity as the female realm. Especially relevant to the situation of the Slovaks in noncapitalist Hungary was the Russian variant of the feminization of virtue. Richard Stites has outlined the "romantic idealization of the Russian woman as the embodiment of Virtue and Maternity," including the concept of the "citizen-mother, the bearer and molder of patriotic sons-of-the-fatherland."[3] This phenomenon was in part positive and supportive since it replaced previous "temptress Eve" and *cherchez la femme* syndromes that were powerful in the Russian church. Moreover, Barbara Alpern Engel has shown that the very glorification of Russian women's idealism, constancy, and self-sacrifice had the paradoxical effect of encouraging a few women to apply their attributed moral abilities to causes quite different from those society expected them to follow, whether as part of the intelligentsia, writers, or even nihilists. The Orthodox emphasis upon Christian self-abnegation and service to others prepared some women to successfully challenge and enlarge the purely domestic role designated for them. Some dropped the Christianity and some kept it, but all of them, instead of being just responsible for the morality of the family, felt themselves responsible for the world.[4] The same sort of empowerment seems to have occurred with Slovak women.

Such internalization and re-application of women's attributed moral superiority was not always positive, however, because some women perceived the extreme hypocrisy underlying their glorification. Domestic women actually had in law almost no power to make decisions about their home or children, and powerlessness breeds demoralization. The other harmful element was the fact that overidealization guarantees failure to live up to the ideal. These negative aspects are taken up in Chapter 6.

The new nationalist heroine could not have developed in the lyric poems by women (or by men about women) in the Štúrist tradition shown in Chapter 2. The lyric heroine was a symbolic orphan weeping at the grave of Mother Sláva, a dancer in the emblematic Slavic *kolo* circle dance, the fairytale sister enduring trials to save her brothers, or in a few examples the mystical lover/spouse of the nation. Though the new heroine was plainly related to these poetic symbols of women as help for males, she required the length and realistic detail allowed by the novel form, or at least by the story and novella forms, for her to develop her own space. She also required the concern with immediacy, social changes, and literary verisimilitude that characterized prose realism.

The Slovak nationalist heroine had parallels in other national movements, of course, and Karolina Světlá's first novel, *První Češka* (The First Czech Woman, 1861), showed a common pattern. Highly romanticized, the heroine abandons her rich Germanized family in Prague, retires to a village, and brings up two sons to fight on the barricades in Prague in the 1848 revolution against Austria. Typically, the city is negatively contrasted to rural life, which stayed closer to Czech culture, and the heroine inspires the actions of others: "not only with love but with pride we must regard her. She aroused our whole countryside in a short time, and the national spirit wafts through every cottage."[5] Influenced by George Sand (whom she translated), Světlá showed all her heroines as "idealized women who were heroic in their self-sacrifice and their purity of emotion."[6]

The appeal of this new kind of heroine is obvious when compared to the traditional moralizing tales of aristocrats with strange fates in foreign lands that were typical of cheap popular reading for young women. The following titles show this character: "Cykáni, anebo Nesst'astný Ferdynand, Pěkný prjklad na wýstrahu mladym lidem" (Gypsies, or Unfortunate Ferdinand, A Nice Example as a Warning to Young People); "Ubohá Marye, Prjbeh pro utrpné čtenářky" (Miserable Mary, a Tale for Sympathetic [Female] Readers); "Sslechetná wdowa" (The Noble Widow); and "Amálie Westonská," an English widow who married a maharajah in Hyderabad.[7] By contrast, the nationalist heroine was local, contemporary, and someone young women could identify with. Moreover, the almost mystical concept of the nation allowed escape from gender roles into a satisfying commonality for women who otherwise would have remained outsiders.

The Slovak nationalist heroine appeared first in texts by male writers, for several reasons. As said in Chapter 2, only a few women poets continued writing past their youth, and a new generation had to build upon the previous one. It was also necessary to develop the new prose genres, as indicated by the first simplistic male stories. At any rate, my interest lies not in priority for the nationalist heroine, but in the way Slovak women writers internalized and transformed it.

Among the earliest examples of the nationalist heroine was a long story "Milan a Milina" in 1862 by a Lutheran pastor, Štefan Križan (1826–1894), which showed a young woman resisting her Magyarized family and finally marrying a Slovak nationalist. Križan shows her (like Marína Hodžová) founding a small women's society, planning a theater group, and speaking favorably of public activities for women, i.e. nationalist activities "suited to their female worth."[8] Milina's meditation is similar to the lyric poems written by women at this time, in that she equates her lover to the nation and identifies with it herself as an orphan:

> When I love the Slovaks, I love Michalovský with them, and in my Milan I love the whole Slovak nation. That's my guiding star, and I'll never let it go, no matter what.... Yes, I love you, my dear nation. Why, I'm your faithful daughter, like an apple from the same tree. You're the large version, I'm the small one: you and I—poor orphans. No one takes care of us, and those who want to care for us, cannot. (1.7: 228)

Among the simplest examples of nationalist prose fiction are two short stories by Daniel Bachát in 1868. In his "Ľudmilka" the beautiful, good, kind heroine refuses a Magyar squire and marries a Slovak schoolteacher; she is seen reading Johana Lehocká's "Slowenka," which although not identified is reprinted in full. In "Bohumil" a young Slovak journeyman dyer refuses a rich Magyar widow to return to his faithful Slovak fiancée, who herself does nothing but show abstract goodness and faithfulness to the nation.[9]

Such simplistic heroines did not appear in the best male fiction. Svetozár Hurban Vajanský (1847–1916) created a variety of female characters ranging from mere male supporters to independent females who are unexpected from the dogmatic editor we earlier saw opposing even the simple women's almanac proposed by Šoltésová and Vansová (Chapter 3). Though he was a conservative who was out of touch with women's new aspirations, his work reflected those aspirations far more than he must have intended. Vajanský's artistic temperament was full of irony, subtlety, and ambiguity, and it is a commonplace of Vajanský criticism that his life and work show the conflict between his wide aesthetic interests and his narrow duty as a Slovak nationalist, between his talent and his restricted opportunity. This conflict gave both depth and desperation to his characters, including his women. As W. E. Harkins has said, Vajanský's ambiguous vacillation "between realism and idealism ... is artistically fruitful and creative," and to our own times his "impatience with the constraints of form seems original and refreshing."[10]

Vajanský's view of women shows two aspects. First was his Rousseauesque belief in women's inherent sacrificial nature and their moral power over men. The novella "Mier duše" (A Peaceful Conscience, 1881) gives his most extreme picture.[11] The argument that women must make superhuman self-sacrifices appears at first ironic, since it comes from the heroine Eugénia, and two male characters play the devil's advocate. The central scene begins with sympathy for the economic and legal disadvantage of women during an outburst of the heroine, who has been abused then abandoned by a degenerate husband:

> "What can happen to a man that is this terrible? If you lose your fortune, you make another. Even if you don't make a new fortune, you're still a number in the world—you need only add zeroes to increase your worth. If you lose someone dear to you, time heals the wound! What loss is too great for a man to forget? Even if the worst occurs and you lose your good name and honor, there's still a way out: the world is wide, and you can begin a new life in the other hemisphere or on the equator. It's different for us. We're no longer what we were." (1: 355)

Eugénia then describes her self-sacrificial love, and her conviction that she is still bound to her husband by this love and by his corruption of her: "What good is legal relief to me, or the forgiveness of the church, when internally I can't free myself?" (358). Later she realizes she is being offered an honorable new life, but her thoughts battle this idea:

> What would she bring to this man who, moved by decency or even pity for her, would draw to himself such a discordant creature who could never again strike a pure tone? Poisoned, she would poison him, destroyed destroy him, and thrown into the pit she would pull him in with her. (372)

The man she loves slowly convinces her she has the right to a new life, but at that moment her husband returns, repentant and tubercular, so she devotes her life to care of him. Despite the male characters' arguments against this self-martyrdom, Vajanský emphasizes his approval in the last line: "Truly, she was superior to all of us with her exalted beliefs!" (382).

This ideal of pathological self-sacrifice was for Vajanský a part of the "eternal feminine." A similar form of women's moral power is shown in the novella *Dve sestry* (Two Sisters, 1882), where the innocent goodness and strength of young Anna miraculously reform a corrupted baron.

The second aspect of Vajansky's view of women reflects the passionate nationalism expressed in the articles and activities for which he was three times imprisoned by Hungarian courts. Believing that Slovaks desperately needed women's sacrificial reforming power, he feared that emancipation would alter traditional family life and thus destroy the only existing base for Slovak culture. This fear made him less favorable to women writers while he was an editor and official of Živena (as indicated in Chapter 3), than his father Jozef Miloslav Hurban had been while editor of *Nitra* in the 1840s (as seen in Chapter 2). Vajanský diminished women's national role to an indirect and supporting one. He summarized this position in a speech at the annual meeting of Živena in 1902. Retrospectively one can see it affecting all of his work, so I have given a long passage here (italics in the original):

> Human society, which from primeval times has been based upon the family, is losing the ground under its feet by casting out family feeling, and building in its place an extreme individualism that allows nothing else, no authority, no limiting bonds at all. Even family love and cohesion are considered chains to be cut and obstacles to be broken so that the individual can enjoy unlimited liberty. Yet we know that

unlimited liberty is savagery, and the fruits of savagery are ruin and death.... Women, the protectors of the familial fires, stand in the front line to defend the fortress of the home, so that destructive individualism cannot tear apart the bond of souls, the bond of simple, rightful interest. Women's blessed, natural conservatism was able to preserve our sacred customs through the ages.... Women's strength is their femininity, their faithful watching over the heritage of the family....

Exactly at present, as I said, tossed about by wild, uncontrolled currents, we Slovaks are seizing upon the family, and only upon the family, like a stone to grasp on the bank of a wild river. Everyone knows how we are exiled from many forums of public life, how our policies lead to no rainbow, how our defenses are falling and our moats filling up. The family is our refuge, and women are the Vestals protecting our family fires. At home we can hear the sweet sound *of our mother tongue*. We call our wonderful language our mother tongue, not our father tongue: see what an exalted symbol this is of female importance, female regard, female historical goodness..., and see how greatly our life is endangered when women betray their beautiful, natural calling. Only in and with that calling can women grow, become liberated, and reach full equivalence to men with their hard, physical, dangerous efforts, works, and battles. In the family fulfilling their beautiful, natural calling, women grow into direct, co-equal, and highly regarded authoritative figures. In their calling they become free, autonomous, and grand![12]

This view of women as the national guardian takes several forms in Vajanský's fiction. The novella *Babie leto* (Indian Summer, 1882) shows a nationalist heroine about whom one of the male characters exclaims, "This is no longer Aphrodite, but already Pallas Athena!" She denounces a turncoat Slovak:

"You're a failure like all your comrades. What good is your life? .... Do you even know you're Slovak?...

No! You lie to yourself. For thirty years you've blinded yourself. Our men were beaten, and we women were left as the objects of your egotistic desire. But we have more strength than you've ever dreamed of!" (190)

Her passionate activity, however, is uniquely motivated because she is the daughter of a Slovak revolutionary in 1848 who was hanged and secretly buried on the hilltop where her dramatic denunciation of the turncoat takes place. Moreover, she does not convert the turncoat to the national cause, and he continues his useless life while she marries a German supporter of the Slovaks.

Some of Vajanský's nationalist women are so limited that we are almost back with Kollár's Mína and Sládkovič's Marína, who existed only in their effect upon men. In the novella *Ľalia* (Lily, 1880) the heroine comforts her nationalist husband:

She did not understand his whole speech, but she felt in her pure soul the dead weight of the battle he had to undertake each day. And when the wrinkles in his anxious brow revealed his voracious pain, she patted his face with her soft hand, and her cheerful smile drove away the worries and pain from her husband's soul. (1: 228)

In the novella *Podrost* (Undergrowth, 1881) the heroine, who has been brought to nationalist beliefs by two young men, calls the nation her lover and weeps that "she was not born a man so that she could quench her soul's thirst by action" (1: 329). But when she falls in love with one of the young men, they laugh at her nationalism, then soothe her by saying, "the noble female heart joins both loves in harmony" (337).

In *Závejmi náruživostí* (Snowdrifts of Passion, 1891) the heroine ruins her life by indecision and passivity, both personal and national, and the hero does the same. They are both Oblomov types—self-destructive "superfluous" people who live without commitment or purpose—but the hero blames himself, not her, and relates only his personal sins, not hers, to neglect of the national cause.

Vajanský's most famous novel, *Suchá ratolesť* (The Dead Branch, 1884), though intensely nationalistic, does not have a real nationalist heroine. The novel's theme is that the dead branch on the national tree is the Magyarized gentry represented by young

Stanislav Rudopolský, who, however, returns to his Slovak roots. The beautiful Mária inspires him in his artistic career as a painter, and he falls in love with and marries the independent widow Adela, but he is converted to the Slovak cause mainly by the arguments and moral example of his friend Albert Tichý. The women's beauty and independence help break down Rudopolský's prejudices and indifference to the Slovak cause, but his conversion is male-inspired and intellectual, not emotional. Mária, in fact, is closer to the classical female muse who inspires male art than she is to Mína or the national sisters who are written of so much in the lyrical poetry of the Štúrist tradition. Even women's helping role was limited in this novel. Nevertheless, Vajanský's women characters are rich and would deserve full treatment elsewhere.

The number of women writers increased rapidly in the 1870's and 1880's, and four women wrote enough to be considered major. As with the Štúrist poets, almost all of these women writers were related to Lutheran pastors or schoolteachers, and since the Slovak national movement, the women's movement, and the women's literary movement were all aspects of one phenomenon, they were usually the same women who were active in the women's organizations and magazines.

Terézia Medvecká Vansová began her writing career in 1875 with a cycle of sentimental poetry like that of the earlier women (Appendix, Nos.118–123), and after her marriage to a Lutheran pastor working in a German area of northern Slovakia she wrote verse and prose in German. She returned to the Slovak language in 1884 with short pieces in the newspaper *Národnie noviny*, and from then on wrote a variety of sketches, tales, biographical pieces, and memoirs as well as several plays both for children and for adults.[13] Five texts are especially interesting.

The story "Supplikant" (Student [asking for alms], 1885) shows the first of Vansová's attractive, spirited, independent heroines.[14] Darinka Trnavská has grown up without a mother and with only a distracted, ineffectual father, so she has had to become independent-minded. Contrasted favorably with a weak-willed beauty and several malicious gossips, she is rewarded with a husband who admires her self-sufficiency:

> I don't want a wife whom I'd have to lead around
> like an immature child and who would in all the
> harder questions of life go to others for answers.

> No, I certainly want a wife who can sometimes stand
> up by herself, and one who when necessary will even
> stamp her foot. (50)

There is no explicit nationalism except a passing reference to the hero's activity in a Slovak youth group (48), and Vansová simply assumes a Slovak society without showing the conflict over Magyarization. This indirect nationalism became characteristic of her work.

At age thirty-two Vansová wrote the first novel by a Slovak woman, *Sirota Podhradských* (The Orphan of the Podhradský Family, 1889), only five years after Vajanský's first novel. Instead of having a typical nationalist heroine, the novel is like the popular Gothic novels in showing a determined young heroine who survives extraordinary adventures by unrealistically but satisfyingly relying on her own strength. The orphan Viola's relative hardness and independence are the fruits of her difficult life as an orphan after her father dies in disgrace, and she is favorably contrasted to a dependent, superficial, manipulative girl. Viola restores her dead father's reputation as well as the family fortune and marries a young man whom she converts to a more noble life.[15] Critics generally agree that Vansová was trying to attract Slovak women readers by giving them the kind of romance that was popular in German and Magyar literature. Thus, she was creating a Slovak heroine indirectly and implicitly.

One of Vansová's few strongly nationalistic pieces was the novella *Hojže Bože!* in 1898, whose title invokes Sládkovič's verse "Hojže bože, jak to bolí, keď sa junač roztratí" (Oh Lord, how it hurts, when the young lads must scatter).[16] It traces a group of male students whose fates range over emigration, early death in poverty, Magyarization, and faithfulness to the Slovak cause. The two men who remain active nationalists have wives illustrating Vansová's ideal women: Ilona, who sacrifices her own young dreams to marry a widowed pastor with children; and Pavla, the wife of a lawyer, who conducts her household quietly but firmly in the national spirit and encourages her daughter Anna to buy *Hlásnik* for peasant families, circulate Slovak and Czech books, and sing Slovak folk songs in public while continuing her education at home instead of in a foreign school.

The elderly pastor, besides representing a Slovak nationalist, expresses Vansová's perception of the chauvinism among most nationalists. He takes a young wife to care for his children and household but lets her know she does not reach his ideal. In a delirious speech after the death of her first child, she grieves over his coolness to her compared to his love for "his darling, his ethereal, high, unreachable ideal" (114). When he overhears her, he feels guilty but defends himself:

> He did love her, though of course in his own strict way. He wanted a wife of such excellence as his ideal had, and she was not capable of reaching that level, as in fact very few women could. (115)

Vansová writes explicitly that he "scarcely agreed with the so-called emancipation of women, and like most of our prominent men believed that women needed little education." Conversation with the bright daughter Anna therefore surprises him, and forgetting she is not a student he encourages her intellectual interests (119). On his death bed, he recognizes the depth of his wife's love, and praises women's love and special nature: "What is our love compared to yours? It is egotism in comparison to your endless kindness and accommodation. We can never reach your level of love!" (123). Then he relates her love for himself to his own love for the nation, without a word of her wider love for the nation though she was herself a nationalist.

Vansová's "Stará piesen" (The Same Old Story, 1898) pictures the classic self-sacrificing spinster "whose greatest joy is to do something for others," and who rears her orphaned siblings and one of their children.[17] Her ward Darina leaves a drunken husband and is thus "declassée, derailed" until she is happily rejoined by him after his reform. Yet the story seems faintly ironic, or tentative and uncertain, probably reflecting Vansová's own uncertainty with the changing status of unmarried or formerly married women. The spinster is favorably contrasted to her widowed sister who lives on false memories of her no-good husband, but Darina wants marriage instead of an independent life as a postmistress. She wants life "at the shoulder of the man of her heart ... absorbed in the care of children and their daily needs" (203–204). She admits to envy at the happiness of a married friend who cites Madame de Staël on love as "everything" for women, at which point the spinster reveals the secret of her own stoic resignation: "We should always compare ourselves to those who are less fortunate, and that way we can avoid dissatisfaction" (205). This cannot have been written without Vansová's irony!

Most of Vansová's heroines were unusually (and probably unrealistically) independent, including the girl Ružena who tries to collect money in support of the women's organization Živena at a Magyarone gathering, and is ridiculed. She is nicknamed a "vixen" in a pun on the title "Vlčia tma" (Night Blindness, literally "wolf's darkness," 1902), which also refers to the affliction of the man she eventually marries. Interestingly, he is a Moravian who understands Slovak nationalism better than the Slovak male characters do.[18]

Elena Maróthy Šoltésová was the next woman writer to publish her works, which consisted of six stories, one somewhat realistic novel, numerous essays, and an autobiographical narrative of the lives and deaths of her two children. Her novel soon received international attention, being translated into Czech in 1897 and Croatian in 1898.[19]

Šoltésová's stories progressed in complexity and in nationalism. "Na dedine" (In the Village, 1881) has a brief scene where a school girl reads to the village women, and "Prípravy ku svadbe" (Preparations for the Wedding, 1882) realistically describes village customs. Šoltésová's novella "V čiernickej škole" (In the Čierna School, 1891) is a long account of the courtship of a schoolteacher's daughter by a young teacher. It shows equal parts of nationalism and romantic love as she inspires him to "feel abler and stronger in doing everything good" (1: 184).

In Šoltésová's novel, *Proti prúdu* (Against the Current, 1894), a beautiful middle-class young Slovak woman captivates and converts a Slovak count who has fallen away from the nation. Šavelský, i.e. Šavel who becomes Pavel, returns to his origins against the current of Magyarization, while she is content to be an exemplary nationalist wife and mother at home. Like Vajanský's novel *Suchá ratolesť* ten years earlier, *Proti prúdu* reflects the nationalist effort to recover the former Slovak gentry and aristocracy, but historically the effort was doomed to failure because most of this social class had become assimilated with the Magyar aristocracy by the seventeenth and eighteenth centuries. Also, the nationalist movement was essentially democratic and could not be made attractive to a cosmopolitan class still clinging to its inherited privileges. Old arguments about this effort peaked when Šoltésová's novel was published, and the effort dropped of its own weight.[20]

The novel explicitly and repeatedly touches on the question whether Savelský is converted by his wife. She claims not to want to determine his views, saying that he started toward Slovak nationalism alone and will continue on his own (5: 130), that she does not want him helpless and dependent before her (5: 158), and that she wants him to change "through his own honor and love of truth" (5: 181). He tells her that despite her effort to be neutral she is in fact partly responsible for his change, because though he observed fanatic injustices that diminished his former idealistic Magyar nationalism, it was his love and admiration for her own unselfish love of her nation that ennobled him (5: 184–187). His Magyar friends too discuss her effect on him and reach Šoltésová's conclusion that she influenced him to change but his convictions are now his own (6: 216–218). We can see here the same equation of love for the nation and for the *ginoch* or *junák* that appeared in women's poems in Chapter 2. Other characters reinforce the idea of mutual support in marriage. For example, Fedora is a frivolous girl until her visits to her husband in prison for his political activity increase her moral strength and self-respect (6: 157), and he in turn "gains moral support from her" (6: 160).

In later stories, Šoltésová shows this same view of marriage as a partnership to which the wife contributes not only moral precepts but their application as well, even in matters of business and public life. For example, in the story "Prvé previnenie" (First Transgression, 1896), the wife asks her lawyer husband to lower his fees for the poverty-stricken peasants and she promises to economize in their household. He answers that "since she understands their situation so well she has a right to speak up about it," and he promises that they have an agreement for life, since "whenever one forgets, the other is responsible to mention it and hold both to the contract."[21] However, in "Popolka (Cinderella, 1898), Šoltésová limits the wife's freedom of conscience in serious ethical questions by creating a husband who allows and is pleased by his wife's independent views and her defense of them, but if he perceived a moral error he would become "the enemy of her independence."[22] In both stories the women foster their husbands' nationalism. This concept of equitable marriage doubtless owed much to the Reformation concept of marriage as "the school for character, ... a partnership in the common endeavor of rearing children in the fear of the Lord and of working together in his vineyard."[23] Šoltésová and the other nationalist women simply added work for the nation to this religious concept.

The third major woman writer was Ľudmila Riznerová, who took the name Podjavorinská (1872–1951). Daughter of a Lutheran schoolteacher in western Slovakia and niece of the bibliographer Ľudovít Rizner, she did not marry and lived primarily from the royalties of her work, particularly its publication in American-Slovak magazines. Her first verses were published in 1888 when she was only sixteen, and her book of lyrics *Z vesny života* (From the Springtime of Life, 1895) was the first poetry collection published by a Slovak woman.[24] Though her poetry was mainly romantic, her prose fiction tended to realism like that of Vansová and Šoltésová.[25]

Besides Podjavorinská's early comic peasant stories about both sexes, peasant women appear as a type of universal heroine capable of independent action. In *Postupne* (Gradually, 1900) a heroic peasant girl unsuitably marries a nobleman but then saves him morally and financially. In "Na záletoch" (Going Courting, 1902) and *Žena* (Wife, 1910), vigorous determined women govern their households as benevolent despots over weak males. Certain of Podjavorinská's texts show an ironic, even satiric point quite different from the direct earnestness of Vansová and Šoltésová. For example, "Záhada" (Mystery, 1905) shows an attractive intellectual girl studying philosophy and a beautiful domestic village girl, but their common friend, a young medical student, "mysteriously" chooses neither of them. Instead, he runs after a scarcely educated, shallow, fashionable girl who has infatuated him.

Podjavorinská's directly nationalistic heroines are especially interesting because, unlike Šoltésová's idealized, abstract women, they show many of the real activities of enthusiastic young spinsters like Podjavorinská herself. For instance, in "Ideál" (The 'Ideal' Suitor, 1896) the man whom Terézia Selenská loves must marry his benefactor's ward, so the forgiving Terézia builds up a picture of him as an ideal nationalist and contents herself with a quiet village life of instilling nationalism in the young pupils of her small sewing school. After ten years, when she visits her old lover and sees the reality of his lazy, irresponsible life, she regrets her sacrifice of her other suitor and faces an old age of lonely disillusionment. She is rescued from this prospect, however, by the reappearance of her other suitor, now a widower who needs a nationalistic stepmother for his daughters. This romantic nationalistic ending belies the realism of Terézia's activities, which copied the small "heroisms" typical of the restricted Slovak life:

> What could a weak woman do alone? She could only teach her young pupils to go their own way instead of following foreign fashions, so that she replaced *Modernblatt* and *Képeslap* with Slovak magazines in several families. By her influence young ladies met together to read Slovak poetry and sing Slovak songs.... (292) The young teacher was not just teaching handwork, but love of mother tongue, music, and literature. The consciousness that she was at least a little useful gratified her. (300)

This same picture of female activities occurs in "Z domova" (From Home, 1898), where a pastor's daughter Božena collects folk songs sung by the peasants, buys and lends Slovak books, and secretly tells fairy tales to the village schoolchildren. She refuses the hand of a young pastor who succumbs to assimilation, and resists her parents' old-fashioned beliefs: "Father always says a woman shouldn't mess with politics, and mother just wants marriage, just marriage!" (362). The story ends with Božena's meditation on the natural way a young peasant couple have fallen in love and married, which is so different from her own complex situation:

> They won't suffer over their unhappy nation, or spoil their days with differing opinions on the nationality problem. They'll just simply, naturally fullfil the role of healthy, living parts of the great body.... But look at us! We sigh for a far-off ideal, maybe unachievable, and condition our personal happiness on it. While we're binding ourselves to this whole effort, to this vain dream that may never come true, we're neglecting and perhaps even losing forever the chance to be useful where we are strong enough and

naturally capable enough to do some good. (383–384)

She goes on to ask the question that must have represented the greatest temptation for young nationalist women — the question whether the national good should take precedence over the good of all humans:

> Who knows whether in my case Mama isn't right? Whether it's not my duty to marry — and marry a man who isn't strong enough to fight for the nation, but still can be a true servant of God for the Slovak people, a decent worker in the field of humanity and goodness? Maybe I'm needed to stand by his side and protect him from falling still lower? To fill the place by his hearth instead of someone who might not guard him and might even push him along the traitorous path? Wouldn't it be a noble deed to return his children to the nation he himself doesn't protect, or even together with him just do good works: counsel, help, love all people without national distinction? (384)

Podjavorinská does not accept this "noble deed," however, and ends the story as the young idealist shakes her head and to calm herself begins reading the reassuring verses of Sládkovič.

These major texts by Vansová, Šoltésová, and Podjavorinská carry the nationalist heroine as far as it went in this period. Several minor writers wrote romantic stories, often with pseudonyms. Among the earliest, Hermína Moštenanová (1845–1933) using the pseudonym "Miloslava Ruslanská," published "Opice čo zkúmatel lásky" (A Monkey as the Test of Love, 1872), where a rich Italian father sets his daughter's suitors to care for a large monkey for ten days to reveal their true characters. The daughter is a pretty dummy with no part in the choice.[26] This tale was still in the tradition of exotic and romantic moral tales that formed the bulk of women's light reading before the advent of the nationalist heroine. Hermína Orphanides (1853–1916), using the pseudonym "Cilka," wrote numerous sketches and slight romantic stories in 1892–1897 for *Slovenské noviny*, the government magazine for Slovaks,[27] and M. Rusnáková, as "Žialica," wrote three high-society love stories in *Dennica* in 1899–1900.[28] Other minor writers commonly mentioned are Milina Laciaková Zochová (1854–

1944), Marína Oľga Horváthová (1859–1947), Marína Ormisová Maliaková (1861–1946), Elena Ivanková (1871–1941), and Oľga Textorisová (1880–1938). Few if any of their stories have been reprinted.

Writing seems to have been a nearly automatic part of nationalist activity, and nationalist women were almost required to try to become writers. This equation of nationalist with writer appears nowhere more strongly than with Izabela Textorisová (1866–1949), whose clear aptitude for botanical research was ignored if not scorned by other women nationalists who urged her to dedicate herself to writing.[29] The unmarried daughter of an impoverished lawyer, she supported herself as a government postmistress, and lived as a "secret" nationalist while helping two sisters gain a Slovak education. Her letters reveal almost paranoid fear in the details of how she disguised her contacts with "panslavs," and they explain the bitterness of her later life.[30] At the insistence of the Czech Slovakophile Vilma Sokolová, Textorisová wrote one story, "Zásvit" (Flash of Light, 1893), using the pseudonym "B. Rudinská," about a Magyarized girl who suddenly discovers and loves her Slovak roots. The heroine resists her parents but leans upon her brother for education and psychological support.[31] Far more interesting is Textorisová's correspondence with Sokolová in which we see a highly intellectual nationalist who read widely (e.g. J. S. Mill and George Eliot), learned five languages, considered herself a feminist, was unsparingly critical of many associates, and avidly followed political affairs though she played no public role. One wonders how many other such women's letters may be lying undiscovered in archives.

The nationalist heroine and her creator wanted to make a difference for the nation, whereas the new heroine we shall see in Chapter 6 sometimes remained a nationalist, but she saw the national cause as a means for her own fulfillment, instead of seeing herself as a means for national fulfillment. Prose fiction, however, was not the only means of arguing for women's rights, and two important essays also show the transition from the concept of women as help to that of women as a class with inherent rights. We turn to these essays in Chapter 5.

NOTES

1. Mary Beth Rose, "Introduction" and "Gender, Genre, and History: Seventeenth Century English Women and the Art of Autobiography," *Women in the Middle Ages and Renaissance* (Syracuse: Syracuse U P, 1986) xiii–xxviii, 245–278. The citation is from xxvi.

2. Ellen Moers, *Literary Women* (Garden City, NY: Doubleday, 1976) 19.

3. Stites 15–16.

4. Barbara Alpern Engel, *Mothers and Daughters: Women of the Intelligentsia in Nineteenth-Century Russia* (Cambridge: Cambridge U P, 1983) Part I and passim.

5. Karolina Světlá, originally Johanna Rottová (1830–1899), wrote voluminously and was very popular for her fiction as well as her activity in the Czech movement for women's education. The quotation is from *První Češka* (Prague: Jos. R. Vilímek, 1948) 293. Božena Němcová (1820–1862), of course, is recognized as the first major Czech woman prose writer, but though she was plainly a Czech nationalist her themes and characters were universal and she did not create a nationalist heroine in the sense used here.

6. *Dějiny české literatury,* Vol. 3 (Prague: ČSAV, 1961) 124.

7. These are titles in a small paperback collection published by Aloizyus Jozef Landfras in Tábor in 1835, without authorship. I have found no scholarship on the subject of popular reading materials before nationalist literature, but it would seem an instructive study.

8. Štefan Križan, "Milan a Milina," *Sokol,* 1.4–9 (1862): 118+. The quotation is from 1.7: 231.

9. For "Ľudmilka" see note 52 in Chapter 2; "Bohumil" was published in *Národné hlásnik,* 1.9 (30 September 1868): 208–212.

10. On these qualities, see William E. Harkins, "Vajanský and Turgenev," *Slovakia*, 30 (1982–1983): 92–99. The quotation is from 96.

11. With Vajanský's work I have used where possible the critical texts now appearing in *Spisy* (Bratislava: Tatran, 1984–). Volume numbers are given in the text with the page numbers. For "Babie leto" I used the earlier collected works *Sobrané dielo*, 2 (Martin: Matica slovenská, 1948): 123–199.

12. Vajanský, "Reč tajomníka," *Národnie noviny*, 33 (7 August 1902): 2–3.

13. Vansová's works were partially collected as *Sobrané spisy*, 3 vols. (Martin, 1919–1922) and 8 vols. (Liptovský Mikuláš, 1941–1947). Where possible, I have cited from the original source as indicated. Her biography was written by Margita Václaviková-Matulay, *Život Terézie Vansovej* (Bratislava: Nakl. Slovenskej Ligy, 1937). An excerpt from *Danko a Janko* was translated into English by Cincura 135–137.

14. Vansová, "Supplikant," *Živena. Národní almanach* 2 (1885): 17–67.

15. Vansová, *Sirota Podhradských*, Vol. 8 of *Sobrané spisy* (Liptovský Mikuláš: Tranoscius, 1947).

16. Vansová, "Hojže Bože!" *Od Šumavy k Tatrám*, ed. K. Salva and K. Kálal (Ružomberok, 1898): 102–124.

17. Vansová, "Stará pieseň," *Slovenské pohľady*, 18.3 –4 (1898): 154–161, 193–209. The quotation is from 200.

18. Vansová, "Vlčia tma," *Sobrané spisy Terézie Vansovej*, 2nd ed. (Martin: Tatran, 1923) 1: 61–131.

19. Terézia Kaššayová, ed., "Personálna bibliografia Eleny Maróthy-Šoltésovej," *Elena Maróthy Šoltésová* (Martin: Matica slovenská, 1987) 195–243. Šoltésová's works were collected as *Sobrané spisy*, 6 vols. (Martin, 1921–1925), which is the text I have used when original texts were unavailable. An excerpt from *Moje*

deti was translated into English by Cincura 132–135. Šoltésová's life and works are summarized in *Dictionary of Continental Women Writers*, ed. Katharina M. Wilson (New York: Garland, in press).

20. For recent work on assimilation of the Slovak gentry, see Branislav Varsik, *Otázky vzniku a vývinu slovenského zemianstva*. One of the strongest condemnations of the effort to reclaim the gentry came in the review of Šoltésová's novel by the realist writer Martin Kukučín; for a summary English treatment of it, see my "Preliminary Notes on Martin Kukučín's Criticism of Americanized Slovaks and his Opposition to the Slovak Gentry," *Slovak Studies* 18 (1978): 153–165.

21. "Prvé previnenie," *Letopis Živeny* 1 (1896): 78.

22. "Popolka," *Letopis Živeny* 2 (1898): 95–96.

23. Bainton 10.

24. Podjavorinská, *Z vesny života* (Ružomberok: Karol Salva, 1895).

25. Only incomplete collections of Podjavorinská's work have appeared, and I have used the latest selection, *Dielo* (Bratislava: Tatran, 1987), which has a complete chronology and bibliography by Jozefína Ballová, 576–589. A biographical sketch was written by Margita Václaviková-Matulay, *Tvorba Ľudmily Podjavorinskej* (Bratislava: Nakladateľstvo Čas, [1942]). "Žena" was translated into English by Cincura 144–160. Podjavorinská's life and works are summarized in *Dictionary of Continental Women Writers*, ed. Katharina M. Wilson (New York: Garland, in press).

26. Hermína Moštenanová, "Opica čo zkúmatel lásky," *Živena. Národní almanach* 1 (1872): 90–95. She was identified by Ormis, *Doplnky* 8: 114.

27. See Rizner for Orphanides' works, 3: 335–336.

28. M. Rusnáková, "Vodná ľalia," *Dennica* 2.5 (1899): 73–76; "Neverník," *Dennica* 3.5–6 (1900): 97–100; and "Čajový večierok," *Dennica* 3.11 (1900): 198–203, 3.12 (1900): 211–212. I thank Dr. J. Ballová of Matica slovenská for these references.

29. Textorisová collected and identified plants in central Slovakia and corresponded with Slovak and Magyar botanists, though her main work remained unpublished. A biography on this part of her life was written by Margita Velehrachová, *Izabela Textorisová: Zo života slovenskej botaničky* (Bratislava: Mladé leta, 1975).

30. Textorisová's letters, dated 1885–1898 besides one in 1910 and the last in 1927, are in the Fond Vilma Sokolová-Seidlová 34/40 of the Památník národního písemnictví in Prague. A few of her letters were given by Sokolová in "Slovenky--naše nejbližší sestry," *Ženský svět*, 1 (1897): 24–25, 146–147, and much later in *Slovenské pohľady*, 45 (1929): 457–467. In February 1886 Textorisová refused to let Eliška Krasnohorská publish a letter for fear of losing the position by which she supported her sisters' schooling, but she wrote a brief article giving the same views, signed "Slovenka" in *Ženské listy* (1886), according to Sokolová 465.

31. Izabela Textorisová, "Zásvit," *Divčí svět* (Prague, 1893) 251–279. Even Šoltésová considered the story unrealistic, *Pohľady na literatúre*, 243. Textorisová had shown her strong self-knowledge earlier when she wrote to Sokolová that she did not have the active imagination needed for fiction (Letter No. 56 dated 18 October 1888).

PART III: WOMEN AS WOMEN

CHAPTER 5: CHRISTIAN EQUALITY OF THE SEXES

The idea of Slovak women as help in the national movement persisted through the period in which women were slowly recognizing their duty to themselves, not only to family and nation. Rather than a complete break with the old tradition, this new recognition appeared as a modification or amplification of the pure nationalist goal. Women's self-fulfillment was often presented as a good for the family and the nation, which of course still amounted to the idea of women as help, but their help almost imperceptibly shaded into an absolute not a relative value. As a result, self-fulfillment of women came to appear as an integral and essential part of national fulfillment, not a means to national fulfillment.

This distinction is critical and can be seen in a comparison of texts. For example, in 1869 Ambro Pietor wrote, "We are sure that women will try to reach that level of humanity Divine Wisdom has honored them with—that level they will have to reach if they wish our nation to free itself from spiritual and material slavery."[1] In 1898 Karel Kálal wrote:

> It is obvious that women should be educated to the highest degree possible (312). When a woman is capable of becoming a physician, let her become one; when she is able to become a professor, let her become one. Man does not have the right to smother the talents given a woman by the Creator (313).[2]

Among women the difference is also seen. In 1846 Johana Lehocká wrote: "Just show us the right path, teach us yourselves since we don't have our own school, and cultivate our spirit yourselves..., and you shall see how we shall awaken and gratefully follow in your footsteps."[3] In 1882 Elena Maróthy Soltésová wrote:

> It is completely proper that women as women should be educated. It is unjust to provide the advantages of education to only one half, the male half, of humanity. We are certain we're not asking for anything unjust, we want nothing that is evil. We don't understand politics, we hate no one, we just want our sacred rights![4]

This change in the view of women inevitably occurred within the Christian framework already seen in nationalist writings. Slovak life had no counterpart of the radical emancipation movement seen elsewhere with such women as Alexandra Kollontai and Emma Goldman. Instead, the classic text for the Slovak writers was St. Paul's Letter to the Galatians: "So there is no difference between Jews and Gentiles, between slaves and free men, between men and women; you are all one in union with Jesus Christ" (3: 18). Though Christian practice was often chauvinist, both women and men invoked theory against practice.

Probably the major essay on women, and certainly the best by a woman, was a long meditative essay by Elena Maróthy Šoltésová: *Potreba vzdelanosti pre ženu, zvlásť so stanoviska mravnosti* (The Need for Women's Education, Especially from the Viewpoint of Morality, 1898).[5] At the beginning of the essay, Šoltésová rejects radical feminism that pits women against men or advocates female control of public life. Then she distinguishes women's internal impulse toward education (their deep-rooted instinct for growth of spirit) from such external factors as increasing need for greater financial independence and employment opportunities. It is the inner impulse which she emphasizes.

Šoltésová's view of men's and women's separate talents is interesting in showing at what point she was still traditional and at what point somewhat modern. Her language and ideas show how closely she was depending on the Christian tradition, partly because the major opposition to education for women was based on Biblical and pseudo-Biblical evidence of women's place. Šoltésová is cautious in defining the extent to which women would be able to function effectively in public life, though her general point is clear that they should be free to find their own level.

She restates the standard claim that for millenia women were in the position of slaves and thereby acquired the personality of slaves. Then she details numerous ways in which men have regarded women as an asset designed to support men, including the pious hypocrisy that this is really for women's great comfort, not men's. The rest of the essay concerns the ways men have prevented the education of women, then complained about their immorality, fickleness, and selfishness. These faults are the inevitable result of an unenlightened mind. On the double standard of sexual morality, with the feminization of virtue through prescription of moral guardianship to women alone, Šoltésová is heavily sarcastic about male behavior. Eventually she asks for the same kind of equal partnership in marriage that she showed in her fiction. Only when a man learns to recognize his wife as a complete human being will there be a moral relation between them, like that of equal friends. From such friendship and mutual improvement (if allowed by society) the ethical level of society will rise.

This essay is Šoltésová's purest statement of her reformist and Christian feminism, because here she rests primarily on the needs and nature of women as such, not on national needs. As noted in Chapter 2, various words used in the national movement indicate how closely the concepts of "national consciousness" (*národné povedomie*), an "awakened nation" (*prebudený národ*), or a "conscious Slovak" (*povedomý Slovák*) fit the modern sociological concept of consciousness-raising. Šoltésová applied these same words to women in such phrases as "conscious woman" and "unconscious woman" (*povedomá žena, nepovedomá žena*). She was asking for more than educational institutions—she wanted new attitudes.

Only at the end of the essay does Šoltésová somewhat narrow her focus to Slovak specifics. She says it is an embarrasing sign of backwardness that such obvious, elementary arguments as she has just given are not yet accepted. Moreover, the Slovak situation could be particularly improved by women's education, because women's effect upon children and all private life is more direct and quicker than men's effect. The essay is given in full below.

> The Need for Women's Education especially
> from the Viewpoint of Morality
> We too, in our out-of-the-way place, hear and read about the so-called emancipation of women, but our information is piecemeal, often exaggerated and distorted. From it we cannot form a complete, clear opinion. We do not know what emancipation really is, since no one has yet educated us either by lecture or book, and instead we hear only contemptuous, sarcastic comments. None of us has seriously gone into the question, first because it is not a burning issue here and we have been afraid that

speaking of the devil would make him appear. Second, however, the so-called emancipation of women is not yet a mature, integrated condition but only a forming and developing one. No one yet knows how it will blossom or what will crystalize, and therefore no one can draw any sure conclusions about it.

The ordinary current view of emancipation is an extreme caricature. Most dubious is the view of women's emancipation as a sort of insane battle of a wife against her husband,[6] which is to say against her calling as a wife—a sort of unthinkable whim to imitate her husband, to bungle inquisitively into his role and ignore her own, to take over his rights without his weighty responsibilities, to take over his public vocation with the conceited belief that the world would be a better place under a woman's rule, and so on. Obviously, such an unthinkable emancipation would be doomed to fail if the idea could even be taken seriously. There is no point in speaking of it, as such emancipation cannot hold up but falls of its own weight with women themselves. Besides, men are not such idiots as to put up with it.

Nevertheless, it must be said that women are increasingly moving in a healthy, moral direction, with their goal first to increase women's education as such, and second to help women's external independence by thoroughly preparing them to honorably support themselves in case of need. This movement is also called women's emancipation—I do not know whether correctly or not, but probably from lack of a better term. It is not just the result of women's caprice, vanity, and overestimation of themselves, as its enemies describe it, but instead the inevitable result of social circumstances. Doubtless it is the necessary state humanity must attain in the course of development. It has exaggerated caricature elements and flaws damaging the movement, but nothing in the world is free of harmful exaggerations or unworthy appendages. It would be unreasonable and unfair to judge the matter as a whole by these unworthy appendages.

This kind of women's emancipation has internal impulses and external causes. The internal impulse is in women's soul itself, which by its own deep-rooted instinct wants to grow, develop, live, and operate in the spiritual realm, just as does the masculine soul—without considering whether the world finds it suitable or not. The external cause is the necessity to find independent self-support, which increasingly falls on women because of their disproportionate numbers and other circumstances creating social and economic burdens. For self-support, of course, *higher* education is not always necessary, but at least the education needed to successfully pursue a purely practical vocation.

The emancipation brought by internal impetus exists primarily in the independent, stable custom of unregimented thought and behavior, and in exceptional education of the spirit surpassing the specially feminine degree. This is particularly true when additionally a woman has such a strong tendency to delve deeply into some branch of science or art that it probably pushes her regular everyday responsibilities into a secondary position. A man of this character would be considered upright, able, and gifted—completely eminent—but a woman, if not condemned, is at least distrustfully labelled "emancipated." Yet such distrust is seldom justified. It indicates a biased desire to change what the Creator of human life Himself decreed, and what in itself is not evil. Of course, the physical and mental[7] structure of man and woman shows a basic difference established by Divine wisdom, which should be left alone since to ignore it or try to smooth it over would be to sin against the truth.

That difference, however, absolutely does not give men the right of domination and exclusive activity in the spiritual realm. Women too are called to this activity, and it has not been given to men's will, nor their power, to decide how far women may go. As long as God's law is not repealed that each woman is also her father's daughter, not only her mother's, and that each man is also his mother's son, not only his father's, then human beings cannot presume to divide and separate the psychological characteristics and roles of men and women in such a way that women never receive men's qualities and roles and men never receive women's. In fact, this would be very undesirable, since such sharply divided sides could have no mutual understanding and so could not contribute to their mutual welfare. Great force of mind in itself without other defects, does not diminish womanliness, just as warm and tender feeling, an attribute of women, does not diminish but instead increases the value of the most manly man.

External emancipation lies not just in a woman's independently supporting herself — since earning her daily bread by purely women's occupations, especially handwork, was never considered improper. It lies in a woman's supporting herself by taking up a profession in public life that until just lately only men undertook. The fact that recently women have interested themselves in the fields that until now were plowed exclusively by masculine strength, has stirred up the sharpest argument and cut to the quick, because it is no longer a matter of principle but of bread and butter. This question is difficult and cannot be answered purely by words, decisions, and opinions, but must await the result of deeds. If women should actually plow into men's economic base to a marked degree, they would disturb the basic plan of the family and the social system. But there is no reason to fear they will go so far. In the public professions women will be able to compete with men only in exceptional, outstanding cases. However, it is already impossible to stop or drive back women who are advancing to new occupations. Deliberate barriers put in their way will not last long; only the barriers of nature can stop them. Thus the whole matter will end up with the most natural resolution: whatever is good, so far as it is good, will last; whatever is not good, will fail. Either women will demonstrate that they are ordained to whatever they undertake and by it they improve the state of society, or they will show that they overestimated their abilities and their behavior contributed nothing materially or morally to society. The first instance will be accepted as advantageous, whereas the second will bring alterations, improvements, reversals, and general experimentation, and thus not come into being.

So much is certain: the chief, normal vocation of a woman within the family and the household will remain untouched, or rather will be perfected as a result of her perfected education, whether she succeeds at an extraordinary vocation or not. The great majority of women will always be drawn to their natural, proper place—they will step out of it only from extraordinary internal or external causes. The former, the internal, are rooted and constant, and they appear and endure at least in the cultured classes under all conditions—though in their purely explicit form in a relatively small number of women. Let this fact serve to calm down those who fear that the current of emancipation will engulf all womanhood. Secondary, external impulses toward emancipation, being called up by external causes, will collapse as a result of basic reforms in society—though likely they will no longer totally disappear.

The purpose of this treatise is to explore at least one line of argument that the first impulse, i.e. internal emancipation with its goal of women's complete spiritual growth, is basically sound and justifiable.

Recently, women growing into self-awareness through advances in their education have charged that men for their own convenience kept women in eternal servitude, material and spiritual dependence, and immaturity. As a result, women developed certain slavish characteristics, remained backward spiritually, and were so to speak crippled. Men have so far answered this charge somewhat superciliously, saying that these are imagined grievances, because women themselves do not know what they want and are deliberately searching for problems. What looks to women like oppression and enslavement is in truth, they say, a natural, necessary condition. The good of the home and family requires that women, whose role is to keep watch over them, strive for only simple feminine virtues, not unnecessary education of the mind that is harmful to their vocation. According to male opinion, it would be best if women showed no interest at all in anything not directly belonging to their natural vocation. The great majority of men believe this way—the right-thinking ones are definitely in the minority.

The majority only want their wife to be beautiful, charming, pleasing in their eyes, and devoted to them body and soul. True education is desired only by the best men, who honestly want to elevate their wife to the ideal. The rest want her ignorant so she will not counter their own autocracy. They require her to have only social skills and external refinement. This is how the aristocratic class of men look on women; as in everything they follow their own pleasure, and see a woman as only an object for themselves, whether spiritualized and idealized or in the lower sense. Into such a frame, then, they place their portrait of all women from the exalted and idolized down through degrees to the most contemned who are expelled from society—all are viewed as an object of masculine favor.

Such a concept of a wife by her husband is above all certainly convenient for her. Nevertheless, however much this idolatry and exaltation may appeal to her, it is not healthy and neither benefits her morally nor gives her steady contentment. It leads her to unthinkable vanity and a mania to please her husband at any price, so that she wants nothing more for herself than external beauty to charm and conquer him. Anxious effort to glorify her exterior person fills the whole mind of a young bride and suffocates all the good fruits of her soul. In short, the fact that a great number of men want a wife to be only an object loving them, builds and fosters in their wives vanity and flirtatiousness to such a shocking degree that their soul goes to ruin. Such a wife, living vainly and anxious only for her husband's favor, ordinarily acquires no internal worth; therefore when her beauty fades and cannot be replaced even by cosmetics, she becomes an unpleasant, unneeded creature lacking respect or love. This tragedy, repeated en masse, will not stop as long as a man sees his wife as only a worker and not a companion, and as long as a wife feels herself to be only someone bound to her husband and not someone awakened to the strength and worth of a self-sufficient person. Thus, when even this kindly concept of woman does not assure bliss to a happy wife in her prime while showered with her husband's love, what of the throngs of women who are not given by nature beauty and charm and who attain no husband's consideration? By such a concept they remain worthless, insignificant, and lacking a mission in life.

The other group of men, those who cannot or will not seek their own comfort in everything but consider what can be most useful, believe that a woman exists not only for her beauty (though they never reject beauty) but also for her material use. They want first of all a housekeeper and, if possible, other helpful labor for themselves. They prize a wife for her ability with material things, and in demanding work of her they often exceed the bounds, so that in the lowest classes a wife is really a beast of burden ordered to work without rest, diversion, or ennobling motives. Even in the better sort of the lowest classes, a wife increases in value by her fitness for work, and if she is also a conscientious mother (though from a higher point of view she is terribly unfit to bring up children), nothing more is asked of her. Any sort of education of the spirit is a disadvantage, not a benefit. In her husband's eyes, every minute spent with a book, for example, would be a sin, because it would decrease her physical, useful work. Here, then, a husband is the ready-made enemy of his wife's education through his conviction that it leads her away from her duty. This enmity unites both categories of men described, though each in his own way. Since those in the higher classes and these in the lower classes of society comprise the prevailing majority of men, their demands and opinions have most affected women's development so far.

From all this it becomes clear that women's charge against men is not unsupported. Nevertheless, the charge does not apply to those classes where men themselves receive no higher education, because the wife is not shorted in relation to her husband. As a whole, it must be said that the sober, ungentle concept of women found among the lower classes, although tough and uncomfortable for women, is healthy and fair as long as it adheres to a decent, moderate scale. All the conditions of life and inevitable necessity point to the fact that women are ordained to work, as Eve was told, not just to bear children. Tenderness and love, wherever conditions exist for them, do not exclude but raise the value of a wife, and give worth and goals also to those women who do not receive a husband's love. Injustice exists only where a man deliberately deprives a woman of exactly that education of the spirt which he fully arrogates to himself as a man.

Such a man energetically argues that he is depriving his wife not from the egotistic motive of keeping her a backward, unself-confident, dependent creature subservient to his needs, but rather in her own interest. A wife, he says, can only be useful and satisfied in a state of spiritual dependence, since only that is natural to her. As soon as she pushes higher and grows out from under her husband's tutelage, she can no longer feel happy. Her salvation, he says, lies not in independent spiritual activity but in modest, comfortable submission to her husband's authority — she can be active at most through a quiet, enriching effect upon him.

This position is insupportable because it unconditionally favors the husband's claims. Admittedly, it may apply to the great majority of women trained to be dependent, but even here it is too one-sided, as if anything could be fair which offers the chance for misuse. Even the argument of unnaturalness breaks down if, for example, an intelligent person should yield in thought and action to a stupid person simply because the intelligent one is the wife and the stupid one the husband. That would be the only conclusion if the position were held consistently, since we all know that intelligence is not owned by men, nor stupidity by women. On the other hand, even the most intelligent, independent-minded woman will happily submit to her husband when he actually earns her devotion by his deserts, not by any rigid rule of male dominance and female submission.

A man and wife are two different halves which together form one whole person constructed so that their mental and physical characteristics mutually support and fulfill each other. The husband is often strong and active — the wife slight, softer, and passive. On this basis the husband takes precedence in all the situations of life and awards himself many privileges over her, but at the same time he should be her responsible protector and supporter, caring for her in all those same situations of life. This is very nice in theory, but here too reality lags quite far behind. Even if the husband can be fully forgiven for this lag on the score of human frailty, from his advantaged position he is still sanctioning himself as a fully independent person, while awarding his wife the sanction of only a dependent person created purely for her husband's will and having no independent status. Certainly this is not right.

In the eyes of her husband a wife is always Eve, created for Adam from Adam's rib, even though such an opinion contradicts his own moral feeling and sense of justice. This opinion has ruled humanity from prehistoric times, and accordingly it formed and fixed social morality and the family order. Women yielded to it, to be sure, from the natural necessity that urged them on—but also from force, and finally from rigid custom. That is, women yielded to the natural necessity of their inborn female role with all its consequences, and this necessity endures eternally so that agitation against it is vain. Second, however, they yielded by force to male domination in the brutal age of humanity, which in truth is not yet completely behind us. Wherever this domination still hangs on, despite Christian enlightenment, morally conscious women are now rising against it. Moreover, because enlightened and just men themselves agree with these women and earlier fought and are still fighting for the woman's side, total male domination has now ceased in principle, at least among the educated classes. Third, women remained dependent by rigid custom because their spirit was backward, their moral consciousness asleep, and their mental ability undeveloped, so how could they possibly resist? By habit and custom they were kept backward, and from this fact was deduced not only the right of male domination, but also the belief in women's inferiority. This belief continues today to a great extent. Husbands do not accept their wives' abilities outside their natural role taken in the narrowest sense, and they want to show this disbelief as justified because it is to their advantage.

Yet the reality is different. Women are showing that under proper conditions they too are capable of the highest education and thus also of extraordinary tasks. Their spirit is as able to grow and be perfected as men's spirit — though there is no denying that the preponderance of intelligence remains on the male side, and in many intellectual missions women will not equal men even when fully developed. But this does not detract from those women who hold their ground very honorably when they are duly educated to the extent of their intellectual capacity.

That a woman is capable of true, genuine education should please not only herself but also precisely her husband, since it is in his interest. An educated husband and an uneducated wife can never make a happy, successful whole — even less can an educated wife and an uneducated husband. Since, moreover, this disproportion is felt more on the educated side than the uneducated, men whose education is unquestionably advanced over women's should do everything possible to keep their wives from falling behind them. Impressing an ignorant woman brings only cheap, doubtful glory. If men are really equipped better than women, not only physically but mentally, they will remain so when compared to an educated woman and thus have no reason to fear her. If men are not superior, the backwardness of a woman will not put them ahead. Indeed, it is easy to look down upon an ignorant woman, but looking down on an educated one requires a man to climb pretty high. This is inconvenient so many men would rather cling to the first kind of woman. This fact directly witnesses against their theory of men's mental superiority.

The education of a wife cannot diminish the education of her husband, but instead together they support and reinforce each other. This is true not only in general, but also in their marriage itself.

A marriage where the wife does her husband's will in everything can be nice and in its way happy for both sides — not where an ignorant, spiritually dark wife yields slavishly to her husband, but where the husband by his superior intelligence, nobility of character, and ability in everything he does, deserves his wife's unconditional trust. Such a marriage is in its way ideal, but it requires an ideal husband and a noble, understanding wife, which an uneducated woman can scarcely be. In general, men would probably like this kind of marriage, but they cannot all be as excellent as needed for its success. They want it, but even on their own side are not supplying that one chief condition, because their frequent great faults keep their wife from being as submissive and devoted as their male ambition demands. In this respect, their wife's ignorance would not help them, because even an ignorant wife sees and feels her husband's faults, and is sharply against them. In fact, her limited sight often sees fault in even the best thing when she does not understand it. Moreover, often she does not see her own faults and considers herself better than her husband. Therefore we have the interesting phenomenon that marriages with the wife in charge, so-called "apron string marriages," which are generally not considered ideal, occur where the woman is ordinary and uneducated, or is sick emotionally. A woman with educated mind and feeling does not rejoice at any mental superiority over her husband. She wants him to be her equal, does not want to make him feel her superiority, and especially does not want to shame him before others, even if she is not lovingly fond of him, because she does not want to make her marriage a target for snide jokes. On the other hand, a mediocre woman eagerly shows her control, and in her moral shortsightedness does not see the bad light she sheds not only on her husband but most of all on herself. All of this clearly proves that true education raises the worth of a woman as a wife, not only as a human being.

If we want to decide which kind of marriage is fairest, we can find it by real observation, not by wilfull, high-flying theories. Reality shows that marriages dominated absolutely in the good sense or the bad by either male or female, are rare—and rarer the more both sides are educated. Thus one must say they are exceptions. As a whole, marriage, whether successful or not, appears to have the natural outline of male and female sides probably equal in power and worth. So the most successful marriage, equally responsible on both sides, can be imagined only when an aware man joins with an aware woman. Both know their responsibilities and always perform them, and both know the rights of the other and in mutual appreciation always consider them. Ordinarily this amounts to true, lasting love mixed with respect. Such love, however, requires an equal measure of moral maturity in both, and so far that equality has not been measured out.

Here we arrive at the most significant point. If I posed the question whether women need and should have full and comprehensive *moral* growth, every reasonable, just person would answer yes with great conviction. It is needed and desirable whether we look at women themselves or at their husbands, their partners. Only when women mature morally can humanity reach its moral adulthood. But what do we see in practice? We see that for ages men controlling the approaches to education, whether thoughtlessly or from prejudice, did not take care of, or cared too little for, the moral growth of their wives. In addition, they always sharply condemned the one-sided morality which they themselves had prescribed for women. Even if men deny as imaginary every charge a woman makes about her servitude, they cannot refute her charge of moral bondage, because unfortunately they have so far supported it to a shocking degree. They somehow take it as unavoidable and feel no guilt at supporting it in practice, even when in theory they are against it. No other question in the relations of men and women shows such disproportion, inconsistency, and ungrateful egotism on the part of the male as exactly the question of female morality.

When I say that men did not take care of or cared too little for the moral growth of a woman, I mean her moral growth as a whole, which develops in step with all other intellectual powers. Not only did men not support it, but so far as they claimed that a woman's vocation made a thorough intellectual education unnecessary and even harmful, so far as they withheld this education, they also withheld her moral growth. Only extraordinary women could break through by their own abilities. Certainly men's conception of morality is well developed, but their practice is very backward. As a result, a woman is left in a moral state of half blindness while she is strictly and relentlessly held to the highest moral practice. This is an anomalous, confused inconsistency. Men claim that a woman, being incapable of moral maturity even with her eyes open, cannot figure out her moral duties. But with a man's leadership she can easily fulfill them while blindfolded! In this way a woman's morality is made external, formalistic, to be practiced not from conviction but by mere rules—thus causing the many superficialities and awful emptinesses of woman's nature which men readily ridicule and sermonize against, not remembering that women acquired or at least continued in these faults under men's tutelage.

Currently, a woman's education, from its very beginning, does not go deeply to the roots of spiritual strength, nor does it sharpen her mind and cultivate her basic moral sense, but instead touches only the superficial. "Make everyone love you, and do nothing for society to be ashamed of" is the paramount rule for a young, developing girl. All motherly advice is directed to this desirable result, since her mother too was brought up this way. If we took this advice to mean everyone loves only what is good and nice, and no one criticizes where there is no fault, then this universal motto would not be bad. But in reality it turns out to be undependable, because it can cover pure hypocrisy and paste on a false glitter. Not everything is good and nice that appears to be, and not everything is damnable that society condemns, nor is everything good that society praises. Therefore, a woman's moral feeling must be seriously, fundamentally developed and her judgment sharpened, so that she herself can distinguish good from evil. Then she can solidly fulfill the above advice. It is amazing but true that women's education is generally flimsy and suited only for superficial routine or skillful hypocrisy, whereas women's role in life is morally important and full of self-denial and responsibility. The fact that even with such irresponsible preparation women still stand up well, often exemplarily fulfilling their difficult role, means that much good in them is innate. Should not this good be fostered and brought to perfection?

So much for morality in general, which means searching for and acting upon the truth, if possible, in all the situations of life.

As far as female morality goes, especially sexual morality, we have a different matter. Women are reared in this morality with conscientious vigilance. Every parent of all classes, simple or educated, as long as he is not degenerate, inculcates it in his daughter, since it should be her most prominent female virtue, and its concept is definite and easily understood. In this sense, even mentally limited women may be and are moral, for such morality can be prescribed like any other exact requirement. Indeed, it is strictly prescribed, since whoever sins against it is despised as a fallen creature and more or less expelled from respectable society. Therefore every parent tries to fortify his daughter so as to deter her from such a possible fall. Of this special morality, then, one cannot say as of general morality that women's education is neglected. But one must still say that neglect of general morality does not serve to strengthen sexual morality. Men themselves in fact sternly demand this morality of a woman, though on the other hand they attack and corrupt her. Well, if she were not attacked she would not need protection and there would be no credit in keeping her virtue—she would have no virtue. A man requires virtue of his wife, daughters, and sisters. His mother especially should be worthy of every honor, because a son always wants to respect his mother. He also requires on principle that his wife be entirely spotless. So far everything is all right. He should now require the same of himself and thereby honor his wife and himself—but what do we see instead?

We see that this same man does not require such moral spotlessness of himself. He lightheartedly gives himself a dispensation. He assumes almost unrestricted freedom in this regard—after all, he is morally superior. Often even his worst trespass is not considered a fault, or at least he is not expelled from respectable society. A man can corrupt the morals of a woman almost without penalty (if he does not brush against a paragraph of the criminal code or is not charged—which anyway would not hurt him much). He need pay no attention to female or male honor, neither considering that this woman whose honor he takes is a wife, sister, and daughter of other men, nor even considering her basic human worth. The proud male, on every occasion self-confidently emphasizing his superiority over women, documents it by the fact that in his unbridled sexuality he allows himself much, indeed everything.

Here, of course, the man would object that he does not sin alone but also the woman sins, and not only he but she seduces him. That objection sounds strange but is characteristic of this kind of man. He willingly forgets his self-proclaimed superiority and turns at once into a pitiful, seduced victim of immoral female snares. Poor thing! But let us ask him: Why does he not show *here* his moral superiority, and why not refuse these temptations of a morally weaker woman? If he were frank he would answer: Because I, knowing what is moral and immoral, presume to give in to my tastes though condemning them on principle, but a woman has an exact rule to follow blindly, so let her stick to it! Let her defend herself against me however she can. When she cannot hold out, then let her fall. Anyway she is unenlightened, morally undeveloped, so it does not hurt her. This is how he would have to answer, because this is how the great majority of men think, unfortunately even those who otherwise want to be called respectable. Even those men who enact laws and establish the social order think this way. So then, let anyone capable of fairness judge whether a woman is in moral bondage to a man. The fact that women of the lowest class suffer most does not diminish the evil, nor men's guilt. Even the most highly placed, respectable woman who has morally fallen the lowest, feels the diminution and insult for herself, because it is not a question of class but of female morality, of the female soul.

Naturally, a woman defiled by a man also defiles the man. Her inevitable revenge will not stop as long as she is defiled. Possibly there are women who are depraved in themselves without the impulse given by a man — though they must be rare enough — but nevertheless that fact does not give men the right to confirm them in their evil, and even less to ruin the women who otherwise would remain virtuous.

It is the deliberate continuation of inequality between the sexes in moral matters, and exactly this inequality, that triggers immorality. The unequal basis and unequal preparation for higher morality cause that shaky foundation which men do not respect in a woman, and which lets them ruin her without scruple. The lower degree of men's punishment for the same transgression against sexual morality, their unequal persecution by society, and their unequal judgment by public opinion—all that is not only evidence of but also an external cause of women's bondage. Men have conferred upon themselves the privilege of immorality without penalty, while leaving the greatest penalty, loss of honor, for the woman sinning with them primarily at their instigation. At that instant, as the strong against the weak and the temptor against the tempted, they gain the secure position of the invulnerable against the vulnerable, so that they can make their predatory attacks against her without fear. Is not this the height of immorality?

Perhaps, however, men are trusting in their manly honor, because certainly nothing should more strongly influence them to save the virtue of a woman than her helplessness—but let men themselves judge whether that honor restrains them from rapacity. After a thousand years men should recognize that they have not lived up to their good opinion of themselves, and they should act as strictly against themselves as against a woman. Doubtless men measured out to her such an extraordinary part of the penalty to help her avoid sin, but here too they should know from a thousand years of experience that bad consequences do not deter people from transgression, especially when these consequences are meted out to only one of the guilty parties, not equally to both.

No matter where we look for a valid reason to punish men and women unequally for their sins against sexual morality, we shall not find it. We shall only find the fact that inequality existed from prehistoric times—the clear sign of it being polygamy. Even in later periods in certain Scandinavian countries, the laws permitted men more than one wife, while women had to keep unbroken faithfulness to one husband under penalty of death. This fact, however, is not evidence of right. At least there is no justification based in morality. More nearly valid is the excuse that exact strictness with a woman is necessary to preserve the purity of the family. If women were permitted all that men are permitted, shortly there would be no proper, single-rooted family but wild animal life. So, may God eternally protect a woman from any erring step against her exalted role as protector of the purity of the family!

But is only the wife bound to this role, and not also her husband? Does the family exist only for the wife — are not its roots, its life, its greatest strengths and joys equally for the husband? How can he strictly bind his wife to preserve the family unbroken while he himself blithely slips out from under this inconvenient requirement, no matter how much he wants his family pure? This is gross personal egotism and unmanly frailty in the "strong-man." Its basic tune is one that men cannot and will not abandon: a woman is created purely for her husband, and the family too exists only for him. The wife should drown her whole being in the family, but the husband, her overlord, can irresponsibly allow himself even immoral lapses. That is probably how he thinks, and despite being morally more mature, he gladly dispenses himself from responsibilities that require any noticeable self-denial. Then he readily puts his wife forward, though she is morally uneducated, to prevent the bad effects of his own laxity. He, strong, through a weak woman sins against his wife and against morality, then orders his wife to stop the disturbing effects of his offenses — and finally as a bonus he throws the responsibility for his errors onto her. This is how it was and still is — completely masculine but absolutely unmanly.

In general, men are morally superior to women, but in this critical sexual question they are not. What is worse, they do not want to be — their ambition does not bear in that direction. As long as a man is not sexually moral, then he is not and will not become the true lord and master of his wife, but instead her defiling tyrant and defiling slave at the same time. He is the exact opposite of the true man, strong-spirited, pure-hearted, before whom every honorable woman could bow down in genuine respect. No one can credit him as a true man, or any sort of exalted being.

From all this it is probably clear enough what kind of impetus exists in women's souls for the internal emancipation referred to at the beginning of this treatise. We must judge whether it is a vain caprice, or a serious intellectual movement, whether a senseless fight of women against men, or a step inspired by the healthy desire to perfect the human condition—their own and men's. Men, of course, claim for themselves the exclusive role of perfecting humanity, but as long as they obstruct women from becoming capable of taking a full part in this work, the part that fits them, these men will not live to see the success they desire.

Only when the whole method and order of education will be directed so that a woman, just like a man, can develop into a moral being, and only when the successful effects of this education make a man regard his wife as also an independent person, or better said as an independent half of a person, instead of someone whose soul he can maim to fit his own needs for fulfillment—only then can there be the desired equality that will basicly improve their sexual morality. Then a man will feel himself under the rightful, qualified moral control of a woman, just as she is under his control, and this situation will in no way be humiliating to him.

True friendship between men and women should be accepted without its having to pass into love, a possibility now dubious to the majority. The fact that such friendship is not yet allowed without suspicion is also characteristic of our moral condition co-existing with the moral immaturity of women. Direct intellectual relations between men and women outside the family circle are needed on both sides. They refine and exchange various intellectual gifts and transmit and enhance diverse spiritual property, by which social pleasures should become more beneficial. In fact, there is a certain intensified charm, because men are not only with men and women with women, but they are mixed without the slightest offense to morality. The saving grace comes from a fundamental barrier built against immorality, i.e. by teaching everyone, women and men, to distinguish good from evil and inculcating love for the former and disgust for the latter. It is no help to build superficial barriers, just for decent appearances, through which in the end immorality can slip comfortably enough. Rewarding intellectual cooperation between a man and woman is generally possible only when they observe morality from their own vital conviction, not from dead rules. This morality is the supreme sign of exalted humanity, because it is attained when the liberated soul leads the body.

No one, I think, not even the most bitter opponent of women's education, would deny that women need moral development. But to a great degree, moral development rests upon mental growth and general education of the intellect, so that anyone who is against women's education involves himself in a contradiction. A woman cannot nourish moral development separately or cultivate it alone, precisely because it must penetrate and govern her whole mind and behavior. One can hardly contend, then, that education damages a woman. Empty education without a moral basis or goal could be harmful, but education aimed above all at moral growth and on this basis supporting further spiritual growth, can only glorify a person, whether man or woman. Therefore, let us not hinder or block the path to women's education in the fear that it will spoil her, but take to it firmly, give it a moral foundation and healthy direction, and above all guide women in a sincere Christian spirit. That is the remedy. Then no one need fear harmful outgrowths of women's education, even of higher education. On such a basis, an educated woman will not become warped even if she independently pursues a male occupation—and after all, only a few women will ever undertake that. I am convinced that even if high schools and universities are founded for women, domestic and other practical training will remain essential and even gain in importance. It is certain that if women's path to the former schools were smoothed, women would still only in exceptional cases go there, while the majority would remain with the nearer, lower, more comfortable level of schooling.

Even the few exceptional women, however, to a certain degree raise the education level of women as such. As a side effect, they permeate the mass of less educated women, just as the male educated class also enlightens the uneducated class. Therefore, such women deserve a stamp of approval as do those men who, not wishing to study or being unsuited for it, go into a simpler occupation. It could be objected that intelligent, educated men, just as they enlighten their unenlightened brothers, can also enlighten women. Doubtless, this occurs and will still occur. For many sharp-witted women the educational influence of the other sex is exactly the most effective. But whoever carefully notices these matters sees that the majority of women, again from the customary convenience or mental laziness which their superficial education fosters, avoid difficult learning and serious intellectual roles until their more capable sisters blaze the way for them. Then they become aware of things women too should know about. As long as only men speak of something, women take it as a male interest alone, especially since most men confirm them in this belief. For these same reasons, the special women's magazines have their rightful place, though they are condemned and ridiculed as absurd by exactly those same men who consider women incapable of education equal to men's.

The authorities justify male disapproval of female intellectual activity, among other reasons, by saying that whenever women began to press forward and meddled in the intellectual roles of men, they feminized the masculine spirit and lowered the intellectual and moral level of society. This is the same kind of charge as that women push men into immorality. If the masculine spirit can be so easily dominated and ruined by the female spirit, where then is its manly power? When a woman has to give up mental activity so as not to ruin her husband's spirit, where does spiritual and moral superiority actually lie? Is it not with the woman? I for my part have a far higher opinion of the male spirit, its strength, and its character than do those men who give such uncomplimentary evidence of it. Feminization of the male spirit has occurred, and with it or after it also the inevitable decline of morals; however, it hardly resulted from true, serious enlightenment of the female spirit, but from an unhealthy, exaggerated outburst. No wonder that, stifled and idle, the female spirit erupted morbidly. Show it the path to healthy growth and it will take it, thus losing by natural means any tendency toward unhealthy eruptions with their bad effects. The male spirit must grow strong and continually succeed in comparison to a *mature* woman — otherwise we shall not believe in its manly power.

These same authorities maintain that from the spiritual view a woman is ordained to an inactive, purely passive role, since she is said to form the fallow, as it were reserve, power of humanity. Such an arrangement would be most convenient for women themselves, if only it could be maintained, and if it did not contradict the mental nature of women themselves and the real conditions of life. Those who take this position seem to forget that everything which only rests without movement or exercise finally must rust out or mildew, and that such a null conversion of strength, bringing little benefit, must be harmful to society. We can best learn of this fact from the Muslims. They deprived their women of all active significance, even denying a woman a soul, seeing her in the narrowest sense as a creature with exclusively bodily worth. She truly just lies fallow, and one sees at once that she gives her nation no nourishment, neither moral nor spiritual, nor even material—except just bodily in begetting children. She is a devoted wife or humble slave of her husband, but not his spiritual companion. The mother of rising generations only by her body, she is not their mother/teacher. As this fallow power spiritually rots away, so also the nation dies out morally. Whoever would investigate cause and effect would certainly find that the denial, imprisonment, and oppression of women's soul simply by inaction is more than the least cause of spiritual infertility and backwardness in the Muslim world.

One can also see how futile is men's conceit that they alone are called to meet the high interests of the nation. With that belief they will not live to see true success. Even vainer would be the conceit of women that they could accomplish alone what men have tried. Only together can we successfully advance, and in fact only when the woman is not a burden hung on her husband's neck but a wife standing on her own two feet in union and understanding with her husband, does she fullfill what her mental and physical talents suit her for. A good basic upbringing should develop those talents and lead to their healthy education. Although even this does not exempt a woman from all individual faults, just as it does not exempt a man from fault, still there is no doubt that education enriches her, moderates her faults, and fills many natural deficiencies.

Christian Equality

For many men, their antipathy to education for women (whether only moral education or training for actual independence as desired by the emancipation movement) results from seeing it as destructive to the pretty image of the strong man and the weak, clinging wife devoted to him. But there is no reason to lament. Actually weakness forces a wife to lean on her husband, so it is this female weakness that he is trying to see as a virtue. He sees in it womanliness eo ipso and gladly tolerates it. The truth, however, is that even the attributed feminine virtues cannot have healthy, vital roots in weakness, but only in strength. From weakness and childish immaturity cannot be born a rich, morally strong character. Only from strength comes everything good. Thus, the ideal of a strong man and a devotedly clinging wife does not disappear when she becomes educated, but is strengthened. That ideal will never die out from a woman's soul, if he does not himself tear it out by his own unworthiness.

Fears that the right relation between husband and wife will be disturbed by her higher education are absolutely baseless. No matter what her educational gains, either morally or in deeds, they will never change by the tiniest bit the fact that any woman, despite everything she accomplishes, will find her supreme bliss only in her husband's love, just as he will find his supreme bliss only in his wife's love. Both will find true contentment only in their established marriage and family life. Women who from choice or otherwise do not marry may use their physical or mental training to gain an unusual occupation which not only secures their income but also gives their lives substance and a goal. They will not be considered useless, oppressed, embittered old maids whom anyone feels justified to ride over with merciless, stupid ridicule, but instead they will become respected, contented members of society. This achievement certainly cannot be considered wrong, but worthy. The institution of marriage itself will be more properly understood when every young girl will no longer blindly push for marriage to secure her material livelihood, or just to escape a dull old maid's life. As the education of a woman should in truth glorify marriage, so her independence should too, because she then will accept marriage not from necessity but from free choice as the desire of her heart, without childishly exaggerated demands and expectations.

Love between men and women will endure through all circumstances and all stages of human evolution, because it is not an accidental phenomenon resulting from human caprice or temporary trends, but an eternal gift to humans from their Creator. With the perfecting of humans, clearly their love should also be perfected. The most perfect and therefore the most enduring love comes less from physical than mental predilection, and is brought to life and sustained by both the man's and the woman's virtues. It is rooted in morality and elevated to morality. The fear that higher education makes a woman incapable of love and devotion for her husband is absurd. In fact, only when a woman is thoroughly and truly educated can the love between herself and her husband become enriched, deepen, and acquire its true heart's warmth.

Just as there can be no harm to a wife's love, there can be no harm to a husband's dignity even if his wife overtakes him in education. The concept of manliness is so surmounting and irrefutable that nothing external can damage it. Even the strength of an advanced woman does not damage it, and yes, she understands it. A woman will always yield to true manliness, and where necessary will give in to it, because it has a strength that builds respect and admiration, dominates without effort, and governs without force. In its righteousness it dominates the feminine soul. A true man by his strong spirit will always have greater effect on a woman than vice versa, and even with equal education she will always receive more spiritual benefits, especially mental ones, from him than he from her. On the other hand, a noble, morally developed wife will always provide more dependable moral support than a man can have by himself. In addition, only a woman with a mature soul can refresh his feelings and reinforce his higher efforts. It is certain at least that no male friend can have so intense a good effect upon a man as a noble, reasonable wife can have—and it is also certain that no woman can so powerfully uplift another woman as can a noble man. In general, a woman receives from a man the gifts of an educated mind, and a man from a woman the gifts of an educated heart—but both require the total development of the soul. Just as a man and woman can fall low morally and spiritually only together, mutually ruining each other, so also a man and woman can rise and remain high morally and spiritually only together, mutually supporting each other. Successful support is only possible with relatively equally developed powers.

It is a shameful sign of our great backwardness that we must still so rudimentarily justify women's education. If education is desirable for humans in general, then it is obviously needed not only for men but women too. Elsewhere this question is no longer even posed, because it is universally agreed upon. Others now question only whether women should study as much as men or in a reduced fashion, whether they should take specialized subjects with the goal of an independent occupation or general studies to raise their educational level, whether women's learning should occur by the methods of men's or by some special appropriate method, and so on. Moreover, stating the belief that women urgently need basic education, i.e. mental development, merely expresses the goal—and from expressing the goal to reaching it, lies a long, confusing, and often meandering path. The hard task for educators will be to lead women to mental growth without stripping them of womanliness, and to perfect the feminine virtues in that growth so that women can later follow their calling more properly. The point is to give women solid training aimed at their feminine calling, and then on this foundation fearlessly to add even higher education. Or if not higher education, then education to help their employability and fit them for practical life—since they will always need that. Here too they can accomplish more with thorough preparation than without it. By their education women will enrich also the lower spheres in which they move through their ordinary responsibilities.

Besides all that has been said here, spiritual education and moral consciousness are especially needed for women as mothers. No one doubts this fact who knows the hard, complicated role of a mother when she is the first teacher of her children and gives the first foundations to their characters. I shall not describe this matter, because no persuasion is necessary. Noble, cultured mothers could regenerate humanity and become the strongest allies and most fundamental support of good schools.

There can be no argument over the need for true education of women, but doubtless much successful and unsuccessful experimentation will occur before we find the right path, before the theorists, psychologists, physiologists, philosophers, economists, and so on, agree upon requirements and regulations to meet the needs of life—including the higher life.

We Slovaks do not have the opportunity to establish our own educational approach as we choose, but confronted by such an important matter we should at least establish our position *in principle*. If in our rigid, extreme conservatism we continue not to want women to look higher than their ladle, needle, and hoe, we shall not spread national consciousness, and we shall not progress at all in education. Just because a lax, immoral education probably does much evil to women, we need not condemn and exclude education guided by a moral, Christian spirit such as I have advocated.

Here at the conclusion, in case I did not show sufficiently clearly the point of this treatise, I emphasize that the education and whole upbringing of women should be founded above all on true Christian religious teaching and vital religious faith. What I am asking for in women's education is really just to follow what Christian ethics itself asks of a person. I am convinced above all else that Christian ethics alive within people raises them to moral heights that no other artificial, purely rational ethics can ever reach. Even where a person rises morally while apparently avoiding Christian ethics, there too it must be at work, though indirectly and unseen, because it holds all the springs of morality. Thus, if everyone ought to cultivate it in their soul, then especially women should. Religion itself, as understood by a ripe soul, is the supreme learning and can raise a woman higher than any rational growth can ever raise her without it. On the basis of such vital, not just formal, religious training, all her abilities unfold including her reason, and she cannot become warped even in the most extraordinary occupation. From this view, for a woman to branch off from the main stream cannot be corruptive, as it widens the boundaries of women's occupations but does not abandon them. In this spirit an educated woman does nothing at all unworthy.

So then in toto: maximum moral development and moral maturity are as desirable for women as men, though in such form as not to rub off the noble feminine attraction from her soul. Only when morally blossoming women are the wives and companions of morally blossoming men will humanity reach that excellence which is in fact its final goal here on earth, and which should fundamentally improve all the living conditions of humanity.

The chagrin which Šoltésová expressed near the end of the essay at having to give such rudimentary arguments to justify the moral effect of education for women, was indeed justified. Yet the conservative Slovak society of her time was not unique in needing such restatement. The history of the women's movement appears cyclical rather than linear when we see the same common-sense principles being repeated. Recent research has (again) rediscovered the *Cité des Dames* of Christine de Pizan (ca 1365–after 1429), who was famous and relatively widely read in her own day and the century after, then forgotten, then rediscovered in French literature in the eighteenth century, forgotten again, but now regarded as one of the earliest women writers concerned with women as persons.[8] Her arguments for women's education against the image of "deceitful Eve" and against male hypocrisy and privilege are strikingly similar to Šoltésová's arguments. One could cite similar passages from Renaissance Christian humanist women writers.

Naturally Šoltésová's expression is more similar to that of women nearer her own time, especially Mary Wollstonecraft, though the influential *A Vindication of the Rights of Woman* of 1792 was not translated into Czech until 1904, and it was not mentioned much in the period of Šoltésová's essay. Šoltésová's idealism and enthusiasm for inner change in women and therefore in society also suggest the utopian socialism of Flora Tristan (1803–1844),[9] but again there is no evidence of influence. Tkadlečková-Vantuchová believes Šoltésová had not read the feminist classics, although Pietor and other men were familiar with John Stuart Mill and certain of the French male feminists.[10] Šoltésová's similarity to other feminist writings likely resulted from common experience, not influence. The long (though minority) tradition of Christian feminism shows the common reaction of devout women puzzled, shocked, or outraged by the contradiction between Christian men's profession and their practice.

Yet some men were also conscious of the discrepancy between theory and practice. Nine years after Šoltésová's essay, the Christian view of sex equality in St. Paul's letter to the Galatians was taken up by a man who condemned its historical abandonment in later centuries. Milan Frič (1882–1966), born in Yugoslavia of Slovak emigrants and educated as an economist in Prague, was one of the Detvan club members of the Hlasist movement under

T. G. Masaryk's influence. Frič's essay from 1907 is given in full below,[11] in part as a more "modern" comparison to Šoltésová's essay of 1898, and in part for its own worth as a contemporary male statement.

On the Woman Question

Today whenever we speak of the woman question, we stand in the ranks of its defenders or its enemies. We are against it, or fighting for it. But we can fight for a new idea, even one with exalted content, only when we are fully familiar with it. Misunderstanding a subject makes us oppose even its core of pure absolute good. Exactly today, when we are living in such stirring times and the whole world is occupied with solving various burning questions, many of them crucial and complex, we cannot be content with superficial knowledge of these matters. Instead, we must devote time to becoming familiar with them.

One of these crucial questions—unfortunately ignored in our society—is the question of women: of giving women rights equal to men's in every respect, and of emancipating women's morality from slavery to men's passion [literally *krv*, blood].

To this point women turn all their efforts—they dream of it, need it, and yearn for it. The history of these dreams and yearnings is an endless chain of pain and despair, sorrow and griefs, affliction and suffering, and the domination of women by men. The chain of this superhuman suffering started with the beginning of humanity. At the dawn of human history we meet with this question, and while we lack closer details of the social life of the time, we can confidently state that women suffered enough to have by now earned a worthier future.

A little clearer light is cast on the development of this idea by Greek and Roman history. But we are disappointed to observe that even in these culturally advanced nations the fate of women was certainly unenviable. Although we do see the glorification of women, it was only formal, only an insulating curtain that veiled the woman calling for help. Females were considered weak and fully subordinate to males. A husband had unlimited power over his wife, and acted accordingly. The homes of the wealthy patricians were full of slaves awaiting every order of their mistress, who was the top slave of her husband, probably with greater rights but at a higher price. Patrician women were not allowed to work and left to their own devices to while away their time, they sought out unworthy amusements. On the one hand it was wealth and boredom, and on the other hand it was poverty which multiplied the number of wanton fallen women—on the one hand sensuality, on the other money.

Into this chaos completely devoid of morality, Jesus Christ was born and Christianity came with the idea of total collective emancipation, the idea of moral purification. Millions and millions of the oppressed in bondage turned their blind eyes to Christianity, and among those millions were many hopeful women—who were disappointed. They hoped for improvement and a better future, but the outcome was unworthy of their dreams and hopes. At the beginning of Christianity, a woman was considered a person equal to a man, but that exalted principle of Christ's gospel, "There is neither male nor female because you are all one in Christ Jesus" (Gal. 3: 28), was later forgotten or neglected.

Women's slavery continued. Women finally realized that they could depend on no one else, and if they wanted to be as worthy as men they must take the initiative themselves. Then Fortune favored them. The French Revolution broke out—that eruption of the age-old stifled pain of injustice, that cradle of freedom for nations, that victory of the humane person over the man/animal. Now women too woke from their long sleep and began to fight for their rights. They did not fight in vain. Since the whole Revolution had a political character, it brought much good to women. They got the right to vote, establish societies, and publish journals, thus attaining freedom and liberty.

They went still further. Dazzled by such a victory, they began to ask for more. Here they came into conflict with the National Convention itself, which by then was no longer willing to give women anything. Clashes occurred, and were fateful indeed. Women were defeated, and the Republic abolished their erstwhile rights and brought back their former condition. Their new situation was worse, and now sadder in that women had brought it on themselves.

This situation lasted until the second revolution, which again raised women from bondage in the dust. The newer actions for women's liberation date from this period. At first they had a slight, uncertain character, but during the second half of the past century as a result of the crushing of women by capitalism, their old position became almost unbearable. Their efforts took on a wider range, more determined character, and more explosive form. To the innumerable enslavers of women was added capitalism, or more accurately the exploitation of female labor. We like to say that employment has freed millions of women, but this freedom is only ostensible; the reality is different. The girl going off to work leaves home, but the wages for her work are insufficient to properly support her. Trying to stay alive she makes extra money—at the high price of her chastity. After all, how can a young girl live in a large city for a monthly wage of 20–25 crowns? Is it not our communal responsibility to bring about reform? Yes, we do want independent women, not dependent on their husbands, and we want to give them the needed means. We do not want the attitude of a woman to her husband to be forced by her instinct of self-preservation, just to secure her future. Instead, we want her attitude to result from her soul's instinct, from her spiritual relation to herself.

The woman question, then, must be understood as a general social question emphasizing the interconnection of all its relations. Indeed, nowhere else do legal, sociopolitical, ethical, psychological, and other moments adhere as in the woman question.

To allow women access to higher education in a modern state is a given; it goes without saying. The mental inferiority of women can no longer be contended by any but blinded women brought up in prejudice, or by men of weak character lacking enough moral strength to compete against women of equal ability. Women should not be humiliated as creatures of a lower order, incapable of a higher spiritual mission. Of course, their age-old bad upbringing and tradition are against them—but not forever. Even today we have women doing intellectual work, to mention only our Šoltésová, Vansová, Podjavorinská, Markovičová, Ľ. G., and others.[12]

Education cannot, and is not intended to, lure women from their natural mission as wife and mother. In fact, higher education for women is actually needed to fill the intellectual gap between wife and husband. Today's average middle-class wife who is entirely dependent upon her husband and has no thought of anything higher, lives in her household as if cursed by a spell. Gossip, constant and useless fussing around the house, extravagance, trumped-up and impractical work, pouring over fashion magazines with expensive clothing, reading of doubtful value, a frantic quest for entertainment—that is the life of such a lady. Her husband either spends his time in a tavern, or sits at home thinking of the "domestic bliss" he lacks.

And what about the upbringing of children? We would have fewer empty "spoiled youth" and dressed-up "silly geese" if their mothers knew something about life. Though their father determines the chief direction of children's upbringing, and the school fulfills his educational plan, it is still the mother's mental and emotional atmosphere that surrounds the child from its first moment of life. Maternal influence remains the strongest, because the mother rears the child's soul. Therefore, deep mental education and emotional refinement of a woman are the basis for a more beautiful family life. Only an educated woman can be a good housekeeper, wife, and mother, and only an uneducated one can be vain, irresponsible, and imprudent.

An educated woman who knows how to earn her own living is not slavish and obsequious, but independent, aware of the load she can carry, and appreciative of her husband. Of course, not all women must be able to earn their living, which depends upon many circumstances. A mother working outside the home may neglect her household and child rearing, and this damage is disproportionate to any profit from her work. However, some women shopkeepers and others away from home all day still have well-run households and proper children, and such should become the rule, not the exception. Awareness that a wife helps bear the common physical load is the path to an understanding husband where no higher spiritual power exists. Just as this fact applies to middle-class women, it applies also to women of the working class.

Women today constitute a secure labor pool that is needed in sales, manufacturing, and almost everywhere. Women own property and pay taxes, so it is only fair to give them a direct vote and thus a hand in settling social questions. This will invigorate our political life. Questions about schools, public health, welfare, morality, and many other matters can be genuinely articulated only by women. Can a man who is profiteering on a woman's labor speak in favor of her better material conditions?

A pressing matter in the woman question involves marital relations and the legal status of unmarried mothers and illegitimate children. An enormous percent of children are born illegitimate. Their conception is not always the result of prostitution or discreet falls from virtue, but rather the result of long-term cohabitation and common-law marriages founded on "psychological sympathy." The illegitimate child is today a subject of contempt, like its mother, as a result of a man's guilt. Here no laws or regulations can help, but only the moral reform of marriage.

We have touched these subjects superficially, but with the conviction that it was high time to speak up. If the woman question is a serious one, we cannot ignore it, and if it is a sick phenomenon, then all human society is sick and we would only delude ourselves if we pursued individual symptoms.

What is our own Slovak situation? The question of women and the proper moral education of women is critical in our country. The prevalent stupefying system of various girls' schools should not satisfy Slovak girls and Slovak women, who are fated along with Slovak men to bear the common burden of national oppression. If we want to survive, we must have healthy, unspoiled growth, and for that we must have educated mothers. We must give them this education ourselves as long as the school system does not.

It is striking that even the economist Milan Frič has little to say about women's lack of legal or political power. As mentioned in Chapter 4, the married woman and mother was idolized as the moral guardian of the family, but she lacked legal authority in marital and parental matters. It seems likely that the constricted position of the Slovaks in Hungary did not foster concern with jurisprudence and parliament, in which they were scarcely represented. Instead, Slovak interest lay where they could reasonably expect to hold some power, i.e. in cultural and domestic spheres.

Perhaps for this reason among others, domestic fiction remained an important means of expression for Slovak nationalists, especially women. As shown in the next chapter, fiction too began to show women as women.

NOTES

1. Ambro Pietor, "Spolok slovenských žien," *Peštbudínské vedomosti* 9 (June 2, 1869): [2]. See also Chapter 3, n.6.

2. Karel Kálal, "Ženská otázka," *Dom a škola* 12.10 (1896): 311 – 315. See also Chapter 3, n.25.

3. Johana Lehocká, "Z Liptova," *Slovenskje národňje novini* 83(1846): 330. See also Chapter 2, n.24.

4. Šoltésová, "Dozvuky k poslednému valnému zhromaždeniu Živeny," *Pohľady na literatúru* 78. See also Chapter 3, n. 19.

5. Šoltésová, "Potreba vzdelanosti pre ženu, zvlášť so stanoviska mravnosti," *Letopis Živeny,* 2 (1898): 154-190. Italics are in the original. It is surprising that such an essay appeared under Vajanský's editorship, and amusing that he published but refused to proofread it, according to a letter by Šoltésová, printed by Želmíra Handzová, ed. *Múdrosť a skromnosť idú spolu* (Martin: Osveta, 1989) 198.

6. In Slovak the words *muž* and *žena* or "man" and "woman" are also commonly used to mean "husband" and "wife" in place of the more formal words *manžel* and *manželka*. The latter words are not used at all by Šoltésová, so the context had to determine whether she meant a married couple or generic man and woman. This seemed slightly problematic in only a few instances.

7. The adjective *duševný* and adverb *duševne* are based on the chameleon word *duša* meaning "soul," but they are also equivalent at times to "mind, reason, spirit, personality, intellect" etc. Thus they must be translated variously as "spiritual, mental, emotional, intellectual, or psychological" according to the context. The religious connotation of our word "spiritual" is often not present at all.

8. Charity Cannon Willard, "Christine de Pizan: The Franco-Italian Professional Writer," *Medieval Women Writers,* ed. Katharina M. Wilson (Athens: U of Georgia P, 1984) 222–363.

9. See S. Joan Moon, "Feminism and Socialism: The Utopian Synthesis of Flora Tristan," *Socialist Women* (New York: Elsevier, 1978) 19–50.

10. Tkadlečková-Vantuchová 43. Other influences were possible, of course, and ideas similar to Šoltésová's were advocated in Russia by M. L. Mikhailov (1829–1865), as summarized by Stites 38–47.

11. Milan Frič, "O ženskej otázke," *Dennica* 10 (1907): 22–25. The original is scattered with italics which are not reproduced here.

12. Frič probably means Ľudmila Boorová Markovičová, wife of a leading Slovak physician and banker; she had written a few minor pieces about language. "Ľ. G." was the young literary critic Ľudmila Groeblová (1884–1968), who later married Bratislava university professor Václav Chaloupecký.

CHAPTER 6: INCIPIENT FEMINIST HEROINES

The nationalist heroine seen in Chapter 4 wanted to make a difference to the nation, whereas the incipient feminist heroine to be taken up here wanted to make a difference to herself and to women as such. Most of the nationalist heroines were married or still young enough to be prospects for marriage, but Vansová's and Podjavorinská's occasional spinster or teacher suggested a potentially different kind of heroine from the partner wives who were usually shown. From this potential difference, a new kind of heroine developed among a few women writers. She showed both positive and negative features, of which I shall first take the former.

Celibacy as an empowering concept of freedom from the opposite sex and from the restraints of parenthood, rather than as a negative concept of denied sexuality, is gaining considerable attention from feminist historians. They now recognize that highly educated abbesses and choir nuns in the great medieval convents and secular women humanists pursuing a scholarly life separate from home and children, can be considered precursors of later "career women."[1]

In the eighteenth and nineteenth centuries, spinsterhood as a deliberate choice by women themselves became increasingly attractive as a way to escape the domestic bonds of "women's place." Examples are varied. In England Mary Astell, a follower of Descartes and John Locke, had "called for a secular religious vocation through higher education for spinsters, women who like herself chose not to marry."[2] In nineteenth-century Russia radical women rejected marriage and family in order to be free for work in the revolution. Although Slovak women had no counterpart to the terrorism in which certain Russian women revolutionaries participated, their sense of self-sacrifice was similar.[3] This is amply shown in their lyric poetry, especially that invoking a mystical marriage to the nation as seen in Chapter 2.

The strongest spinster heroines in Slovak nationalist literature appeared with the fourth major writer, Božena Slančíková (1867–1951), who used the name Timrava. The daughter of a Lutheran pastor and schooled only at home, she lived her whole life in the two small towns in southeast Slovakia which appear in her more than fifty stories and novellas published from 1893 to 1926.[4] She wrote light verse while young and two plays late in life, but she is known primarily for her two categories of stories. Classic tales portray the hard life of the peasantry with realist or even naturalist objectivity and sardonic humor, and unusual psychological portraits show young girls in inchoate rebellion against women's established position. Both categories of stories are combined in Timrava's masterpiece, the long novella *Hrdinovia* (Heroes, 1918) condemning World War I. Her work has been widely praised despite its difficult style, though little has been translated.[5]

Timrava occasionally created minor fictional figures representing nationalist endeavors, for example the aunt in "Strašný koniec" (An Awful Ending, 1912) who encourages her romantic ward to marry an unglamorous but nationally sound schoolteacher. The major figures, however, are extended portraits of nationalist spinsters in Timrava's two autobiographical stories. Taken together, they can be read as the bildungsroman of a young writer who is plainly patterned upon the young Timrava, and who grows up under the influence of a spinster nationalist mentor to become a spinster nationalist mentor herself. These two stories also provide the only portrait of a woman writer in Slovak literature of this period.

The novella *Všetko za národ* (Give Your All for the Nation, 1926) shows Hana Čepčinská (financially independent and deliberately single) as she inspires and provokes the young girl Viera into becoming a nationalist writer. In real life the mentor was Ema Goldpergerová (1853–1917), and the events shown occurred around 1893–1894 though Timrava dated them just before World War I, perhaps to mask their closeness to her own family.[6] Čepčinská considers her spinster status as a sacrifice for the nation:

> "You may be sure that the good of all nations, not just our own tiny one, rests on the shoulders of women! But for us Slovaks it's especially true, because our men are being lost." .... (2: 622). "I chose not to marry because I wanted to live independently of everything. I denied myself." (2: 624)

The novella was retrospective, written when Timrava was 55–56 years old. Perhaps she could not imagine a woman's life as happy without marriage until she had lived such a life herself. The view of celibacy as nationalist sacrifice was here more benign than her earlier view had been in the other autobiographical work she wrote.

This earlier story shows a young woman writer facing a harsh picture of the single life. In "Skúsenost'" (Experience, 1902) the young writer Marína is bashful and introverted like Timrava herself, though she has already published several stories and is well known. She becomes a paid companion to a wealthy egotistic, manipulative widow. The story was based on Timrava's actual stay in Dolný Kubín in 1900, and despite considerable cutting before publication it caused a small sensation for its scornful satire of the widow and Slovak society.[7] It is usually treated as a small *roman à clef*, but for my purpose it is most interesting as an autobiographical portrait of a woman writer and her response to her position.

Marína is unsure how to behave as a writer or even as an intellectual in a society that itself had little idea how to react to a woman writer and intellectual. She has yearned to meet two leading nationalist male poets, but when she does she stammers and has nothing to say to them. When a toast is made to her as a promising writer, she angrily says she "was held up to scorn" (1: 461). When some of the men invite her to join them after dinner, she goes instead into the garden with another young woman, where they pick flowers for their hair and go out alone on a romantic canoe ride. Yet she complains then and afterwards that the men ignored her. The metaphorical death of Marína's expectations of the leading nationalists is paralleled in her sad memories of a former lover and in two brief episodes showing a happy bride and a self-assured fiancée in contrast to Marína's loneliness as she faces the spinster's life ahead of her. Supporting details include a dying single girl and the lack of family mourners at the funeral of a celibate priest. As Marína finds that she can neither answer nor accept the widow's constant petty criticism, she returns home. Obviously the story tells of a "failed quest," but its ending turns it from failure into victory. Fighting off despair and determined to go her own way, Marína will pursue her own kind of nationalist activity.

If we consider Marína to be the grown-up version of the teenage writer Viera in *Všetko za národ*, then the two stories show a bildungsroman of first the uncertain adolescent with her spinster mentor, then the lonely but determined young writer, and finally the serene nationalist who is prepared to mentor others. Timrava's acceptance of the ideal of nationalist activity allowed her to create what feminist critics rarely find in women's literature: a novel of development mirroring a society that supported a woman's growth from childhood to personhood in her own right. In the terms used by Nancy K. Miller, this is an "euphoric" text, not a "dysphoric" one, because of the "heroine's integration into society."[8] More often the opposite is shown: as Annis Pratt says, "by necessity, the orderly succession of stages characterizing the male bildungsroman is disrupted since the role requirements for women are antithetical to maturation."[9] In the absence of a supportive society, a female character's development appears as interior withdrawal, a "voyage *in*."[10] Timrava's woman writer, however, continues her public career and becomes integrated into society by her "outward voyage," despite whatever personal conflict she may feel during this life.

These nationalist spinsters can be read as incipient feminists in having satisfyingly resolved their desire to empower themselves through their desire to help the nation. They are still close to the pure nationalist heroine, but they show a new sense of selfhood. They represent a positive response to women's social and national position. Most of Timrava's work, however, embodies the negative responses of victimized women. Timrava's life as a single woman, financially dependent upon her mother's pension or her brother's support, and located far from the nationalist center in north central Slovakia, gave her an outsider mentality that forced her to see the world in economic terms, not national ones.

Even her stories about marriage are filled with the agonies of the marriage market, where a young lady who has no dowry must marry a widower with children, or a peasant girl must marry her cousin whose family's fields adjoin her family's fields. Timrava's more than fifty stories show a controlling concern with mammon, i.e. the power of money and property to determine human lives. The peasants idolize their land and value everyone by their ability to drudge like beasts with no higher concern. Among the gentility and small town intelligentsia who populate the other category of Timrava's stories, this economic concern often ends the same way. The plots are like those of Jane Austen in turning entirely on how to make a suitable marriage, but the bright, sensible girls do not wed handsome heirs as do Austen's heroines. Many of Timrava's girls are rebellious, at least inwardly revolting against the necessity for a marriage of convenience. These genteel heroines see themselves as victims of a materialistic world. They sense that society is disordered and want to strike out somehow against a system that victimizes them.

This inward rebellion takes various forms. Anna in "Strašný koniec" (An Awful Ending, 1912) sees herself as the "dowryless victim of a cruel world" because she must accept marriage to someone less than her dreamed-of ideal (2: 266). She sees clearly that the problem lies outside herself and does not accept the blame for having been born poor and plain. In "Nemilí" (Unpleasant Suitors, 1899) Sabína feels herself at the mercy of fortune as she is playing cards, hearing and using the word for drawing a card, *vydať*, which is also the word for a woman's marriage (a different word is used for a man's marriage). This word *vydať* becomes in her thoughts symbolic of drawing a mate, or being drawn, in the game of marriage and life, and she feels as passive and helpless as a tarot card (1: 361–368). Superstitious and fatalistic in other ways, she accepts as true a dream that she will marry a disliked widower, and she consults a gypsy fortune-teller about her future husband.[11]

Even where a heroine internalizes and lives up to the required "perfection" of the ideal woman, she is not entirely misled and oblivious to its falseness. In one of Timrava's longest novellas, *Veľké šťastie* (Her Great Good Fortune, 1906), Otila represents the official ideal as she prepares to become the ornamental wife of a middle-class husband, "beautiful, calm, womanly" (1: 628). She has fully internalized the code and accepted it as her own personality, thereby becoming a placid, statuesque egotist. Sensing the emptiness of marriage to her ideal suitor, Otila would be willing to accept the young village minister for his moral superiority, but only if he idolizes her as the code prescribes. Since he does not, she accepts the man she considers the empty ideal. Interestingly, this text also uses that same male ideal to indict these standards. Meditating on his dull future with Otila, he admits to himself he would prefer the explosive peasant girl who was taken as a baby to be a ward of Otila's mother, if only he "were a lower being himself" (1: 735–736).

Marta in "Boj" (Battle, 1900) forces herself to save her father from financial ruin by her marriage to a wealthy, consumptive artist, and Timrava rewards her by the artist's death and a second marriage to her former suitor. This reward, however, is ironic because she now has tuberculosis herself. Again, the code does not bring happiness.

Perhaps Timrava's most striking characters represent the women for whom idealization did not have a positive effect because they could not turn it to a personal cause. They suffered the negative effects of glorification in personal despair and self-hatred at an outside-imposed identity. Barbara Heldt has called this syndrome "perfection or doom" because failure to live up to the ideal brings moral ruin.[12] In "Bez hrdosti" (No Self Respect, 1905), Milina even takes to drink because of her hopeless love for an egotistic wastrel: a good woman should not feel an unworthy passion. Joža in *Vel'ké šťastie* is supposed to marry her late father's middle-aged friend to provide a haven (peace of mind as well as economic security) for herself and her mother. Joža does not refuse, but she procrastinates and becomes a "meddling, willful, obstructive old maid" (2: 636) despite her open-hearted efforts to help others. Her marriage cannot meet the romantic ideal of two young people who are both suitable and in love (as Otila's marriage outwardly seems to meet this ideal in the same novella), so Joža deliberately flouts the standard of womanly calm and decorum. These "doomed" characters (irrational, uncontrolled, and self-destructive) are called mischievous, headstrong, self-centered, undisciplined, and even mad by those around them who see only how they reject the standard role. They are minor examples of the "madwoman in the attic."[13]

In Timrava's complex pictures of women being drawn like tarot cards, women penalized for following the code, and women doomed by imperfection, it was the social structure at fault, not the individual women themselves. In recognizing this fact about her work, Slovak Marxist literary critics made their most perceptive contribution to the study of women writers. In their reassessment of Slovak literature in Marxist-Leninist terms after World War II, they re-emphasized Timrava, who had not been widely popular earlier, probably because of her naturalist cynicism and lack of idealistic nationalism. Her theme of mammon and obsession with property was eminently suitable for Marxist analysis, and she was easily placed in Maxim Gorky's category of "critical realists":

> those writers coming from a bourgeois society who did not separate from it enough to reach the position of the organized working class, but whose longing for truthful expression led to their exposing the inability of the bourgeoisie to secure a just and happy social structure. Since these writers could not really overcome their class limitation, they did not know how to resolve the contradictions they pictured artistically in their works..., but at least they gave the signal to rebel.[14]

Many of Timrava's stories catch what Kusý calls that "stage of development when the patriarchal relations still held together, when the villagers still believed in unchanging social classes, but already the next step in development could crack this apparent idyll" (475). Hungary was undergoing the industrial revolution with major economic dislocations and modernization as the rural economy slowly changed into a more urbanized and capitalized society, and these changes are much more deeply embedded in Timrava's stories than in those of Vansová, Šoltésová, or Podjavorinská.

The critic Alexander Matuška relates these economic changes that made the property and dowry arrangements of marriage baldly apparent, to the development of Timrava's rebellious females. When she began publishing in 1893, as Matuška says,

> emotional relations and love were presented sentimentally and bloodlessly or as a pathetic, patriotic exaltation: the pale, ashy, sexless erotica shown in the works of Vajanský, Šoltésová, and Vansová. This corresponds to the half-hearted understanding and application of emancipation in the developing Slovak urban society, where women were steadily being drawn out into public and national circles, but where still at least theoretically the romantic cult of woman persisted, and where a woman was becoming a partner but still remained above all a good match.[15]

Timrava's heroines go through the "school of disillusion" about love, which becomes sharper for them because in their society love carries the meaning of life. This disillusionment became the key to Timrava's understanding of bourgeois society, because through it she saw the falsity of the ideology of love which her heroines believe in:

> Love is not just the central point of marriage, because it also gives the very fullness of existence. As moral personalities women want to be able to decide their destiny themselves. Life loses its meaning for them when they find they are not free, and their pure feeling cannot win and cannot avoid betrayal. Therefore life becomes repugnant and not worth living. It is true that from their disillusion they arrive at a "soberer" view of life and become resigned to the prosaic conditions around them, but their resignation is always prepared for attack, always prepared to assail social lies and falsehood. It is they, not the men busy earning their bread, who are the bearers of antisocial rebellion.... It is not the presence of naive, conventional girls yearning for love and being disappointed, but the presence of such figures as Marta in "Boj," Milina in "Bez hrdosti," and Joža in "Veľké šťastie," whose reaction to the rule of money allows us to say that the daydreaming of young girls uncovered for Timrava the basic antagonism which she distinguished as symptomatic for the bourgeois and the would-be bourgeois society: the antagonism between dream and reality. (503–504)

This is a significant perception and biographically accurate to Timrava's outsider mentality that allowed or even forced her to see much that her more nationalistic Slovak contemporaries missed.

Timrava's heroines can be related to those in other literatures. As Matuška says, they "are historical, socially contemporary class types" (529). Timrava's protesting females were new to Slovak literature, but they are typical figures who were presaged in Austen's country houses or parsonages and who appear on the Brontes' heaths, in George Eliot's drawing rooms, and elsewhere. Timrava's pervasive irony is also significant. The desire for equity in marriage underlay the rebellion of much women's fiction, and inevitably the discrepancy between premarital ideals and marital reality was shown ironically.[16]

Because of this typicality Timrava's stories may also be read fruitfully in terms of age-old symbols: the green world of nature, the ideal lover, rape trauma, marriage as enclosure, the odd woman or witch, and the wise old woman who is seeress and mentor. Archetypal criticism is particularly helpful with those stories which (like so much nineteenth century fiction by women about women) show a perplexing, tiresome self-absorption and undeveloped or underdeveloped illogical, contrary minds and personalities. Some of Timrava's characters' amorphous anger at the world is insufficiently focussed for us to feel sure it is rooted in their recognizable social basis. Therefore such stories are not always successful as literature though they are revealing as sociology. This aspect of Timrava's work can be reached aesthetically through its most basic archetypes as they transcend the uncertainty of her social picture and evoke the resonance of myth.[17]

Such analysis is particularly helpful with Timrava's rebellious heroines who went beyond the nationalist heroine by perceiving that the opportunity to work beside men for the national cause did not solve economic problems, that nationalists too (of both sexes) could be hypocrites and materialists, and perhaps that the initial joy of self-sacrifice and abnegation was short-lived. This was not just a chronological matter of outgrowing nationalism. For some women the opportunity to work for the nation was simply never attractive because they were apolitical. This aspect of Timrava's work has been related to Slovak Modernism.[18] Like Vajanský's fiction Timrava's whole canon would provide a rewarding study.

Such a picture of women doomed by the social structure they lived in continued in the work of Hana Lilgová Gregorová (1885–1958), daughter of a nationalist family in Turčiansky Svätý Martin. Her marriage in 1907 to the important critical realist writer Jozef Gregor Tajovský (1874–1940) gave her a literary household that helped complete her self-education after grade school.[19]

In her first book of stories, *Ženy* (Women, 1912), Gregorová was probably reacting against the idylically happy wives and mothers shown in nationalist fiction including some of the works of Vansová and Šoltésová, but she most strongly contradicted the male picture of women as dependent creatures of high feeling and no mind. Besides the work of Vajanský treated in Chapter 4,

Koloman Banšell (1850–1887) had clearly advocated this view in "Emancipovaná" (Emancipated Woman, 1872), which caricatured the new independent woman.[20] His heroine, Štefánia Odolinová, is given sympathetic traits as a member of the nationalist gentry, and she becomes a governess to support herself after she refuses to marry for money. Her experience as a single woman, however, teaches her to reject "equality with men. Women gain equality only by love" (85). At the end her happy marriage has taught her that

> to shine in family piety, nobility, tenderness, love, care-giving, work ethic—being exemplary in every respect: this is worth more than a doctorate. We women emancipate ourselves, *when we worthily fulfill our mission as wives and mothers*. For this we shall be blessed by our family, community, nation, state, and church—and our wreath will not wilt like the wreath given to Sappho. (89)

Banšell viewed "independence" as counter to "woman's emotional nature," and he showed women suffering the penalties of sorrow and illness if they went against their nature. In contrast to this view, Gregorová showed penalized wives and mothers suffering from that very role which was supposed to insure their happiness. In almost every story the heroine is victimized by this prescribed role.

Gregorová's earliest published story, "Prvá obeť" (First Victim, 1910), established her typical pattern. A young girl's stifled yearning for education, frustrated by her family and community, eventually leads to her moral ruin according to the double standard. Oľga Biela wants to become a teacher, for which her family calls her "lazy, ungrateful, frivolous, unfeminine, abnormal, contrary" (94–95). Refused schooling, she finds self-study too hard, moves alone to the city, works as a governess, then falls prey to her naive imagination of the sympathy of an actor who seems to promise all she has wanted of life. Eventually she commits suicide. A similar fate threatens an illiterate young girl forced to go begging with her blind father in "Po žobraní" (Begging, 1912), and a bright servant girl whom poverty grinds down in "Slečinka a služka" (The Young Miss and the Servant Girl, 1912).

Publication of these stories in 1912 created a storm that partly resulted from Gregorová's grim picture of victimized women, but it also engaged an ongoing controversy between the Martin and Hlasist nationalists over the way to fight Magyarization. Gregorová's "Prvá obeť" was first published in *Dennica* under the editorship of František Votruba, one of the chief Hlasist critics of Vajanský, and her collected stories came out with the same publisher. It is no wonder that Gregorová's book was attacked by the editors of *Národnie noviny*. The book's reception was also harmed by a specific controversy between Vajanský and Gregorová's husband Tajovský over realism in literature, with Vajanský desiring the kind of idealized picture presented in his own work, and with Tajovský asking for almost naturalist detail as in his own work and that of Gregorová.[21]

The book *Ženy* was defended in a review by Elena Maróthy Šoltésová on three grounds. It was truthful in showing women's rightful desire for education; in unhappy marriages women undeniably suffered more than men since they usually had no other outlet for their minds and emotions; and fallen women were punished more severely than their seducers.[22] These were all points Šoltésová had earlier made in her long essay on women's right to an education (Chapter 5). Šoltésová also defended Gregorová personally because her dedication of the book to her husband who supported her efforts and encouraged her to become a writer proved that she wanted a moral kind of emancipation (131).

Gregorová was certainly a nationalist in her interest and support for the Slovak national cause, but her work showed little of the typical nationalist elements. She was already close to a feminist as we see clearly in her later stories and novels. This later work, however, belongs to the new era of Czechoslovakia when the nationalists' battle to get away from Magyarization had been won.

Both Timrava and Gregorová were transitional writers who continued some of the practices of their predecessors but who also suggested the nature of future developments in looking at women as a submerged class. With these two women, the importance of nationalism in the development of Slovak women writers decreased, if it did not end. Other means of identity and other sources of encouragement came into existence as Slovakia was modernized in the twentieth century. In a sense, the importance of women writers in the national movement also ended, because by the time new major writers developed, the national movement itself had changed within the different conditions of Czechoslovakia on the new map of Europe after World War I.

NOTES

1. Marilyn J. Boxer and Jean H. Quataert, eds. "Overview, 1500–1750," *Connecting Spheres* (New York: Oxford UP, 1987). See especially the essay by Olwen Hufton and Frank Tallett, "Communities of Women, the Religious Life, and Public Service in Eighteenth-Century France" 75–85.

2. Boxer and Quataert, "Overview, 1500–1750," *Connecting Spheres* 46.

3. Barbara Engel, *Mothers and Daughters,* Chap. 10 "The Personal versus the Political."

4. Standard biographical information is given by Ivan Kusý, "Timrava (život a dielo)," *Timrava v kritike a spomienkach: Sborník* (Bratislava: Slovenské vydavateľstvo krásnej literatúry, 1958) 260-283. This collection of memoirs and literary criticism reprinted everything available on Timrava to that time, as well as several new articles; hereafter cited as *Sborník*.

5. Timrava's lack of formal schooling is reflected in idiosyncratic grammar that made editors "improve" her style in the first collected works of 1921–1945, but a critical text was prepared for *Zobrané spisy,* ed. Ivan Kusý, 7 vols. (Bratislava, 1955–1959) and the shorter selection *Timrava,* 2 vols. (Bratislava: Tatran, 1975), which I have used. In English, part of "Ťapákovci" appeared in *The Linden Tree* (Prague: Artia, 1962) 307–310 and in Cincura's *Anthology* 138–144. Six stories translated by myself are in preparation. Timrava'a life and works are briefly summarized in *Dictionary of Continental Women Writers,* ed. Katharina M. Wilson (New York: Garland, in press).

6. Timrava, "Všetko za národ," *Timrava* 2: 577–726.

7. Only part of the manuscript is now extant (see Kusý, ed. *Zobrané spisy* 2: 406–420, so the story cannot be seen in detail though its outlines are clear.

8. Nancy K. Miller, *The Heroine's Text* (New York: Columbia U P, 1980) xi.

9. Annis Pratt, *Archetypal Patterns in Women's Fiction* (Bloomington: Indiana U P, 1981) 34.

10. See the essays edited by Elizabeth Abel, Marianne Hirsch, and Elizabeth Langland, *The Voyage In* (Hannover, NH: U P of New England, 1983).

11. For a close examination of this story, see Eugen Pauliny, "Štruktúra Timravinej poviedky Nemilí," *Sborník* 674–693. First published in 1947, Pauliny's essay is structuralist, not Marxist-Leninist.

12. Heldt 28–29 and passim.

13. Sandra M. Gilbert and Susan Gubar, *The Madwoman in the Attic* (New Haven: Yale U P, 1979).

14. Ivan Kusý, "Timrava (K periodizácii jej diela)," *Sborník* 474–475.

15. Alexander Matuška, "Timrava," *Sborník* 497.

16. See, for example, Heldt, "Introduction," *Terrible Perfection*; Miller, *The Heroine's Text;* Abel, Hirsch, and Langland, eds. *The Voyage In;* as well as Judith Lowder Newton, *Power and Subversion: Social Strategies in British Fiction, 1778–1860* (Athens: U of Georgia P, 1981), and the references listed in these sources.

17. Archetypal criticism provides a relevant frame of reference even without its Jungian underpinnings. Besides Annis Pratt's *Archetypal Patterns,* see also important theoretical articles in Estelle Lauter and Carol Schreier Rupprecht, eds., *Feminist Archetypal Theory* (Knoxville: U of Tennessee P, 1985).

18. Michal Gáfrik, "Timrava a slovenská moderna," *Slovenská literatúra* 15 (1968): 174–179.

19. Gregorová's works have not been collected, but were reprinted in various selections including *Oživená nádej*, ed. Karol Rosenbaum (Bratislava: Tatran, 1985), which I have used. Her short story "Dobre mu tam bude..." was translated into English by Cincura 160–166.

20. Koloman Banšell, "Emancipovaná," *Živena. Národní Almanach*, 1 (1872): 67–89.

21. These controversies are detailed in the articles given in *Jozef Gregor Tajovský v kritike a spomienkach: Sborník* (Bratislava: Slovenské vydavateľstvo krásnej literatúry, 1956). See also *Dejiny slovenskej literatúry*, 4 (Bratislava: Veda, 1975) 176–198.

22. Šoltésová, "O 'Ženach' Hany Gregorovej," *Pohľady na literatúre* 131–136.

CONCLUSION

My treatment of nineteenth-century Slovak nationalism began seven years ago as a literary historical study of a phenomenon existing in the past with a special effect upon women who were looking for a new wider place in their circumscribed world. Chapter 6 therefore ends with the belief that the women writers emerging with increased opportunities in the free state of Czechoslovakia after 1918 require a different kind of study.

These concluding remarks do not retract that position. Yet in the light of the 1989 revolutions all over what was formerly called undifferentiated "Eastern Europe," nationalism again appears as a strong force in the late twentieth century. The large powers turned it into the aggressive and pernicious forms of colonialism and fascism, but the small states without power to impose upon others apparently still find in nationalism an explanation and defense of their individual identities. Thus we should not have been surprised that particular national consciousnesses served as bulwarks and antiseptics against the totalitarian force of communist systems that were perceived to be infectiously foreign as well as oppressive and nonfunctional.

What will women make of this new situation? Hesitantly I would still believe that women no longer need nationalism as a means to their identity as women. The rush to "westernism" that was immediately apparent in the 1989 revolution has already brought the first signs of deliberate, conscious feminism. As an explicitly recognized and named women's movement forms, it will doubtless broaden the reference and range of women writers and develop autonomous women characters beyond those figures typical of the incipient feminism that was born in nineteenth century nationalism.

What shape might these women characters take? Perhaps a prophecy about one possible shape can be suggested by a persistent trend in twentieth century women's literature. I have elsewhere analyzed Oľga Feldeková's character Žofia in the novella *Veverica* (Squirrel, 1985) as a mythic and cyclic nature symbol for the Slovaks and Slovakia which follows the tradition of Slovak lyrical prose and also Latin American magical realism.[1] This symbolic female character is a sort of obverse of the apotheosis of women as Slavdom or Slovakdom by Ján Kollár in *Slávy dcera* and Andrej Sládkovič in *Marína*. The same mythic tradition appears in the exalted epic symbolism of Margita Figuli's expressionistic *Tri gaštanové kone* (Three Chestnut Horses, 1940).[2] It can be read perhaps in the early lyrics of *Červený mak* (Red Poppy, 1932) by Maša Haľamová,[3] and certainly in the later lyric symbolism of vineyard, clay, and carpenter shop in *Trvanie* (Duration, 1979) and *Víno* (Wine, 1982) by Lýdia Vadkerti-Gavorníková.[4]

Such pervasive emphasis upon nature imagery in Slovak literature, as well as the current widespread repugnance toward anything resembling Marxist theory, suggests that certain Slovak women critics might naturally gravitate toward the archetypal school of feminist criticism and historical analysis rather than to the social and historical materialist school. In fact, the work of the Bulgarian-born French semioticist and psychoanalyst Julia Kristeva, with her profound interest in the maternal and her understanding of Slavic and Orthodox views of women, may well speak with particular clarity and intensity to the new feminists of east central Europe at their current intellectual and emotional moment.[5] Be that as it may, we can expect interesting comparative studies of eastern and western women writers which will now be possible with detailed corollary studies of literature in both areas.

NOTES

1. "National Antiheroes: Symbolism and Narrative Voice as Coded National Identity in Oľga Feldeková's *Veverica*," in *Modern Slovak Prose Fiction since 1954*, ed. R. B. Pynsent (London: Macmillan, 1990), 205–214, and "Recent Prose of Hana Ponická and Oľga Feldeková," in *Recent Developments in East European Literature*, ed. Celia Hawkesworth (London: Macmillan, in press).

2. Margita Figuli, *Tri gaštanové kone* (Martin: Matica slovenská, 1940).

3. Maša Haľamová, *Červený mak* (Prague: Leopold Mazáč, 1932).

4. Lýdia Vadkerti-Gavorníková, *Trvanie* (Bratislava: Slovenský spisovateľ, 1979) and *Víno* (Bratislava: Slovenský spisovateľ, 1982).

5. For example, particularly Julia Kristeva's seminal essays "Le Temps des femmes," *34/44: Cahiers de recherche de sciences des textes et documents*, No. 5 (Winter 1979): 5-19, and "Hérethique de l'amour," *Tel Quel*, 74 (Winter 1977): 30–49, which is titled "Stabat Mater" in later editions and translations.

APPENDIX TO CHAPTER 2:
VERSES BY SLOVAK WOMEN, 1798 – 1875
by
Marianna Prídavková Miráriková
Slovak Academy of Sciences, Bratislava
Czech and Slovak Federal Republic

The verses of Slovak women poets between 1798 and 1875, in the brief period of three quarters of a century, were circumscribed by two factors: the minimal opportunities women had for formal education and the dynamic changes occurring in the standard Slovak language.

As a result of the first factor, the great majority of women writers were educated in the homes of Lutheran pastors and teachers, since, as is well known, the Slovak intelligentsia was primarily composed of nationalist clergy, and the households of the celibate Catholic clergy held no wives and daughters.

These writers must also be seen in the context of Slovak language changes, which Eugen Pauliny has summarized as follows:

> A nationwide language in Slovakia began developing during the middle ages with the formation of Slovak cities and a Slovak-speaking gentry class whose members were the first to use the local language as a universal medium supplanting its dialectal status. In the fifteenth century this development continued through acceptance of the Czech language as the written equivalent of the standard spoken language of the Slovak nationality. From the sixteenth century on, despite use of the Czech language but also on its basis, two linguistic forms began to be used: Western and Central Slovak, which were closely intermingled. From the sixteenth to eighteenth centuries Lutherans continued with the traditional Czech, whereas Catholics accepted Western Slovak as the basis for the standard language. Anton Bernolák proceeded to codify this language as the indigenous standard Slovak. For various reasons... his movement was not accepted nationwide. It was the movement of Ľudovít Štúr, proceeding from Bernolák but based upon Central Slovak and maturing in more favorable circumstances, which culminated the drive that had lasted several centuries.[1]

Thus, for several centuries in Slovakia, besides the local cultural language and besides the use of Latin, various forms of Czech were used as the standard language. For a short time German was also used, but despite the strong pressure of Magyarization the Magyar language was not used by Slovaks as their own even though it later became the state language.

The almost complete absence of schools for Slovak girls was, naturally, an obstacle to literary activity by women. Although these women's verses are usually of little aesthetic value, they give evidence of Slovak conditions and the cultural accomplishment of the authors. Certain poems are about romantic love or morality, but primarily they are nationalist poems or adaptations of folk literature, often written with the didactic intention to stimulate activity in the national movement. The situation was somewhat different for men, and at this time Slovak accentual poetry boasted of distinguished representatives in Samo Chalupka (1812–1883), Andrej Sládkovič (1820–1872), Janko Kráľ (1822–1876), Ján Botto (1829–1881), and others. Naturally, without formal schooling women could not be expected to compose poetry based on classical prosody and length of syllable, as written by Ján Hollý (1785–1849). Nevertheless, women's verse inevitably reflects the century-long conflict over language and literature.

The first known Slovak woman poet, the wife of a Slovak Lutheran pastor and writer who was superintendent in Prague for four years, Rebeka Laučeková Lešková published a didactic poem in the collection of the Czech poet and Catholic priest Antonín Jaromír Puchmajer (1769–1820). She was then the only female representative of Puchmajer's poetic cirle. Published in the last year of Lešková's stay in Prague, the poem is in Czech. A second poem of this same year, 1798, by Mária Kubiniová is closer to Western Slovak *(predkow, chod'te, prawú, swú)*, as is the poem attributed to Estera Šuleková *(krome, wěrjm, smela, horj, pred, moge, twoge, mogi)*. The verses of the gentlewomen Judita Kiselyová Ruttkayová, Judita Ruttkayová Majerová, Katarína Kiselyová, and Terézia Vitališová (1800–1830) are written in the Central Slovak which later became the basis for the standard language. The versions published in *Slovenské pohľady* in 1894–1895 by Rehor Uram, however, may not be entirely accurate to the lost originals.

Language development can be observed directly in the work of a single author. Johana Lehocká published two Czech-language poems, "Podkřiwánsky wlastenec" and "Slowenka," in the collection *Nitra* in 1842. Lehocká's three other Czech poems, "Sen," "Lipa," and "Hrob," were not released by the Magyar censor in 1843. In that same year, however, the Štúrists agreed on the codification of the standard language, and in 1844 editor Jozef M. Hurban was able to publish Lehocká's "Hrob" in *Nitra*, the first book in the new standard language. Hurban simply translated Lehocká's Czech poem into Slovak without a note to the fact, regarding it as a natural development. Lehocká's last poem, "Peseň labutia," was published in 1852 in Slovak.

The collection *Nitra* in 1842 also had Czech verses by "Rosália and Amália" and Zuzana Reguliová Moravčíková, as well as by Zuzana Šoltýsová, who from 1849 on, however, wrote in Štúr's Slovak. "Sophia" and "Slowenka Sitňjanska" also wrote in Štúr's Slovak in 1846. In 1861 Karolina Pulíny still wrote two devotional poems in the Czech with Slovak elements that was used as the Lutheran liturgical language, but thereafter all her poems were in Slovak.

By the 1860s women from all parts of Slovakia were writing poems, many of them using pseudonyms. Their styles reflect the linguistic development and stabilization of norms that were occurring, although it is difficult to judge how extensive editorial changes may have been.

Many of the pseudonyms that women used still remain undecifered. Moreover, those decifered may not be certain, because the same Christian name can belong to two authors; for example, the pseudonym Milina can belong to Antónia Emília Rumanová and also Milina Lohinská, or the name Milina Lohinská may itself be a pseudonym for A. E. Rumanová. We also do not rule out the possibility that certain verses with women's names were really written by men.[2]

The following 123 poems probably cover most of the poetic output of Slovak women published from 1798 to 1875. We have not systematically searched all of the periodical literature of this period, and by the late 1860s much more work by women was appearing, so we are doubtless less than complete for at least the later period. Very few of these verses have been reprinted since their original publication in short-lived magazines and newspapers, and most are now difficult to find outside Czechoslovakia, where in fact many are available in only a few libraries. Several verses have been printed only in a modernized version, and two have not previously been published. This fugitive status made us decide to reprint the whole collection.

The verses are given chronologically except that where the author wrote more than one work her pieces are grouped together in their own chronological order. Known biographical information is given as well as bibliographical data. The poems are referred to by number (e.g. Appendix, No.1).

The texts are reproduced without change (except a few obvious misprints). With the verses written in Czech or Czech with Slovak elements, the old spelling shows the following differences from modern Czech: *w=v, ss=š, g=j, ně=ňe, au=ou, ůu=ú*, and *j=í*. In the Czech poem by Rebeka Lešková, prepositions are written together with their objects. The verses written in Central Slovak and later in standard Slovak show the abandonment of the old spelling and consistent replacement: *g=j, ss=š, w=v*, and *j=í*. They show *uo* and the diphthongs *ja* and *je*, and *d* is distinguished from *ď*, *n* from *ň*, and *t* from *ť*. In the 1840s *i* was not distinguished from *ý*.

The women are listed with their names in currently correct Slovak spelling, though many surnames were not declined in the past.

ABBREVIATIONS USED   (full reference in WORKS CITED):

Biog. odd MS	Biografické oddelenie Matice slovenskej
Ency. slov. spis.	*Encyklopédia slovenských spisovateľov*
Krč.	Krčméry's *Dejiny literatúry slovenskej*
Miš.	Mišianik's Bibliografia slovenského písomníctva: *Doplnky k Riznerovej Bibliografii*
Orm.	Ormis's *Doplnky a opravy k Riznerovej Bibliografii*
Riz.	Rizner's *Bibliografia písomníctva slovenského*
Slov. biog. slov.	*Slovenský biografický slovník*

Rebeka Laučeková Lešková (1773–1856)   "R—a L—ową"

Bohuslav Tablic's identification of this author in 1812 was neglected or denied until Václav Jílek restored it in 1927. See Chapter 2 and notes 36–38 for details and a summary of Lešková's life; see also *Slov. biog. slov., 3: 393.* Daughter of Martin Lauček and wife of Štefan Leška, Lešková with her single known verse became the first woman poet in the restored Czech language and the earliest uncontested woman poet from Slovakia. According to Jílek (267), these verses were set to music by Jakub Jan Ryba in *Neue böhmische Lieder*, which however we have not confirmed.

1. Wýstraha předswůdcy wssem pannám (A Warning to All Young Ladies against Seducers)

> Pozorugte sbedliwostj,
> Panny, swůdcůw podwodných!
> Wládněte swau stydliwostj,
> Střezte se těch nehodných,—
>
> Kteřj wasse srdce čisté
> Chytře khřjchu swáděgj,
> Mluwjc řeči gako gisté;
> Wssak se wám gen wysměgj.
>
> Necht' wám oni co chtj twrdj,
> At' to mjsta nemjwá;
> Neb y mysslenj gjch smrdj,
> Jako mrcha čerwiwá.
>
> Onit' wassich ctnostných ussj
> Posskwrňugj mnohými
> Řečmi, kteréž nepřislussj—
> Zapyřte se přednjmi!
>
> Onit' wasse oči ctnostné
> Odctnosti a swětlosti
> Budau lákat kpřežalostné
> Ohawnosti, ktemnosti.
>
> Zgara wsaumrak rádi chodj
> Naprocházku sděwčaty;
> Newinnost gich chytře swodj,
> Tot' zwyk gegich proklatý.

Wlétě, když gest horko welmi,
Wedne někde spáwagj,
Podwečjr pak gako sselmy
Lowit wycházýwagj.

Napodzym pak pozahradách,
Sstěpnicých a winnicých
Chodjwagj pozlých radách.
Newinnosti sskodjcých.

Wzýmě swůdce nagme saně,
Kužjwánj sanice,
Sedneli mu děwče naně—
Oklamá se welice,

Proklatj a zlořečenj
Buďte ctnosti zhaubcowé!
Připrawte gim odsauzenj,
O wy zemsstj saudcowé!

Neboť wpannách swaté gměnj
Potlačugj přebludně;
Mluwjce, že swaté nenj,
Mámj khřychu bezstudně.

Wjnem hřjchů opogenj
Budauť často mluwiti:
Wjno to ge sladké!—chtěnj
Zlé chtjc wpannách zbuditi.

Y to slowo stwořitele,
Genž dj: Ploďte, množte se!
Přewrátj ctným pannám směle,
Kbjdě gegich, kzhaubě swé.

Neboť rauchem lásky prawé
Zastjragj chlípnost swau.
Když wnich, gako zwjře drawé,
Chlípnost řwe, tuť lásku lhau.

Protož, Panny utjkeyte
Předswůdcy, co můžete,
Prawé lásce ruku deyte:
A tak ssťastné budete!

> R — a L — owá
> *Nowé básně*, ed. Antonín Puchmajer
> (Prague, 1798) 141–143.

Mária Kubiniová (17? –18?)   No pseudonym

This poem is dated 1798 in Kollár's *Národnie zpievanky* and obviously deals with the French wars. As indicated in Chapter 2, Mária Kubini has not been specifically identified among the many members of this gentry family in north central Slovakia.

2. Pjseň Insurgentská (1798) (Song for the Militia)

> 1. Nu gen chlapci neženatj
> Nedegte se ponúkati,
>   Koně si rychtugte,
>   Šable pripasugte,
>   Maširugte!
>
> 2. Choďte šťastně a bogugte,
> Wašich predkow následugte,
>   Králowé uherský
>   Býwali šťastliwj,
>   Wy probugte.
>
> 3. Sbite Francúza na zkazu,
> Ukažte zmužilost prawú,
>   Buďte wěrnj králi,
>   Swogeg wlasti stálj.
>   Pro swú sláwu.
>
> 4. A gestli z wás který padne
> Co se stati může snadně,
>   Na geho hrob nápis
>   "Hic miles quiescit"
>   Napsat dáme.
>
> 5. Gestli šťastně zwjtězjte,
> K nám se zase nawrátjte,
>   Budeme wjtat wás,
>   A weselý bál zas
>   Obdržjte.
>
> 6. A tak wšecci naši milj
> Choďte šťastně wen z kraginy,

> Tam wás gedna Dáma
> Insurgentom známa
> Očekáwá.
> *Národnie zpiewanky*, ed. Ján Kollár,
> Vol. 1 (Budapest, 1834) 44.

Estera Šuleková (17? –18 ?)   No pseudonym

Ján Kollár identified Estera Šuleková as an author known to him without citing her work, but this poem is accepted as hers because of its acrostic. Rizner (5: 267) lists her without further data. Her family was literarily active (*Ency. slov. spis.*, 2: 175) and well known, as indicated in Chapter 2, but the standard sources give no information on her own life. Anecdotally it is said the poem was probably sent to Kollár before 1791.

3. Skrytý pohled lásky (The Secret Glance of Love)

> 1. *E*i Milý můg, Milý můg
> Gak mne zklamal pohled twůg!
>   Ei zklamal mně welice
>   Tak že i moge ljce
> Plače, Bože politug!

> 2. *S*talo se to pro tebe
> Můg Milý že gen w sobě
>   Musjm lásku dusiti,
>   Aniž komu zgewiti
> Gi nesmjm, krome tebe.

> 3. *T*obě se gen zdůwěrjm,
> Že si sprawedliw wěrjm,
>   Nebo sem tě poznala
>   Když sem tě milowala
> Že mi chceš býti wěrným.

> 4. *E*i kdyby gá to smela
> Wygewiti do cela
>   Co se děge w mém srdci,
>   Gak horj láskau wraucj,
> I tebe bych pohnula.

> 5. *R*áda na tě mogjma
> Hleděla bych očima,

>   Než to zgewně činiti
>   A na tebe patriti
>   Nesmjm pred domácjma.
>
> 6. *A*le i w ten čas moge
>   Hledj oči na twoge,
>   Když obracené negsau
>   Predce oni twoge gsau
>   Wěr, Milý, obidwoge.
>
> 7. Šuhag kdybych wůli twé
>   *U*tratila sliby swé
>   *L*itug mé nemožnosti,
>   *E*i netrap mogi duši
>   *K*dy tě milugi wěrně.
>
>   *Národnie zpiewanky*, ed. Ján Kollár,
>   Vol. 2 (Budapest, 1835) 208–209.

Judita Kiselyová Ruttkayová (b.? – after 1830?) No pseudonym

Rehor Uram collected these poems (and those of the next three women) and published them in "Zemianski veršovníci slovenskí," *Slovenské pohľady*, 14–15 (1894–1895), though they were written in 1800–1830. Rizner lists these women without further data. The women's manuscripts (now lost) were said to be in the possession of Samuel Medvecký in Zvolen, and Uram's manuscript identifies Ruttkayová as the wife of Daniel Ruttkay in Banská Štiavnica. In a few poems, her authorship is not clearly distinguished from that of the next woman with a similar name, presumably a close relation. The published verses are easily available in major libraries, so here we give only the first lines serving as titles, lines left out of the printed version, and two previously unpublished poems (Nos.5,16). We have followed the order given in Uram's manuscript, which differs from the printed version, and indicated where authorship is unclear. The manuscript is in the Archív literatúry a umenia Pamätníka slovenskej literatúry, Sig. B 392. Unlike the preceding three works, these verses are in Slovak, though the extent of Uram's linguistic changes is unknown.

> 4. Ach, na čo že mám na svete živá byť,
>   Sig. B392; *Slovenské pohľady*, 14,11 (1894): 686.

5. Trávička zelená kade já chodievam,
lebo ju já často slzami polievam.
Ústa mi spievajú, oči sa mi smejú
ale od srdiečka slzy sa mi lejú!
Nie preto já spievam, by veselá bola,
ale preto spievam, by žiale zabola.
Žiale moje žiale už ste mi namále
ako ta rosička na zelenej tráve.
Ešte tú rosičku vetríček oduje
a mňa zarmútenú nik nepoľutuje.
Bože môj, Bože môj, zarmútený svet môj,
každej je veselý, len mně zarmútený.
Škoda našej lásky, že sa nám tak tratí,
kto nás rozlučuje nech mu Pán Bôh platí!
Koho som najradšej na svete videla,
toho šuhajička nechať som musela.
Za kým som najradšej dvere zapierala,
tomu šuhajkovi som sa nedostala.
A za kým som nikdy ani nemyslela,
teraz ma taký vzal, čo som ho nechcela!
  Previously unpublished, Sig. B392.

6. Nechoď k nám šuhajko, neradi ťa majú,
Čo by si ma pýtal, veru ma nedajú.
Sig. B392; *Slovenské pohľady*, 14.11 (1894): 686.

7. Nechoď k nám šuhajko, neradi ťa majú,
ani mi zapierať za tebou nedajú;
Sig. B392; *Slovenské pohľady*, 14.11 (1894): 686–687.

8. Kľajú ma, bijú ma, šuhajko pre teba,
Sig. B392; *Slovenské pohľady*, 14.11 (1894): 686–687.

9. Falošný si, milý, falošné srdce máš,
Sig. B392; *Slovenské pohľady*, 14.11 (1894): 687.

10. Zaplakalo dievča predo dvermi stojac;
Sig. B392; *Slovenské pohľady*, 14.10 (1894): 625.

11. Ach, milá, premilá, keď ti mám povedať:
Sig. B392; *Slovenské pohľady*, 14.11 (1894): 687–688.

12. Veď som ťa ulapil, čo rybku vo vode,
Sig. B392; *Slovenské pohľady* 14.11 (1894): 688.

13. Trávička zelená, ktože teba sožne?
    Slovenské pohľady, 14.11 (1894): 688.
[The fourth and fifth lines were not printed:]
Dajže ma, mamičko kedy ma pýtajú:
keď ružička kvitne, vtedy ju trhajú!
    Sig. B392.

14. Všetko sa mi, všetko včera večer zdalo,
Sig. B392; *Slovenské pohľady*, 14.11 (1894): 688.

15. Hore, dolu idem, na seba nepozrem,
Sig. B392; *Slovenské pohľady*, 14.11 (1894): 688.

16. Mať moja uprimná, povedala si mi,
    že sa ja vyplačem kde ma nik nevidí.
    Pravdu mne mať moja, pravdu povedala,
    žeby šuhajkovi navždy pokoj dala.
    Mala som ťa mala verne za milieho
    ale som poznala, že si nič dobrieho!
    Previously unpublished, Sig. B392.

17. Prechodí sa milá smutná po hájičku,
Sig. B392; *Slovenské pohľady*, 14.11 (1894): 688–689.

18. Chodievali by k nám,
Sig. B392; *Slovenské pohľady*, 14.11 (1894): 689.

19. Každý pes mládenec,
Sig. B392; *Slovenské pohľady*, 14.12 (1894): 753.

Judita Ruttkayová Mayerová (b.? –d. after 1830) No pseudonym
Rehor Uram's manuscript identified Majerová as a resident of Batizovce in eastern Slovakia. Nothing else is known of her, though she may have been a daughter or sister-in-law of the preceding woman. Uram also published poems by "Ezechiel Ruttkay," and study of family archives might be fruitful.

20. Ach, srdiečko moje, čo že ma tak bolíš?
Sig. B392; *Slovenské pohľady*, 14.11 (1894): 687.

21. Nechoď šuhaj ko mně,
Sig. B392; *Slovenské pohľady*, 14.12 (1894): 753.

Katarína Kiselyová (b.? – after 1830)   No pseudonym

Apparently a relative of Judita Kiselyová Ruttkayová, she is otherwise unknown. Obviously both were members of the same gentry family with its seat in Liptov, and family archives might be helpful. Her two poems differ from the others in evoking the long tradition of satire on women.

    22. Stodolôčka deravá a zlá žena k tomu,
    Sig. B392; *Slovenské pohľady*, 14.10 (1894): 627.

    23. Dajte pozor, mládenci, a múdre sa ženie,
    Sig. B392; *Slovenské pohľady*, 15.3 (1895): 192.

Terézia Vitališová (b.? – after 1830)   No pseudonym

Nothing more is known of this woman either, except that she was a member of the Vitališ family with its seat in Vitališovce in Liptov. Poems by "Gregor Vitališ" were also published by Uram. Uram's manuscript shows several variants not given here.

    24. Stalo sa mi stalo, čo sa mi malo stať,
    Sig. B392; *Slovenské pohľady*, 15.3 (1895): 189–190;
    [The printed version divides this poem into two.]

    25. Povedzže mi, povedz, sivá holubička,
    Sig. B392; *Slovenské pohľady*, 15.3 (1895): 190.

    26. Ach, já zarmúcená [dated 1818]
    Sig. B392; *Slovenské pohľady*, 15.3 (1895): 190–191.

    27. Rozhovor dvoch zamilovaných
    Sig. B392; *Slovenské pohľady*, 15.3 (1895): 191–192.
    [The printed title is "Rozhovor dvoch milých."]

    28. Zavzali sa na mňa ľudia
    Sig. B392; *Slovenské pohľady*, 14.10 (1894): 627.

    29. Ty si myslíš, že neviem,
    Sig. B392; *Slovenské pohľady*, 15.3 (1895): 191.

Unknown Authors   "Rosália and Amália"

J. M. Hurban says only that the two young ladies composed the verses jointly and requested anonymity, *Nitra*, 1 (1842): 395. They have not been identified.

    30. Pjsně Slowenek   (Songs by Slovak Women)

od Rosálie a Amálie

Pod Tatrami wětřjk
Čerstwý, zdrawý wěge,
A Slowenská pjseň
Gak angelská zněge.

Slowenštj otcowé!
My wás rády máme,
Keď nás před Maďarem
Bránj waše rámě.

Slowenská řeč čistá
Má široká mjsta,
Co krag swěta půgdem
Slowenskau řeč nagdem!

Slowenštj študenti
Wěrné srdce měgte,
A lásku k národu
Wšude zachowegte!
   Nitra, 1 (1842): 122–123.

31. Bjelý tulipán w prostřed zahradě,
Djewče přemýšlj gak geg dostane.
"Ach Bože, Bože, Bože gediný!
Gak geg dostanu ten kwjtek milý?"
"Ráda ten kwjtek ráda bych měla,
Ráda bych k němu i přeletěla"
Rádo by djewče kwjtek dostalo,
S šuhagcem rádo by se smlauwalo.
"Dwéře wrzagj na té zahradě,
Newidjm tě dnes drahý poklade."
   Nitra, 1 (1842): 123.

Zuzana Reguli Moravčíková (b.? –1861) "Slowenka Rymawská" and [?] "Wlastimila Rymawská"

   Rizner (4: 309) gives only the pseudonym "Wlastimila" for the first two poems, but "Slowenka" was identified as Moravčíková by Ormis in his *Doplnky* 114. We thank Dr. Jozefína Ballová of the Biog. odd. MS for information on this identification, details of which Ormis published in *Obzor Gemera*, 7 (1976): 191–192. Born in Klenovec, Zuzana married Ján Moravčík, a nationalist though a state official. Ormis believes that "Wlastimila" might be Zuzana's sister, Emília Reguli; both are listed as subscribers to *Nitra* in 1842. The third poem below was prepared for the second volume of *Nitra* in 1843 which was not passed by the censor. Found in J. M. Hurban's literary remains, it was published by Rudo Brtáň in 1965, but we have used the original text which is in the Archív literatúry a umenie a Pamätníka slovenskej literatúry in Martin, Sig. 29 K 48.

32. Slowenka (Slovak Woman)
    od Slowenky Rymawské

S Wepru[3] zjra smutně
    Truchliwá Slowenka,
A pri zwučné lutně,
    Bolestně upj, lká:
        Ach wlasti má, wlasti,
        Co se s tebau děge?
        Stogjš nad propastj,
        Nepřjtel se směge!

Žalug srdce moge,
    Gako když wlasti kwět
Wytáhl do boge
    Na ten Turecký swět;
        Neb cos utřjmala
        Od těch Tureckých dob,
        To ti nynj giný
        Chce wložit w chladný hrob!

Kdyby hrdost, wjra,
    W srdcjch našich byla,
Tatra, genž umjrá,
    Zase by ožila:
        Kdyby Wlastu bjlý
        Kůň po wlasti nosil,
        Slowák odrodilý,
        Sám by se nj pýšil!

Než zpěwem panenským
    Wztek se neskrocuge,
Ramenem hrdinským

Wrah se gen zuzďuge;
    My můžem gen hráti,
    Pjsnj stjhat winy,
    Struny probjrati,
    Zwěčnit cnostné činy,
Ne sic tak, gak wěčných
    Zwukŭ Sláwy-dcera,
Genž w zpěwjch nebeských
    Zem i nebe merá;
    Zpjwegme přec nynj,
    Aspoň gako wjme,
    Neb posléze i my
    Wlast swau oželjme!
            Nitra, 1 (1842): 124–125.

33. Potěšenj (Consolation)
    od Wlastimily Rymawské

Děwy milé, děwy šwárné,
    Nechme dél smutnými být,
Nechme ty nářeky marné,
    Poďme wěnce, kytky wjt,
Bljže chrámu Lady čilé,
    Gegžto stjnj swatý hág,
Krášlj nezábudky milé
    Hlučného potúčka krag.

Tam si otcŭ, bratrŭ wěrných,
    Zpomeneme krutý bog,
Genž wytáhli w řadech pewných
    Zlomit zrádných wrahŭ wog;
Tam se srdce sepne wýše
    Kde zřj lásky wěrné kwět,
Na miláčka zpomnj tjše,
    By se wrátil zdrawý zpět.

Ach ty srdce co tě kogj?
    Blahost lásky newinné!
Cjtjm že tě nic nezhogj
    Gestli on tam zahyne;
Chci wšak trpět a nehřešit —

Pǔgdu nezábudky klást
Na hrob geho, a se těšit,
Neb za wlast mřjt gestiť slasť!
Nitra, 1 (1842): 142–143.

34. Hlas Nitranky (The Voice of a Nitra Woman)
    od Wlastimily [Rymavská][4]

Po slowenském kraji
Čistá woda plyne,
We slowenském háji
Zpěv Slowenek hyne.

Ey milé Slowenky!
Hynaut mu nedejme,
Ale jak Wlastenky
Po haji zpívějme.

A wy šumné děwy,
Milené Nitranky.
Neste Nitře zpěwy,
Rúže, tulipanky.

A to srdce čisté
Wlasti nechať bije,
Pro niž mnoho jistě
Statných synů žije.

Ey a tímto citem
Slowákůw milujme,
Ey a tímto srdcem
Zrádce jen litujme.

Šwarní jsau mladenci
Co Sláwu milují,
A tito Wlastenci
Lásku zasluhují.

Naše láska čistá,
Jejich činy prawé,
Povznesau dojista
Nitru k zlaté sláwě.
(Fond J.M. Hurban, Sig. 29 K 48)

Anna Zuzana Šoltýsová (? – ?) "A. Š–vá."

Rizner (5: 235) says she was the wife of the Lutheran pastor in the north central Slovak village of Važec, apparently Michal Šoltés (1802–1862). She was unique in this period for usually signing her full name.

35. Žárliwost (Jealousy) od Anny Zuzanny Šoltýsowé

Tam kde Křiwán a kde Tatry strmj,
A z nich řeka po skalinách hřmj,
Tam i gedna dědinečká ležj,
Okolo nj bystrá řeka běžj.
W nj bydljwal Lidomil srdečný,
Dobrý, milý, upřjmny a wděčný;
Geho srdce lidj milowalo,
Láskau k člowěčenstwu plápolalo;
Poddanj geho šťastliwj byli,
Neb gárma gak ginj necjtili,
On gen radil, rozkazy nedáwal,
Ano radu dobrau od nich bráwal.
Ginj se hned, když gen mohau ženj,
Než on nechtěl slyšet o ženěnj;
Proto "by si děwče k boku swému
Swolil" lidé radjwali gemu.
"Žena žiwot muži oslazuge"
Tak mu každý ženbu přechwaluge,
Gemu wšak to nechtělo se zdáti,
Neb slýchal zase mluwjwati:
Gak ženičky manželů sužugj,
Žiwot nesladj gim, než zhořčugj.
Pokud gsau panny milostně hledj,
A když se wdagj škaredit wědj.
Než posléze zunuwal mluwenj
Lidské, a nabral chuti k ženěnj,
Tichau chtěl mjt, proto tichau hledal,
A osud mu tichau milenku dal.
A když byli manželstwjm spogeni,
Nastal gemu žiwot utěšený.
Zdálo se mu že gen nynj cjtj,
Že teprw teraz počjná žjti;
Než osud byl k němu nelaskawý,

Wsel žárliwost w srdce Boleslawy,
A tá blaho gegich rušit znala,
A to tjm wjc, čjm wjc se zmáhala.
Boleslawka obrazy si twořj,
Že geg' manžel k giným láskau hořj;
Že se před nj on gen přetwařuge,
Zatjm ne gi, než giné miluge.
Posléz newj se už přemáhati,
A dá se mu trpce domlauwati.
Manžel powědomý swé wěrnosti,
Dáwá odpowěd plnau hořkosti.
A to znowa trápj Boleslawu,
Tak že newj ani kde má hlawu.
Chodj sem tam, gakby zpitá byla,
Práci činj gak by nečinila.
Když ge sama pláče, wzdychá, taužj,
Gen se trápj bolestně a saužj.
Manžel se na to žalostně djwá,
A od dlauhých wzdechů se mu zjwá,
Ale předce chce gi potěšiti,
A tak gewj lásky swogj city;
Wěrnost swau k nj mocně doswědčuge,
Sebe gen gj samě poswěcuge.
Ale žárliwost gest had stohlawý,
A ten žere srdce Boleslawy,
Čjm ho wjc porážj manžel cnostný,
Tjm se wjce wzteká neljtostný.
Sláwka wždy gen na muže dorážj,
Hněwem lásku wydobyt se snažj.
Manžel citliwý to nemůž nésti,
Proto klesá pod gármem bolesti.
Twáře geho obledagj rázem,
Gako kwěty opálené mrázem.
Sama Sláwka se mu znechutjwá,
Když gi wždycky gen slza poljwá.
I žiwota se mu odnechtělo,
Posléz zchradlo celé geho tělo.
Sláwka widauc že gest toho wina,
Ruce—ale pozdě—k nebi spjna,
Lituge, že muže newinného

Sama klade do hrobu chladného.
Prosj muže — ale darmo prosj,
Nebo slza už mrtwolu rosj.
Tu procitne žárliwé swědomj,
Sem tam běhá, zaufá, ruce lomj,
A tepe se w hlawu, trhá wlasy,
Wolá zpátkem pominulé časy.
Newrácj se časy, hrob se bljžj,
Nemůž ona snést swědomj tjži;
Žárliwost swau hlaupau neskrotila,
Ta manžele i gi pohřbila.
O by prawda této udalosti
Byla lékem proti žárliwosti!!
      Nitra, 1 (1842): 118–121.

36. Chwála Tater (Praise of the Tatra Mountains)
    od Anny Zuzanny Šoltýsowé

Tatra prý gen sjdlo zimy,
Hnjzdo neaurodné,
Omrzlé, a cestugjcjm,
Obtjžné, neschodné.

Ale práwě to gest dobře
Že také gsau Tatry,
Nech k nám negde, třebas nikdo,
Nech gen přigdau bratři.

Slowan, věrný syn přjrody,
Na Tatrách okřege,
Neb se mu w austřety krásná
Přjroda usměge.

Tu geg plesa, tu wýšiny
Zowau ku plesánj,
Tu prameny, wodopády
Péče pryč zahánj.

Naše Tatry nebesáhlé
Wůnj kořjnkowau
Plnj powětřj, a kogj
Duši pautnjkowu.

A we Tater lůně temném
Gasné zlato blýská,
Při něm si i náš odpůrce
Negedenkrát wýská.

Tatry naše, Tatry wěčné
Magj zpěwů tisjc,
A Slowenka, swau Slowenskau
Pjseň nedá za nic.

I my sme tu byli w lůnu
Tater nebetýčných,
A na těchto nezábudek
Nabrali si sličných.
Nitra, 1 (1842): 126–127.

37. Zradná straka (Traitorous Raven)

1. Na ploťe straka rapotala;
Ej! čože matki žalovala?
  Žalovala, žalovala:
Že som na Janka pozerala,
  Pozerala.

2. Na ploťe straka rapotala;
Ej! čože matki žalovala?
  Žalovala, žalovala:
Že som sa s Jankom shovárala,
  Shovárala.

3. Na ploťe straka rapotala;
Ej! čože matki žalovala?
  Žalovala, žalovala:
Že som miljemu pero dala,
  Pero dala.

4. Na ploťe straka rapotala;
Ej! čože matki žalovala?
  Žalovala, žalovala;
Že som miljemu pišťok dala,
  Pišťok dala.
  A. Š—va.
Domová pokladnica, 3 (1849): 269.

38. Ňespravedlivá hana (Unjust Pursuit)

1.Šuhaju, šuhaju!
Luďja ťa haňajú;
  Ale ňemáš hani,
Akú ťi dávajú.

2.Zaspjevaj slávičku,
 V zelenom hájičku;
  Já len tvoja budem
Muoj drahí Jaňíčku!

3.Daj mi Bože ten dar,
Za ktorí ťa prosím:
  Len toho šuhajka,
Čo ho v srdci nosím!
        A. Š—vá.
Domová pokladnica, 3 (1849): 269.

Johana Lehocká (1810–1849)   "Miloslawa" and "Želmíra"
Daughter of a small town official named Matej Vyšný and of Eva Kusá, in 1830 she married Ján Lehocký, a Štúrist and nationalist Lutheran minister in Liptovský Trnovec (*Ency. slov. spis.*, 1: 381–382; *Slov. biog. slov.*, 3: 374, 379). See Chapter 2 and notes for selections from her letters and her contemporaries' praise. Of her three poems not passed by the censor in 1843, Hurban published a Slovak version of "Hrob" in 1844, so we have given his version as well as Lehocká's original Czech text (Nos.41a–41b). The other two poems were radically changed in Brtáň's version in 1965, so we have given only the original texts which are in the Pamätník slovenskej literatúry, Sig. 29 K 48. The last poem was published by Hurban after Lehocká's death, and the pseudonym "Želmíra" was decifered by Ormis in his "Novozistené pseudonymy z polstoročia 1842–1893," *Bibliografický sborník*, (Martin, 1962): 206. Presumably Lehocká began writing poetry in Slovak instead of Czech at the same time she began writing letters in Slovak (May 1844—see Chapter 2).

Básně (Poems) od Miloslawy

39. Podkřiwánský wlastenec (A Patriot near Mt. Kriváň)

Pod Křiwáněm u studánky
Zarmaucený ginoch seděl,
Temným okem zaslzený
Wzhůru k černým mrakům hleděl.

Mrtwé ticho panowalo,
Gen w dálce se hrom ozýwal;
Geho srdce zkrwácené
Neljtostně bol rozrýwal.

Wedlé něho w tráwě bugné
Ležj lýra nastruněná,
Wzdechy wjtr z nj wywádj,
Skalnj wrácj ge ozwěna.

Mladjk lýry se uchopj:
Ach Bože můg wšemohaucj,
Wraucně zapěl, "wyslyš nynj
Srdce mé želem hynaucj!"

"Pakli zhynu w oné bauři,
Gen to mi deg ugištěnj,
Že můg zhanobený národ
Dogde geště oslawenj!

A w tom náhle, gako diwem,
Tmawé mračno se rozprášj,
A s Křiwáně giž gasného
Djwenka se lehce wznášj.

Ke smutnému ginochowi
Letné kroky namjřila,
W rukau gegj skwěl se wěnec,
Aby ho gjm owěnčila.

Cosi sladce mu šeptala;—
W tom se ohledne mládenec,—
Mžikem zmizne děwa krásná,
Na čele mu nechá wěnec.
   Nitra, 1 (1842): 128–130.

40. Slowenka (Slovak Woman)
Gak bych gá neměla být Slowenkau?
 Wšak sem se pod ljpau zrodila,

Slowenská mne máti kogila,
Naučila prawau být wlastenkau.

Teď obýwám ono mjsto krásné,
    Kde Wáh swými hučj wlnami,
    Pjseň Slawská zněge Tatrami,
Křiwáň ljbá slunce zlatogasné.

Sama přjroda mně k tomu wáže,
    Řeč swau nade wšecko milowat,
Ač i zákon lidský gináč káže.

Dřjwe si dám srdce wyrwat z těla,
    Nežbych se od tebe wzdalowat,
Neb tě zradit, národe můg, měla!!
        Nitra, 1 (1842): 130.

41a. Hrob (Grave)

Půlnočnj giž wětry dugj,
Tatra sněhem gest pokryta;
Přjrodu w sen ponorugj
Gegjch usta mrazowitá.
        Wše giž pusto — lúky, pole.
        I mau duši nowé bole
        Rozrýwagj w geseni.

Kwětiny, čo gemně kryly
Hrobku matky mé milené
Mrauce hlawky naklonily,
Dechem severu zmařené;
        Ani hognau byť oživené
        Slzau dcery trúchljcj.

Drahá! Ty spjš sladce w hrobě
Prosta wšech bolů i strastj.
Nežádáš-li mjť pri sobě
Dceru swau w nebeské wlasti?
        Kdo zná? — snad giž w garnj době
        Sázeť budau na mém hrobě
        Ljpu Sláwowé wďečnj?
Fond J.M. Hurban, Sig. 29 K 48.

41b. Hrob od Miloslavi

Pounočnje uš vetri dujú, —
Tatri sňehom sú pokritje, —
Prírodu v seň zamorujú
Fujáki ich mrazovitje. —
  Šetko spustlo — polja, lúki, —
  Moju dušu novje muki
      Rozrívajú v jaseňi.

Kvjetki, čo krásňe šaťili
Hrob matički milenej
Bolňe hlávki nakloňili
Dechom Tatri stuďenej;
  Aňi hojnou porosenje
  Nemuožu biť oživenje
      Slzou céri smuťjacej.

Drahá! ti uš odpočívaš
Zbavená šetkej trpkosťi —
Či po cére ňetúžjevaš
Tam blaženej vo večnosťi?
  Kto zná? — či mi v jarňej dobe
  Ňebudú saďiť na hrobe
      Lipu Slávovja vďační. —
            Nitra, 2 (1844): 158.

42. Sen (Dream)

Snilo se mi, snilo, sestry moge drahé!
A zde wám odkrýwám moge sněnj blahé:
Procházela sem se po kwetnaté lúce
Zamyšlená držjc Slávy dceru v ruce.
Náhle sem se octla w přerozkošném hági.
Bylo gitro krásné a den prwnj w mági.
Do stjnného háge sem gá zablúdila;
Wšade rostly růže kudy sem chodila.
Střjbrné potúčky gemně šepotaly
Pestré kwjtky ragskou wůni wydáwaly:
Stromy pyšnorostlé rastolestmi chwěly,
W krowjch a w oblacjch ptáci pjsně [ptácj] pěli.[5]
I začne sa we mně cosi ozjwati:

"Jak by milo w ragi tom bylo býwati!"
W tom se opru o strom. Náhle zrak můg zočj
Jak se čtyři panny kolo ljpy točj.
Bjle přioděna byla gegich těla,
A wěnec ljpowy krášlil gegich čela.
Rozuměla sem gjm slyšjc gegich hlásky,
We čtjrech nářečjch pěly soběslawský.
Tá ljpa košatá byla čtyrokmenná,
U wrchu vzágemně w gedno zapletená;
Na neyvyššjm wlála wrcholci zástava
S nápisem: "Za krále a Slovanů práva."
Nedaleko odtud stál oltář kamenný,
Slawskými ginochy wůkol otočený.
Co za slavnosť měli tagno mě zůstalo,
Ale srdce gegich radostj plesalo.
Náhle slyšjm hlasy na mne wolagjcj:
"Proč ty také negdeš w kolo plesagjcj?"
W tom sem procitnula z tichého usnutj.
O byl to sen blahý, ne k zapomenutj!!
Fond J. M. Hurban, Sig. 29 K 48.

43. Ljpa (Linden Tree)

Na pahorku ljpa stogj,
    Stara, stoletá;
Můg duch, můg duch w nj se kochá
    Ku nj zalétá.

Neb z gara mne těšjvala
    Dítě nevinné,
Půvabu vždy dodavala
    Me hre dětinné.

Když se v létě v plném kwětu
    Nynj usmjwa,
Letu mysli me dodáwá;
    Duch nj okřjwá.

Neb ona je strom Slowanský,
    Strom [swatý] otců swatý,[6]
Kwět gegj mě upomjná
    Na wěk gich zlatý.

V geseni když oprcháwá
　　Postesknu sobě,
Neb mi nechtě na um přigde,
　　Že sme w porobě.

A když gegjm ljstjm swadlým
　　Wicher zmjtáwá,
Tak se mi zdá, že to s námi
　　Zlý swět pohráwá.

Ale gá se nic nelekám,
　　Žel zpěvem kogjm,
A pod ljpau takto zpjwam
　　Ku sestrám svogjm:

Buďmež wěrné rodu swému,
　　Rodu slawnému
I když strašné bauřkau hrozj
　　Černawy gemu.

Tak nás ljpa šumem wonným
　　Bude owjwať,
A na nás se i w geseni
　　Milo usmjwat.
Fond J.M. Hurban, Sig. 29 K 48.

44. Peseň labutia (Swan Song)
　　od Želmíry

Veje vetrík, veje
　　Po tráve zelenej:
Nevyveje smútok
　　Z duše zarmútenej.

Na zelenú trávu
　　Napadla rosička;
Vari ju kropily
　　Moje sivé očká.

Slniečko zasvieti,
　　Rosičku osuší,
Ale kdo navráti
　　Pokoj mojej duši?

Žiale moje žiale
    Kedy ma necháte?
Var mi ani v hrobe
    Pokoja nedáte?

Zasvietil mesiačik
    Na moju tvár smutnú,
Ale mi nezotrel
    Z oka slzu mutnú.

Nechaj mi mesiačik
    Slzy v očach mojich,
Veď ten za kým tečú
    Nezvie nikdy o nich!
    Slovenské pohľady, 3.22 (1852): [1].

Unknown Author   "Ľudmila K"

Like Nos.34,41a,42,43, this poem was prepared for the unpublished *Nitra* of 1843, and it was not printed until 1965. Brtáň suggests without evidence that the author might be Ľudmila Koléni ("Torzo Nitry 1843": 512), possibly the daughter of Daniel Koléni (see Riz. 2: 393; *Slov. biog. slov., 3, 140,* and Orm. 77). We have used the text from Hurban's manuscripts.

45. Žalost a potěcha Nitranky (Despair and Comfort of a Nitra Woman) od Ľudmily K.

Ó wy sestry, sestry milé,
Dcery Slowenska zpanilé,
Slyšte moje stěžowání,
Wizte i mé radowání.

Jak se to jen nyní žije,
Cítí, mluwí a pracuje?
Zmatek jen a přewrácení
Panuje w tom žiwoření.

Mnohý, jenž se synem Wlasti
Zowe, zawrhuje cnosti,
A při tom zlosti nemilé
Šije, kuje potmešile.

Než oko mé i těch widí,
Kteří za swou Wlast se stydí,

A co jen slowenským sluje —
To on všecko potupuje.

Než my takých nemilujme —
W národnosti stále stůjme;
Nejsau oni lásky hodni,
Odrodilci nehanební.

Než zní i hlas národnosti
Sláwa Bohu na wysosti!
Mnohý žije pro samu cnost,
Aby oslawil národnost.

Národnost swau zastáwají,
Ač i v nenáwist padají,
Mnozí, a ti nech ať žijí,
Těm nech naše srdce bijí!

Kdo tak národ, Wlast miluje,
Kdo pro ně wše obětuje,
Ten zasluhuje korunu,
Od wšech Slowenek pletenou.
Fond J.M. Hurban, Sig. 29 K 48.

Unknown Author   "Slovenka Sitňjanska"
Rizner (5: 110) lists her with no further data, but she must have lived near Mount Sitno, perhaps in Banská Štiavnica. It is one of the earliest poems by a woman in Štúr's Slovak.

46. Pjeseň (Song) od Slovenki Sitňjanskej

    Dolinuočka moja!
        Tak ťa huorki krijú,
   Ako keď ňevestu
        Do venca zavijú.

    Oj huorka zelená!
        Samá jedlovinka,
   Taká mi vizeráš
        Ako z rozmarínka.

    Potuoček bistručkí,
        Len samá čistota.
   Veselo ces našu

Dolinku hrkotá.
* * *

Dobre nám je, dobre
 V dolinuočkach bivať,
Čistá tu voďička,
 Radosť ju je píjať.

Milo v tích dolinkách,
 Milo sa i spjeva,
Keď ťichí vetríček
 Od Tatjer povjeva.

Tatránske sestrički
 Čože ňespjevaťe?
Veť vo mňe spevavú
 Ťjež družičku máťe!
* * *

Keď si ja zaspjevam
 Hňeď mi je veselo,
Čobi ma hňeď ako
 Srďječko bolelo.

Hoj, drahje sestrički,
 Nuž si len spjevajme!
Že sme mi Slovenki
 Svetu poznať dajme.

Spjevajme, spjevajme
 Tej našej roďiňe,
A to v uťešenej
 Našej Slovenčiňe!

Slovenskí spjevajme,
 Po Slovenskí lúbme,
Slovenskím junákom
 Vernú lásku slúbme!!!
Orol tatránski, 2.50 (1846): 393–394.

Unknown Author "Sofia z Oravi" and "Žofia"

Rizner (6: 263) lists all three poems under "Žofia z Oravy" with no further data. Possibly she was Sophia Medvecká, a gentlewoman who had collected folk songs for Ján Kollár's *Zpievanky*.

47. Smútok (Sorrow) od Sofie z Oravi

Slňječko zachodí, rosa poprcháva,
Očká celkom vischlje, hlávka je bolavá,
Smutno to slňječko pod večer zachoďí,
Ale v božej sláve za rána sa roďí;
Ja veselo líham, dosť spokojno spávam,
Predca som zmorená keď z posťjelki vstávam.
Zakvita lalija ňiže nášho domu,
Čo mi je z lalije ňemám ju dať komu.
Ružička červená milá vuoňa tvoja,
Čože mi z ružički keď ňemám pokoja.
Odtrhňem rozmajrín, vložím ho do žbánka,
Čo mi z rozmajrína keď tu ňemám Janka.
Odišjeu za hori, kďe vodička ťichá,
Ťažko túžim za ňím, smutno srdce vzdicha.
Už i tje ptáčatka len málo spjevajú,
Ešťe ňebožjatka v smútku vizdichajú.
Príjď že skoro zpátkom dušička zlatuška,
Veru ťi reč dobrú pošepňem do uška.
   Orol tatránski, 2.37 (1846): 289.

48. Básňe od Žofie (Poems by Žofia)

 Slávnosť jara (Spring Celebration)

   Už sa lipa pučí
   V zelenom hájičku,
   Spev slovenskí hučí
   Na poli v lesíčku;
   Príroda sa buďí,
   Ptáctvo žije, plesá,
   Stvorca zvelebuje.

   Nože sestri milje
   Zasveťme že i mi
   Slávnosť kveťeninu
   Slovenskími zpevmi,
   Ňechme žjalou márních,
   Poďme blížej k lesu
   Radosťi a plesu.

   Tam potuoček hraví

Lučinou sa trasje
Kvjetočki objíma
A ďalej sa ňesje,
Z tích voňavích kvjetkou
Ti mi natrháme
A z ňích sebe vjenkou
Pekních naspletáme.

Prví veňjec ťebe
Vesno naša milá,
Bi si z krási svojej
I nám uďelila.
Vencom z bjelich lalij
Zdobíme ťi čelo,
Bi svoj čo v zrkadle
Obraz v ňom viďelo.

Druhi veňjec k pocťe
Tím naším rodákom
Z pomjenok a ruží
Tím hodním Slovákom.
Bo stromi bobkovje
Pod Tatrou ňerastú
Ňemuožme vás venčiť
Leč kveťinkou sprostou.

Treťí veňjec ťebe,
Matko naša drahá,
Bi si cérki svoje
V lono svoje vzala,
Veňjec z ňezvadljeho
Zvijeme ťi kvjeťa,
Bi sa tvoje jemu
Podobalo žiťja.
  Nitra, 3 (1846): 142–144.

49. Slovenkám (To Slovak Women)

Slovenki, Slovenki
Čo tak tvrdo spíťe,
Kedi že sa zo sna
Svojho prebuďíťe?

Veť nad našou Tatrou
Už počiná svitať,
A vi ňeideťe
Ďeň so spevom vítať?

Čo vás sestri moje
Smutnjeho potkalo?
Či vám mať umrela?
Či čo sa vám stalo?

Pustje sa bez spevu
Tatránske dolini,
Ako bi vimreli
Slovenskje ďjevčini.

Ach veť nám umrela
Tá naša mamička,
Už ju vjac ňezbuďí
Tá naša pjesňička.

Ňebojme sa sestri,
Mať nám neumrela,
Mať nám neumrela,
Len tuho omdlela.

Prečo že omdlela? —
Od velkjeho žjalu,
Že ju opusťila
Jej roďina celá.

Leťme že už leťme
Matke do náručja,
Ňech nás aňi streli
Od ňej ňeodlúča.
  Nitra, 3 (1846): 144–145.

Karolína Puliny (b.? –1888)   "K.P., K. Pulíny"

Rizner (4: 183–184) lists her, but biographical information comes primarily from notes to her poems. In *Sokol*, 2 (1861): 169, her father was given as Nathanael Pulíny, a Lutheran preacher in Budikovany, whose father Samuel "Paulini" was later identified as a Lutheran preacher in Bohemia (Miš. 7,231). Otherwise, her relation to the literary Pauliny family is unknown. As a sickly child she lost both parents at once, then lost her guardian NN Spišiak, a Lutheran senior in Gemer, and from the shock "became dumb" for twelve years. Cured by a homeopath, she again became dumb at his death and lived with her sister Amália, wife of the Lutheran pastor Štefan Homola, according to a note sent with her poems to *Sokol* by "H.Tisovský," i.e. Gustáv Hostivít Lojko, husband of the writer Zuzína Lojková (see Nos.83–94). She died in Vyšný Balog in Gemer (*Národnie noviny*, 7 February 1888). Mikušťáková (97) found the first hymn below, which is not listed by Rizner.

50. Přjkré žiwota časného sau cesti (Harsh are the paths of mortal life)

>Přjkré žiwota časného sau cesti,
>Po níchž moc Božj ráčj nás zde wésti,
>Plač kwjleni, Wssudy gen znj,
>Kam se obrátjm čeká mě nesstěstj.
>
>Rodj se na swět k bjdě a k trápenj,
>Gak neybjdněgssj, tak slawnj, wznessenj,
>Koho Bůh chce, Časem tresce,
>Milosrdenstwj nad tisjce činj.
>
>Těžce ge cestau trnowatu gjti,
>W údolj plače pokoge nagjti,
>Než zřjdil wsse, Bůh w radě swé,
>Ruže bez trnj nemohau kwětnauti.
>
>Leká se srdce w strachu a w bolesti,
>Hrůzy když walj se s trpkau nerestj,
>Wssak úfá duch, Že mocnj Bůh
>Může ochránit i w mořské propasti.
>
>Aposstole wždy gen w Pána daufali,
>U wjře stále boge přemáhali,
>I w skutcjch swých, Diwů plnjch,
>Duchem swatým sauc posilnění byli.
>
>Popřeg ó Bože! údatnost w sauženj,
>Wssem, kteřj k tobě obrácegj zřenj,
>By po bogi, Sme w pokogi,
>Mohli řjc také slowj Pawlowými:
>
>"Bog sem bogowal do mého skonánj,

Wjru sem zachowal, dobré swědomj
Zatjm dána, Mi od Pána
Bude koruna w geho zasljbenj."
                    K. P.
Ewangelické cjrkewnj nowiny, 2.13 (1861): 104.

51. Gežjssi Milý Pane (Jesus, Dear Lord)

Gežjssi milý Pane,
    W tobě skládám naděgi swau,
W twé wssemohaucj schraně,
    Pomoc gen nagjti mohu,
W sauženj unawenj,
    Skljčeni bogem nemocj,
    Pod tjži omdléwagjcj,
Ty dáš gim občerstwenj.

Přemilý Spasiteli,
    W tobět se kogj mé srdce,
W zármutku těssiteli,
    Genž hogjš raněnjm těžce,
Rány těžkých bolestj,
    Wzhlédniž i na mne když me křjž,
    Tlačj mnohých neřestj tjž,
Buď při mne s twau milostj.

Wjm, že žádné stálosti,
    W swětě nič nemůže mjti,
Buď radost neb žalosti,
    Moc twá wsse ráčj změniti,
I neytěžssj trápenj,
    Byť gakkoli dlauhé bylo,
    W němž mnohé srdce kwjlilo,
Dogde gednau skončenj.

Ač plynau dnowé mogi,
    Gen w tjži plné žalosti,
Milost twá Pane, kogj,
    Dussi skljčenau w úzkosti,
Wždyť wěřjm tomu práwě,
    Ze nyněgssj utrpenj,
    Genž znássjme, rowné nenj

Oné budaucé sláwě.
K. P.
Ewangelické cjrkevnj nowiny, 2 (1861): 112.

52. Smutný los národa (The Sad Fate of the Nation)

Bystro si potokom vlnka skáče,
Veselo si spieva krásno vtáčä;
Len švárna dievčina
Má drahá rodina
Horko plače — horko plače.

Čo sa ti, dievčatko, ach čo stalo,
Že si tak žalostne zaplakalo?
Povedz mi len predca,
Čo do tvojho srdca
Žiale sialo — žiale sialo?

"Drahú matku mi chcú usmrtiti,
Všetkého dedictva pozbaviti,
A milú rodinu
V osudnú hodinu
Usmrtiti — usmrtiti.

Po dedictve najskôr mi čahali,
Že matka usnula, sa kochali,
Deti ešte mladé,
Sirôtky[7] v zahrade,
Omámili — omámili:

"Či je to váš zámok na tej stráni?
Dajteže nám kľúč od jeho brány,
Poberte i vaše
Ozdoby najkrajšie
Poďte s nami — poďte s nami!"

V tom sa milá matka prebudila,
Deti i majetok si bránila;
Ale čata celá
Zlého nepriateľa
Matku mučí — matku mučí.

Dospelí synovia hlas slyšali,
Hneď z cudziny domov pospiechali,

Už bojujú dávno,
A bojujú slávno,
Či zvítazia — či zvítazia?"
         K. P.
Sokol (ed. P. Dobšinský), 2.22 (1861): 169.

53. Milá bola i mne... (Dear to Me Too...)

Milá bola i mne reč maďarská,
Kým nám netrpela reč slovanská,
Kým pre ňu nátisky, ukrutnosti
A divé neprišly surovosti;

Ale ak sa začala zvyšovať,
Všetky národnosti potlačovať,
Nepriateľsky naproti ním zúriť:
Musela sa nevinná krev zbúriť.

Ozývalo sa tisíce hlasov:
Nechcem nič mať s tou slovenskou chasou,
Slovanská reč je len pre delníkov,
Nie pre pánov, len pre služebníkov.

Z rodu slovanského narodzený,
V okolí slovanskom vyrastený
Odrodilec predca pyšno svedčí,
že, vraj, nerozumie slavskej reči.

Zablúdilý ten syn len to hlása:
Nach zahynie tá slovanská chasa,
Netreba jej práva slobody dať,
Maďarčinu treba zvelebovať.

Čože srdce pocíti Slováka
Pri rečnení takého mudráka?
Nad tým bludom horko zažalostí,
A reč svoju miluje z vrúcnosti.
         K. P.
Sokol (ed. P. Dobšinský), 2.22 (1861): 169–170.

54. Žalostne sa dívam... (Despairingly I Watch...)

Žalostne sa dívam do sveta šíreho
Na utiskovania národa milého.

Kdekolvek sa ozve milý hlas slovanský,
Všade ho sužuje nepriateľ tyranský;
Zlobivý závistník rozsieva rozbroje,
Milý pokoj mení v neprestajné boje.
Falešný zradca nás chce vpútať v okovy,
Lež verný syn kráča v boj proti vrahovi,
Nedesí ho búrka, kráča si zmužile, —
Premení i búrku čas v jasnejšie chvíle,
Vyjasní sa nebe, vyjde slnko jasné,
Rozvijú sa stromy aj kvetiny krásne.
Máš pomoc u Boha, Slávia premilá!
Zkvitneš časom i ty jak ruža spanilá.
Nechlúbi sa syn tvoj mrtvými pokladý,
Hrdinsky dobýva duchovné základy.
Sriebra, zlata v obeť na tvoju ozdobu,
Národ náš, nekaždý dá ti pre chudobu;
Ale prosba vrúca z srdca úprimného
Vyslyšaná býva u všemohúceho.
Za to i ja pred ním na kolená padám
A večer i ráno toto jedno žiadam:
Zdržuj ťa Bôh mocný, národe môj drahý,
A zdarom korunuj tvoje krásne snahy.
              K. P.
Sokol (ed. P. Dobšinský), 2.22 (1861): 170.

55. K Slovenkám (To Slovak Women)

Hej Slovenky! tu je už čas krásneho svitania,
Všetko, čo žije, budí sa už z dlhého spania.
Východ slnka predchádzajú papršleky skvelé,
Hore sa, k novému žitiu, Slovenky spanilé.
Reči našej ľúbezný zvuk najmilšie nám zneje,
Šírim Slovenskom keď živo duch slovenský veje;
Kriesi zo spania k životu, z tmy k svetlu jasnému,
Nech zneje vždy medzi nami k rozkvetu krásnemu.
Milujme národ náš milý z uprimného srdca,
Sbierajme spanilé kvietky do krásneho venca;
Našej drahej MATIČKE ho k úcte položíme,
V prostred šírej Slávie ju osláviame.
Marný slávoblesk cudzoty oko nech nemámi,
Verné srdce nepokalia bludné sveta klamy;

Držme sa milej svojeti; pracovať, žiť i mrieť
Za ňu a jej zvelebenie — nad to väčšej cti niet.
1865.   Karolína Pulíny
           Sokol, 6.1 (1867): 338.

           56. Pravda (Truth)

Trvám od počiatku sveta, idem cez všetky veky,
Nekonečné moje letá, budem trvať na veky.
Bývam ja po celom svete, prejdem všetky krajiny,
A predsa ma nepoznajú po dnes mnohé rodiny.
Putujem ja neustále, navštevujem každého,
Kto ma rád privíta, vlúdne prijme do domu svého.
Milujem nad všetko pokoj, učím ľudí k svornosti,
A za to ma mnohí majú vo veľkej nenávisti.
Mám vždy mnohých nepriateľov, kďe koľvek sa obrátim,
Za to ja ale česť nikdy ani smelosť netratím.
Bars mi mnohí aj hrob kopú, radi by ma pochovať,
Ale ma predsa nemôžu docela zamordovať.
Keď ma jeden vek pochová, v druhom zase ožívam,
Jednym k radosti a druhým ku strachu sa ozývam.
Nikomu nič zlé nerobim a tak sa ma ľakajú,
Že predo mnou ľudia dvere i okná zamykajú.
Neraz sa už mnohé hlasy v predesení ozvaly,
Žeby sa ver radšie s čertom nežli so mnou vítaly.
Mám prístup nie len k chalupám, lež i k trónom
           kráľovským.
A prenikám i oblohu až k vyšinám nebeským.
Dlho hľadím na tú krivdu, čo sa tu v svete deje,
No konečne i môj ortiel hromozvukom zavzneje.
           Karolína Pulíny
           Sokol, 7.1 (1868): 18.

57. "Čas vše mení" ("Time Changes All")

Odhodlanosť verného Slovana,
    Žiaden čas a hrúza nezmení;
Vernosť k rodu pravdivej Slovenky,
    Žiaden čas a búrka nezmení;
Ráz a rýdzosť rodu slovenského,
    Žiaden hatišerif nezmení.

K. Pulíny
Sokol, 7.6 (1868): 150.

Amália Launerová Huľuková (?1845/46–1891) No pseudonyms
   Rizner (3: 22) lists her verses with no further data. She was identified as a fifteen/sixteen year old orphan in Krupina when she began sending riddles and verse to V. Pauliny-Tóth for *Sokol* (Liba, *Listy Hodžovej* 103–104). She became a member of the Matica, and married a Lutheran teacher, Ján Huľuk. She died in Čaba (*Národnie noviny*, 11 November 1891).

   58. Potecha (Consolation)

Pilo vtáča, pilo vodu pilo na kolaji,
A Anička nariekala za milým po háji.
Pokerúc to vtáča pekné pyšťok zamočilo,
Toľko raz si dievča švárné líčká zarosilo.
Nepi vtáča na kolaji vodu zakalenú,
Nech aj očká Aničkyné nariekať prestanú.
A vtáčatko vyletelo, k hajíčku sa hnalo:
A dievčatko sivooké nariekať prestalo.

Žalo dievča, žalo trávu, žalo ďatelinku
Keď nažalo, obzeralo širokú dolinku.
Na doline na širokej šuhaj seno vozí
A milá sa Janíčkovi z ďaleka pohrozí:
Šuhaj, šuhaj na doline, čo si ma opustil,
Ej čože to bol za kňaza, čo ťa J a n k o m krstil?
Nedbám, nedbám môj premilý, bárs ma aj zabudeš;
K druhým pôjdeš na vohľady a môj predca budeš.
Nedbám, nedbám môj premilý, bárs si ma i zabou;
K druhým pôjdeš na zálety a k oltáru so mnou.
   Amália Launer
Černokňažník Letopis na rok 1862 (1861): 79.

   59. Sokol (Falcon)

Ponad Tatrou svitá, slnce jasno svieti;
Na slovenské nivy letí Sokol sivý
      Pozrieť slavské deti.

Hučí pieseň, hučí dolu dolinámi,
Hučia vrchy, hole: "vítaj nám Sokole!

Víťaz medzi nami."

Tá Krupinská brána pekná, malovaná;
K nej že sa rodina, tu šťastná hodina,
Vítaj úsvit rána.
        Amália Launer
        Sokol 6 (1862): 196.

Ant. Emilia Rumanová Bachátová (1841–1884) "Milina Ruman" and possibly "Milina"

Rizner (4: 293) lists her as the daughter of a Lutheran teacher. In 1862 Marína Hodžová praised her acting in community theater (*Listy Hodžovej* 67,73), and as the wife of superintendent Daniel Bachát in Budapest she had a prominent position among Slovaks. Rizner (3: 213) lists separately the poems by "Milina," but we have tentatively attributed them to her. If she did in fact write the last poem here, she returned to poetry in 1879 after a long pause.

60. Komparácie z grammatiky Černokňažníkovej (The Comparative in *Černokňažník* Grammar)

Pekne je, keď dievča čistotne sa šatí,
Krajšie keď i srdca krása ju bohatí;
Najkrajšie keď pekná, rozumná devenka
S hrdosťou všiad vyzná, že je ver — Slovenka.

Milé je dievča, keď vrelo sa zaľúbi,
Milšie keď rúčku junovi prisľúbi;
Najmilšia však býva v svete ľúbosť taká,
Keď dievča zaľúbi šuhaja — Slováka.

Dobre je, keď dievča viac rečí hovorí,
Lepšie keď slovenskú nimi nezpotvorí;
Najlepšie však, ktorá nimi sa nechľúbi,
Druhé rada vraví, svoju ale — ľúbi.
        Milina Ruman.
        Černokňažník, 1.22 (1861): [3]

61. Slovenkám (To Slovak Women)

Pekné vence vy viť znáte
Z kvetov krásnych, rozmanitých;
Lež jeden veniec neznáte

Krajší všech, vámi uvitých.
Nezáleži z jaroplodných
Rúž a nezabúdok krásy,
Ale z národovcov hodných—
Jenž nevädne v žiadne časy.
Posnážte sa ľubé devy!
Sestry priznajte sa k rodu,
Nech zvestujú naše spevy
Národa zlatú slobodu.
V pleť e sa do venca samy,
Vstúpte do Sloveniek kola—
A krajšia bude budúcnosť
Ako tá minulosť bola.
           Milina Ruman.
Černokňažník Letopis na r.1862 (1861): 80.

62. Lietali sokoli (The Falcons Were Flying)

Lietali sokoli
Nad našim Kriváňom,
V tej slnečnej žiare
Jasno-pekným ránom.

Tú slnečnú žiaru,
V ktorej sa kúpali,
Celému Slovensku
Slávne zvestovali.
       Sokol, 1.5 (1862): 84.

63. V zime (In the Winter)

Biely sniežik poletuje,
Clivo, smutno v okolí;
Keď pozriem do tej pustoty
Až ma srdce zabolí.
Lež čím smutnejšie tam vonku,
Čím viac tam von chumelí,
Tým krajšie mi na kozúbku
Horí ohník veselý.
Na kozúbku ohník horí,
Ach, tak milo svieti sa;
A pri ňom moje vretienko

Ach, tak rezko vrtí sa. —
Pradiem, pradiem länik biely,
Pradiem ho tak veselo,
Keď ho zpradiem, keď ho potkám
A vymočím na bielo:
Potom budem strihať a šiť
Na košieľku milému,
Na košieľku, na svadebnú
Ženichovi svojemu.
Milina
Sokol, 1.5 (1862): 165.

64. Kvety moje (My Flowers)

Kvety moje, pekné kvety!
Rada si vás pestujem,
Veď si vo vás pekné kvety
Osud ľudský malujem.
Mnoho slastí v srdci kvitne,
A mnoho jich uvädá;
Sťa na ruži jeden lístok
Pučí — druhý opádá.
Milina
Černokňažník, 2.12 (1862): 92.

65. Šuhajovi (To a Young Man)

  Detvianska výša jak to velebné
    Zo zelenej tvojej hole
  Hľadeť za rána na neprehledné
    To naše slovenské pole —
Tam som raz z rána sama zastala
A divné zjavy z razu zbadala,
    Vznášať sa v mlhových chmúrach —
Postavy junov, čo umom pästʼou,
Krvavým potom, mukou, nerestʼou
    Za rod náš válčili v búrach,

  Jedon balvány skál stocentových
    Pratal preč mocným ramenon;
  Iný diamanty zo skál žulových
    Dobýjal v znoji plamennom;

Zas iný skaly Kriváňa mrvil
A jich na piesok drobunký drvil
    Na chodník pekne zhladený;
Iný zas čistil potôčky vedy
Aby raz zmizly slovenské biedy
    V jich kryštálovom prameni.

Hoj to sú chlapci, perál belejší
    Tíško šepnem sama sebe,
Jích zápal ohňov sopky vrelejší
    Ztrhne na zem celé nebe;
Ti sa neboja, útrapnej práce
Tí z našich chatrč ztvoria paláce,
    Z pustiny rajské zahrady,
Tí sa Šťastene v službu nedali,
Ale jej z ruky opraty vzali —
    Vydobyli si jej hrady.

Medzitým, čo sa duša tak teší,
    Prejdem rukou volné vlásky —
Čo vidím — hore sihlinou spieši
    Šuhaj ku mne s citom lásky —
Ja mu pokážem na tie postavy
A pýtam sa ho, nech mi vyjaví,
    Či chce vstúpiť v jejích rady,
Či aj on vstave zaprením seba
Mohutnou rukou plamene neba
    Schvátiť pre svoj národ mladý?

Lež čo zkúsila som, drahí moji,
    Bola to smiešna robota,
Do neba nesmie, ohňa sa bojí
    V duši i srdci holota!
I drsná púť ho života straší
Hladu sa bojí, práca ho plaší
    Do boja: rameno slabé:
Tú ja nevole hnevným pohnutím
A prísnym bielej ruky kynutím
    Odpravím to chlapä chabé:

Nie si ty — rečiem, k búram života
    Slovenského odchovaný,

> Teba vetrík, jak zástavku hrota
> > Krúti v štyry sveta strany.
> Keby skaliny—chlebíčkom boly
> Tu bys sa pásol na našom poli—
> > Preč mi—obraz ľahkej plevy,
> Komu svetácke blesky, čačíky
> Tak ľahko zmútia mdlé pochopíky,
> > Nezaslúži lásky devy.
> > > Milina
> > *Orol*, 10.1 (1879): 25.

Unknown Author   "Zlatina"
Rizner (6: 208) lists this poem, but we have no further information.

66. Moja Láška (My Love)

Modro-jasné nebe tmavý mrak sastierá,
A deň unavený večerom umiera.
Zhaslého dňa zora viac sa nepozlátí,
Slza vyronená nikdy sa nevrátí;

Nevrátí sa mladosť, mrtvého srdca cit,
Zhaslého veku dej, zklamaný blahobyt;
Nezkvitne už veniec, bars ho panna vije:
Tak aj moja láska—nikdy neožije.
> > Zlatina
> > *Sokol*, 1.5 (1862): 140.

Unknown Author   "Anička"
Rizner (1: 37) lists this poem, but we have no further information.

67. Rada matkyná (A Mother's Advice)

> Padá listie z jalšoviny,
> Do studienky padá;
> Tašla som k nej na vodičku,
> Začrela som hada.
> So strakatým hadom v žbánku
> Bežala som k mame,
> "Čuj mamičko moja milá,
> Hada v žbánku máme."

Lež mať moja mi radila:
"Nechaj dcérko hada,
On je plný jedov škodných —
A tys' ešte mladá.
Choď na druhú studienočku,
Kde si sokol sedá;
Ten ti vodu nezakalí,
Z nej nebudeš blädá.
Sokolík je vtáčok milý,
Ten ti neuškodí:
Za sokolom obráť oči —
Hada hoď do vody.
   Anička
 Sokol, 1.5 (1862): 165.

Marína Hodžová (1842–1921) "Marína"

Her biography is given in Chapter 2 and notes; see also *Slov. biog. slov., 2: 349–350*. Rizner (2: 109, 3: 151) does not identify Hodžová as author of the one poem he lists (No.67). The militant poem she wrote in December below was not published until 1963 with her correspondence. See also our speculation that Marína Hodžová may have written the anonymous "Dumka" (No.81 below). Mikušťáková (109) attributes to Hodžová a humorous prose sketch in *Černokňažník*, 14 (1864): 107, which is signed "Marína."

  68. 7.12.1862

Hor sa bratia! hor do boja!
Ruky si podajme,
ta sa na vrahov národa
nášho poberajme!

Nič nás neodstraší od toho,
žiadna strasť, nehoda,
heslom naším nech vždy bude:
Národ a sloboda!!

Dosť dlho sme už úpeli
pod jarmom poroby.
Znášali krivdy, nepravdy,
nepriateľa zloby.

No netrpme viac rabstvo to,
putá roztrhajme!
Sväté právo rodu nášho
odňať si nedajme!

Skalopevná viera v Boha,
nádej, láska k rodu
vydobyjú nám víťazstvo,
pravdu a slobodu!

A keď i mnohý z nás padne
v boji spravodlivom,
celô Slovensko zavolá:
Sláva verným synom!
   In *Listy Hodžovej*, ed. Peter Liba, 86.

69. Duma (Meditation)

Smutného zvonu trudný zvuk
 Doniká v cintorín tichý,
Kde v šum vetra večernieho
 Miešajú sa temné vzdychy.

"Kamže vzdychy, city chcete,
 Azda v pustý, chladný svet?
Ach úbohé! zostaňte tu;
 Pre vás tam prítuľku niet.

Čierne chmáry, vetry, zima,
 Ach desno je na tom svete;
Jasné iskry, útle kvety
 Tam zhasnete, uvädnete."

Takto devica nešťastná
 City svoje v srdce vinie,
V nich žije, umiera s nimi,
 Duša, srdce, žitia hynie.

Blädá deva v cintoríne
 Nemo hľadí zrakom mutným,
Rozbolenú hlávku kloní
 Tu ku hrobom čiernym, smutným.

Duša chorá, hroby tmavé, —

Mrazný vietor svetom veje,
A v tych hroboch pochované
Jej túžby, city, nádeje.
             Marína
        Sokol, 4.7 (1865): 125–126.

Unknown Author   "Mína Kováč"

Rizner (2: 438) has no further information, but gives her name as "Kováčová." It is not inconceivable that the author could have been Pauliny-Tóth himself, who is known to have used the pseudonym "Mína" (Riz. 4: 29), though "Mína Kováč" is also listed twice among those who solved the puzzles in *Černokňažník* in November and December, 1861.

70. Na Sylvestra 1861 (On New Year's Eve 1861)

No tak teda s Bohom, s Bohom
Roku minulosti,
Šťastlivú ti cestu prajem
I ja do večnosti.
Rok môj, rok môj, či to cítiš,
Či ti je známo tiež,
Že ranný ples roda môjho
V slávu večnú nesieš.

Ach nie, ty necítiš, nevieš,
Bez citu si minul,
Bez citu si rok môj milý
Do večnosti vplynul.
Do večnosti? kďe je ona?
Či v zemskej ohrade?
Čo je večnosť? — ona je to
"Vždy a vždy a všade."

Hoj veľké sú to hranice,
Myseľ sä mi točí —
A lež prvé svitne ráno,
Rok môj do nich vkročí.
Nuže vkroč len rok môj milý,
Čas ti mieru strihá;
Keď ta vletíš, zpýtajže sä:
Kde je ľudstva kniha?

A hneď vpíš do nej zlatými
Znakami — nech svety
Predošlé i budúce tam
Žiara jich osvieti —
Vpíš to dnuká rok môj milý
Čo si videl, zažil,
Žes' svedkom bol, jak sä Slovák
Za životom snážil.

Vpíš dnuká, že i nad Tatrou
Jasné hviezdy svieťa,
Že duch jarý matky Slávy
Nad Beskydom lieta.
Vpíš to do svätej knihy ľudstva:
Že i nám už svitne deň,
Čo zbrieždil rok: osemnásť sto
A šestdesát i jeden.
    Mína Kováč
Černokňažník, 2.1 (1862): [lst p].

Unknown Author   "Tomónia Haff"
Rizner does not list this name, and it is uncertain whether it is a pseudonym. The verse is unique in being heavily sarcastic and satiric, and possibly was written by a man. The name may be Greek (*tomé*) for *cutting* or *needing cutting*, and *haff* is the Slovak equivalent of "bark, bark."

71. Milá — milému (Lover [f] to Lover [m])

Namiešaný, ty si moja potecha a chlúba!
Máš tie ústka jako vráta, krivé jako trúba;
Zúbky drobné jak lopaty;ušká za somára;
Vlásky jako sviňské škuty; nôžky od komára;
Očká jako kocúr; líčka jako stará handra —
Ale čo ťa čerti vezmú, pekná si ty švandra!

Mnoho si sa nepoučil, to je pravda stará,
Hneď to čuší jako ryba, hneď do sveta tára,
Z bieleho a zeleného papiera rád čítaš,
A pri tom na hunno-skythskú mienku rád sa pýtaš,
Ale ja ťa držať nesmiem predca za somára:
Keď ťa páni silou mocou tisnú za phar-hára.[8]

Čistotný si tiež nie nazbyt—azdaj ako hviezda—
Každý vie, že dosial špinceš do vlastnieho
   hniezda;
A kde sa ti jaká pravda do oči zablyští,
Pľuvneš na ňu a sťa kuvik jazyčok tvoj spyští—
Lež časom aj to sa spraví, lebo každý jistí,
Že sa ti môj najmilejší práve—rozum čistí.

Ale kto by teba vedel ospievať dôstojne?
Ledaby sa húb najedol a gebuľky hojne,
Pani líšku v srdci nosil, v kotrbe otruby,
A poriadok celý v svete obrátil na vruby.
Slabý ohlas tvojich zásluh buď celému míru
Pieseň táto kým len bude o gebule chýru,
Budúcemu nech potomstvu ešte sa rozsieva,
Keď ti dávno starý Dunčo na kare odspieva.
   Vďačná Tomónia Haff.
      Černokňažník, 2.35 (1862): 280.

Unknown Author   "Opustená"
   Rizner (3: 331) lists her but we have no other information.

72. Sirota na hrobe matkinom (An Orphan at Her
      Mother's Grave)

Odstri sa odstri—príkrovie tmavé—
   Ta hrudka z matkinej hrobky suchá:
Až jej boskom, na pery sinavé—
   Vtisnem iskru žitia z môjho ducha.
Necítiš—mati!—na hrobci tvojom,
   Zem mokom sĺz dcériných už zpitú?—
Predsa ťa len ľadovým závojom,
   Sen smrtný tríma večne zavitú?—
Ulož ma náhla k nej smrti rana!—
   Oj ulož ma drúžka usmievavá!——
Bo s ňou byť—je žiť raj Lybana——
   Bez nej však život——smrť mi zdĺhavá.
Vstaň mati!—vstaň!—bolesť vo mne horí!
   Tma myseľ múti—hlávkou previeva;—
Slza žiaľu—očko už umorí:
   Poď—mati—poď! dcéra ti omdlieva.
      Opustená

Sokol, 2.13 (1863): 293.

Milina Lohinská   No pseudonyms
Rizner (3: 103) lists her with no further data. She also contributed puzzles to *Sokol*.

73. Žiaľ (Sorrow)

Pri potôčku stála, vodičku si brala,
Do nej pozerala, žalostne plakala:
    Ako tieto vlnky kalným tokom plynú —
    Tak aj moje časy ím podobne hynú: —
    Ako tie ružičky obtrhané vädnú —
    Tak aj moje líčka im podobne blädnú.
        Milina Lohinský
        Junoš, 1.7 (1866): 106.

74. Moje kvety (My Flowers)

Pod oknom zahradka,
V tej zahradke kvety —
A rannie slniečko
Milo na ne svieti.

Ach svieť len slniečko
Nech mi pekne kvitnú,
Veď mi o nedlhý
Èas zase zakvitnú.

Tešievam sa s nimi —
Keď ma smútok tlačí,
Keď mi ubližujú
Moji utrháči.
        Milina Lohinský
        Junoš, 1.8 (1866): 120.

Unknown Author   "Hronka"
Rizner does not list this verse, and we have no further information.

75. Potecha dievčiny (A Girl's Consolation)

Sedela dievčina pod zeleným stromom
A slávičok spieval smutným hlasom na ňom.

Žiaľ jej slzy ronil, z očí sa jej kradnul —
A v slze tu i tu na skalie odpadnul. —
Hoj! nerob mi žiale, slávik, tvojím spevom —
Bo nemám radosti nikde pod tým nebom.
Smutnú ja mám mladosť na tomto údolí,
Žijem zarmútená beze srdca vôli:
Srdiečko ma bolí, slzy z očí tečú —
Moje mladé časy žiaľom sa mi vlečú;
Žiaľom sa mi vlečú, srdce zarmucujú,
Lebo mi priatelia život podrucujú.
Jaj, priatelia moji! čo len z toho máte —
Že mi sužovaním do srdca strielate?
Ale len súžujte, ako ste súžili
život môj lesťami Vy priatelia milí! —
Veď sa Vás nestrachám — zostávajte zdraví —
Mám inde potechu: v mravnosti báj pravý.
    Hronka
     Junoš, 1 (1866): 135.

Emília Vadászfyová (? - ?)   No pseudonyms

Rizner (6: 93) lists her without further data. She was presumably from Spiš.

  76. Ohlas zo Spyša (A Voice from the Spiš Region)

Duch môj vo mne zaspal, ktože ho zobudil?
Drahý brat slovenský, čo po Spyši chodil.[9]
Duch môj čo tvrdo spal, už počína vstávať,
Svoj slovenský národ počína poznávať.
Duša moja spala, viacej spať nebude,
Svoj slovenský národ vždy milovať bude.
Môj slovenský národ, veru ťa milujem,
Za teba národ môj život obetujem,
 Prečo sa Slováci v Spyši maďarčili?
Preto že v Rožňave do školy chodili.
Na Spyši pánici tak sa shovárajú:
"Jo reggelt, pán bratko, akože sa majú?"
Bo spyšskí pánici sotvaj pár slov vedia,
Myslia, že Maďari všetci na nich hledia.
Na Spyši pánici reč tú zahodili,
Zapovrhli reč tú, v ktorej sa zrodili.

Oni všetci len tak po maďarsky vedia:
"Neviem po slovensky; neviem čo povedia."
Nechoďte Spyšiaci do školy v Rožňave,
Bo sa odrodíte našej matke Sláve,
A čo vám už potom zo všetkeho príde
Keď v Spyši nenašská reč panovať bude?
Milí bratia, sestry! stáli zostávajme,
Krásnu reč slovenskú v uctivosti majme.
Ty Bože pomôž nám takto pokračovať,
A tú reč slovenskú ďalej upevňovať;
Aby panovala po celom Okolí,
By sme verné deti matky Slávy boli.
    Emília Vadászfy
       Sokol 5.1 (1866): 35.

Unknown Author   "Eva z pod Baby, E.J."
    Rizner (1: 367) lists her without further information. She also wrote two short articles about the new women's organization and signed the initials "E. J.": "Ohlas zpod Baby," *Národní hlásnik*, 2.8 (August 1869): 242–243, and "Ohlas zpod Baby k sestrám Česka," *Národní hlásnik* 2.9 (September 1869): 271. A note to this first poem identifies it as a response to the poem by Emília Vadászfy above. The quotation is from Kollár's *Slávy dcera*.

    77. Ohlas z pod Baby (Response from Mt Baba)

    "Bez pastýrek co jsau Arkady?
    Co jsou ráje, v kterých není Evy?"

Sestrička slovenská tam hen z pod Kriváňa!
Buďte mi v "Sokolu" mile privítaná!
Keď som ja Váš "Ohlas" v "Sokolu" čítala,
Zase jednu sestru v národe poznala,
Sestru to Slávie, čo národ neznala,
Lež poznajúc chybu k verným sa priznala:
Potešila som sa; veľmi mi je milo,
Že sa Vaše srdce k národu hlásilo.
Musím sa Vám musím teraz prihovoriť,
V dôvere slovenskej srdce Vám otvoriť.
Tie neverné sestry reči a národu,
Čo sú verným dcéram na hanbu, na škodu,
Oj keby tie sestry bludné, neveriace,

Tiež obrátily sa na Evy kajúce;
Daj že to, môj Bôže, by sa obrátily,
K našej sa zástave húfne prihlásily.
Národ náš zaiste nevidíme skvitnúť,
Pokým budú sestry za cudzinou lipnúť;
Hlaďme, by si matky za povinosť vzaly
By v národňom duchu synov vychovaly!
Nech že za cudzotou mamičky nebažia,
Deti slavsky učiť, to nech si neťažia;
Nech nedržia pri nich maďarky, nemkyne,
By jich odcudzily sprosté varovkyne;
Tým rečiam nech nikdy prednosť nedávajú,
Bo tak hneď materskú reč zanedbávajú.
Vy dcéry Tatier, čo ste už mamičky,
Prímte slovo srdca od svojej sestričky:
Nech že si nelení nikdy žiadna matka
Vštepovať hneď tú cnosť do srdca dieťatka:
By si milovalo reč svoju vždy vrele,
A svojmu národu oddalo sa cele;
Nuže od malička tie svoje detičky
Takto vyučujte, slovenské mamičky.
Bože dobrotivý! poprajže nám sily,
Aby sme národ náš nad všetko ľúbily.
    Eva z pod Baby
     Sokol 5.3 (1866): 117.

78. Národní veniec (National Wreath)

 Švárné dievča, slavské dieťa
 Nasbieralo sebe kvieťa,
 Kvietky krásne, utešené!
 Bielé, modré i červené.
 Ukladá jich do ručinky,
 Nevinné to konvalinky,
 Jasno-modré fijalôčky,
 I červené smrkalôčky.
 Oj vy kvietky premilené!
 Vy ste moje potešenie,
 Milé ste vy tro-sestreniec,
 Uvijem vás v jeden veniec.
 Mať príroda vás zrodila,

Vôňou sladkou napojila,
V jednom kríčku prebývate,
Rúče sa vy znášavate.
Drahé dcéry Slávy Matky!
Berme z toho príklad taký:
Z tých nevinných milých kvietkov
Ako žiť sestra so sestrou.
Jedna matka nás zrodila,
Slavským mliekom odojila,
Milujme sa buďme svoje,
Nedeľme sa tak na dvoje.
Nehanbme sa za otčinu
Za tú slovenskú rodinu;
Lež hanbme sa odroditi,
Reč a rod svoj potupiti.
Usilujme-s' uviť veniec
Zo slavskych verných dievčeniec:
Národ náš ním ozdobíme
A dobre mu poslúžime.
 Eva z pod Baby
  Sokol 6.1 (1867): 22.

79. Naša vďaka (Our Thanks)

Čože nám to zase tá milá brať naša
V našom Hlásnikovi, čo za pravdu hlása?
Oj hlása nám hlása, deň k tomu určený
Pre blaho národa: by sa panny ženy
Sišli všetky spolu o tom rokovaly:
Ako by si dcéry národne vzdelaly.
Tá matička naša za dobré uznala,
By si dcéry rodu k sebe pripútala
Primäla ku práci a učinlivosti,
Tak sa na nich ešte dožila radosti.
Oj matička naša! chceme mať tie cnosti,
Vrelo sa milovať, plniť povinosti, —
Čože sa to stálo? čo to za príčina:
Že sa shromažďujú ženy do Martina?
Ako by sa stalo nejaké zjavenie:
Že ich toľká túha k mestu tomu ženie;
Alebo zábava, hostina nejaká?

Ich ku tomu sjezdu tak radostne láka.
Inšia ich zaviedla k tomu dobrá vôľa:
Ešte viac, ako by, hostina tam bola.
Synia dobrí matke chcejú uviť veniec,
Zo slávskych, a verných rodu to dievčeniec.
Veniec neuvadlý nech Jej čelo krási;
Kto ale ten základ národa si spási:
Tomu nak z úst zneje naších trikrat sláva
Pokial bytu nášho na svete zostáva.
  Živio! Sláva! Sláva!
   Eva zpod Baby
 Národní hlásnik 2.9 (1869): 270–271.

80. Pri kolíske (In the Cradle)

Slovenka som rodom Slovenka ma mala,
Nad mojom kolískou mať mi tak spievala:
Hajaj že mi belaj dieťatko moje ty,
Keď vyrastieš hodnou buď verná svojeti.
Nepovrhni matkou, tou čo ťa zrodila,
Zpomni, že ťa mliekom slovenským kojila;
Aj reč tú vždy miluj ktorú ťa tvoja mať
Po prvô v kolíske naučila poznať.
Ľúb si dcéra moja, ľúb svoj národ milý!
Bárs aké by búrky nad tebou krížlily.
Maj vždy tieto cnosti milô moje dieťa!
Pošle ti mať Sláva z raja peknô kvieťa.
Kveťa ti vpletieme do pekného vienku
Čo i pred oltárom ozdobí Slovenku.
Vďačne junoš verný poda rúčku pravú
Takejto neveste čo ctí matku Slávu.
Verný syn národa nehľadá len zlato,
Lež ten poklad srdca klenót drahší nad to.

— — — — —

Vyrástla som v pannu, žitia ma tešilo,
Ešte viac že srdce za národ môj bilo.
Tie spevy, čo matka v srdce mi vspievala,
Oj žiadna by mi moc zo sveta nevzala!
Aj modliť sa modlím, ako ma učila,
Za národ môj drahý mati moja milá.
Rada ja zasielam prosbu k Hospodinu,

By potešil čím skôr slovenskú rodinu!
— — — — —

Od útlej mladosti nechže si každá mať
  Učí synov, dcéry, národ svoj milovať.
Veľa, veru veľa aj od nás závisí
  Ako deti svoje jak vychováme si,
Potom už zlí ľudia nemajú tej sily,
  By nám deti naše rodu odcudzili
Keď že si tak matka pre národ nelení,
  Niva jeho skvitne, a sa zazelení,
Potom nám len bude ako nám nebolo,
  Keď synia i dcéry stanu v rodné kolo;
Tak skôr vstane rod náš, akoby zomretý
  Iste že ho vskriesa verné rodu deti.
      Eva zpod Baby
Národní hlásnik 2.11 (1869): 346–347.

Unknown Author   "Marína z pod Kohúta"
    This poem is not listed in any of the bibliographies, and we have no further data. One wonders if it could have been written by Marína Hodžová, because its depression is like that she expressed before leaving for Germany (No. 69), and in 1867 she had to leave for exile with her father in Silesia.

81. Dumka (Meditation)

Vej vetríčku, vej večerní,
Odvej ťažké žiale moje,
Vzdych mojej túžiacej duše
Vezmi na krídelka svoje.
Ružový ker zelená sa,
Šumný puk sčestia rozkvitá,
Kedy že sa už rozviješ,
V ružu plnú, lásko skrytá. — —
    Vo Veľkej Revúci
    Svitať už počína
    Veselo si spieva
    Slovenská družina.
    Veselo si spieva
    Šuhaj i dievčatko
    Ako pod Muráňom

Veselé vtáčatko.
Hoj už v našich krajoch
Duše dorastajú
Či si už veselo
Slovensky spievajú.
Šuhajci veselo
Do skoku spievajú,
Lebo už národa
Katom odzváňajú;
Ale deva túži
To dvoje si praje:
Národ zvelebený
A s milencom ráje.
      Marína z pod Kohúta
        Sokol 6.1 (1867): 23.

Unknown Author   "K—š."

This is not listed in any of the bibliographies. The initials do not indicate a feminine ending, but many Slovak women at this time did not decline their surnames.

82. Radosť Slovenky (Joy of a Slovak Woman)

Vitaj že nám okamženie blahé,
   Vitaj slávy jasná dennice,
     Aj, uplynulo let tisíce
Čo čekáme svetlo tvoje drahé.
Vitaj slnce slobody a práva
   Slnce bratskej lásky, jednoty,
     Ty lámeš nepriateľské hroty,
Ktorým v obeť daná bola Sláva.
Vitaj slnce slovanskej osvety!
   V blesku tvojom pozná brat brata,
A nesvárov umlknú klebety.
Ach rada bych do jednoho vienka
   Sviazať to, čo radosť je svätá,
Ktorú cíti tatranská Slovenka.
      K—š
Sokol 6.10 (1867): 313.

Zuzína Zajacová Lojková (1848–1886)   No pseudonyms

Rizner (3: 106) lists her with the information that she was the wife of Gustáv Hostivít Lojko (1843–1871); see also *Ency. slov. spis.*, 1: 391–392. He was studying in Vienna at the time she wrote her complex poem mingling national and personal love (No.85). Her poem "Lúčenie" is an elegy at his death. Lojková was widowed at age twenty-three and reared her three daughters without remarrying. She continued to write prose but apparently not poetry.

83. On a ona (He and She)

"Nechceli ťa za mňa dať
Ani otec ani mať,
    Ani celá rodina,
    Sama si si Marka
      Príčina!"

"Keď ja tvoja nebudem,
Banovať ja nebudem,
    Lebo ja mám druhého,
    Susedove Janka —
      Milého!"
        Zuzína Ružena Zajac
        Sokol 6.9 (1867): 282.

84. Zverbovaný (Conscripted Lad)

"Nenariekaj milá
    a nehub si oči.
veď ma nepovezú
    ďalej od Levoči!"

"Ach! veď ťa povezú
    až hen do Prešova,
budem ja nariekať —
    Janko duša moja!"
        Zuzína Ružena Zajac
        Sokol 6.10 (1867): 299.

85. Dumka (Meditation)

Ľúbim národ, ľubim teba,
Čo že mi je viacej treba? —

Národ ľubiť to mi je česť,
Teba drahý — milovať tiež!
Dumky moje nevyzraďte,
S kým sa rady zabávate;
Národ drahý ľubte zjavne,
Len milého — toho tajne.
Vy spanilé, útle kvietky,
Čo tak smutne pozeráte?
Či večerní snaď vetríčok,
S takou túžbou vyzeráte?
Slniečko za vrch sa skrýva,
Vetrík tichý viať počína: —
Kvietočky už veselé ste?!
Už viacej nie ste zvädnuté,
Prišlo vám už potešenie,
Za ktorým tak túžily ste!
Tu vám je už aj sestrička,
Tichá — chladná to rosička;
Duje vám už čez doliny,
Ten čekaný, drahý milý!
Pri vás bavím sa tak rada,
Keď som v žiaľoch zadumená:
Pre teba — drahý národ môj
Druhé pre teba — milý môj! —
Dumky moje leťte krásne,
Zvelebujte národ hlasne;
Zvelebujte jeho krásu,
Dokial máte ešte času!
Príroda spí — odpočíva,
Či len o mne — milý sníva?!
Príjemnejšie tebe, sladký sníčok snívať,
Nežli mne v cudzine tejto pustej bývať!
   Zuzína Ružena Zajac
    Sokol 6.11 (1867): 346.

86. Pierko kvetov (A Nosegay for a lover)

Večierkom v zahrade prechodí sa deva,
Zelenú trávičku slzami polieva;
Trhala by kvety, vila by pierečko
Keby ho privinúl šuhaj na srdiečko.

Ale deva v žiaľoch kvetov natrhala,
Potom z ních pierečko pekné viť začala;
Najskôr nezábudku, tak bielu ružičku,
Klinčok a rozmarín, zelenú myrtičku.
Keď ho dovíjala, slzou ho zkropila
A potom hovoriac k srdcu pritlačila:
"Komuže pierečko dostaneš sa — komu?
Komu milé budeš, ja ťa len dám tomu!
Koho by s' tešilo, toho tuná nenie,
Preto smutná nemám žiadne potešenie!
Zavievaj vetierku na vysokej skale,
Asnáď ty vyduješ moje ťažké žiale —
Veľa je tých žiaľov na mojom srdiečku,
Sním že mi z ních Bože! aspon polovičku!
Avšak mnoho času od tedy ubehlo,
A pekné pierečko od tedy už zvedlo.
Zvedlo s' mi pierečko zato ťa len nechám,
Nechať zvie môj milý, že ho ja rada mám,
Keď príde, na dôkaz lásky ta mu ho dám!"
   Zuzína R. Zajac-Lojkován
    Sokol 7.4 (1868): 107.

87. Vzdych (Sigh)

Noc je tmavá noc je tichá
Za kým moje srdce vzdychá?
Duch môj letí za túžbami,
Sťa ten vetrík dolinami.
život môj je túžba samá,
Len v nej duša sa mi hráva;
Srdce moje v nej radosť má,
Nádej vieru ona mi dá.

A na nebi hviezdy jasné
Trblietajú sa tak krásne;
Na mňa smutnú a samotnú
Rozlievajú žiar ligotnú.
Vetríčok už utichuje
Ticho — pokoj všiad panuje;
Dobrú noc ti národe môj! —
Hospodine, chráň — spas ľud svoj!

Zuzína R. Lojko
Sokol 7.4 (1868): 116.

88. Sirota (Orphan)

Tam prostred cintera
    Či vo večer tichý,
Tam na jednom hrobe
    Počuť ťažké vzdychy;
Počuť ťažké vzdychy
    Či búrka panuje,
Tam na hrobe matky
    Dcéra horekuje:
"Čo mňa po tom svete?
    Tu mňa nič neteší,
Moja celá radosť
    V tomto hrobe leží!"
Ťažko zahrmelo,
    Hviezdy sa pokryly,
Ťažšie však z úst devy
    Slová sa prúdily:—
"Ty dobrá matička
    Musíš v hrobe ležať,
Nemohúc sirôtke
    Ku pomoci bežať!
Nečuješ už viacej
    Nadzemské hrmenie,
Ani moje vzdychy,
    Ni vrúcne modlenie."
Zahrmí okolo,
    Deva sa zobzerá,
So slzavým okom
    Šerú noc premerá.
"Tu na hrobe zvädnem
    Sťa odtrhnutý kvet,
Bože môj! už pre mňa
V svete radosti nie!"
        Zuzína R. Zajac–Lojková
           Sokol 7.6 (1868): 189.

89. Zmena (Change)

Pozri, milá dcéro! tu na toto kvieťa,
Jako sa rozvíja — rosa v ňom trblieta;
Však pomni, že prídu búrky hromobitia,
Čo i jeho krásu v šíry svet uchytia!
       Zuzína R. Lojková
         Sokol 7.8 (1868): 253.

90. Hrom (Thunder)

Na zožatej roli,
  Kde prv žito bolo,
Krútilo sa detí —
  Krútilo sa kolo.
Matka, keď na strane
  Kláskov nasbierala —
"Deti poďme domov!"
  Na ne zavolala.
"Počujete hrmí!" —
  Matka na né volá
A deti zplašené
  Rozbehnú sa z kola.

Slniečko sa skrylo
  Pršať už počína,
Poberá sa domov
  Chudobná rodina.
Matka detí štvoro
  Idú domov smutne,
V tom pred jích očima, —
  Blesk strely sa zkrútne.
A hrom zarachotí
  I zašumie lístia —
Matka, štvoro detí,
  Dušičky vypustia!
       Zuzína R. Lojková
         Sokol 7.11 (1868): 340.

91. Žiaľ Slovenky (Sorrow of a Slovak Woman)

Zapadlo slniečko za vysokú hoľu,
A Slovenke očká zalialy sa v bôľu:
"To moje srdiečko tuho zaviazané,

Nad slovenskou vlasťou celé vyplakané." —

""""Ty mladá Slovenka, nač slzy vylievaš?
Prečo že si radšej v smútku nezaspievaš?
Oj spievaj si, spievaj! vylej žiale svoje,
Veď je spev jediné potešenie tvoje!

A keď si zaspievaš, vzdýchni k Pánu Bohu,
Ach, veď je on dobrý, splní túžbu tvoju;
Za čím srdce tvoje vzdychá v noci, vo dne,
Nad tým Pán Bôh mocný raz predsa rozhodne!""""
   Zuzína R. Z. Lojková
   Živena. Národní Almanach 1 (1872): 22.

92. Matkina prosba (A Mother's Prayer)

 Medzi dvoma kolískami
  Sedí mladá matka,
 Bielou rukou v pravo v ľavo
  Dve dcérušky hladká.

 Podriemkujú, necíťa už
  To hladkanie matky:
 "No, búvajte, nevinniatka,
  Snite sníček sladký."

 Zamyslená hľadí na ne
  A slzy vylieva. —
 Jedno sebou práve trhlo,
  Druhé sa usmieva.

 "Dieťa moje! čože búra
  Nevinné sny tvoje?
 Že aj v spánku strhuješ sa:
  Snáď znáš sveta boje?"

 Bože svatý! Teba prosím,
  Len to mi daj z nebe,
 By z nich dobré vychovala
  Mne, národu, Tebe!

 Spite, spite! — Ach, neviete,
  Aký to dar boží,
 Tiché spanie, komu osud

Smútok v srdce vloží!
>> Zuzina R. Z. Lojková
Živena. Národní Almanach 1 (1872): 43–44.

93. Oželená sirota (The Despairing Orphan)

Nad potokom chlapček sedí,
Zamyslený doňho hľadí,
  Ako vlny žblnkotajú,
  Čo si ony povedajú.

"Tebe potôček môj krásny
A tebe mesiaček jasný,
  Vám sa ja tu posťažujem,
  Moje biedy vyžalujem.

Dávno ja už nemám otca
A dávnejšie nemám matky;
  Dávno ja už nepočujem
  Slová: poď sem, syn môj sladký!

Ach ten svet zlý, ten svet planý,
V tom svete ľud neuznaný!
  Keď mi duša plače, stená,
  Svet tam pre mňa miesta nemá!"

A vlnôčky žblnkotaly!
To si ony povedaly:
  Čo zlý svet vykonať nechcel,
  Že to ony vykonaly!
>> Zuzína R. Z. Lojková
Živena. Národní Almanach 1 (1872): 48–49.

94. Lúčenie (Farewell)

Všade ticho, všade voľne
Ach, len srdce bije bôľne!
Večer tichý je, vábivý,
Ale pre mňa smutný, clivý. —
Všade ticho je a voľno,
Ach, len v srdci bije bôľno!
Jarní vetríček povieva,
Ruža kvitne, slávik spieva;

> Radosťou sa všetko smeje:
> Len moje vädnú nádeje! —
> Srdce, obráť city k Bohu,
> Veď on splnil túžbu mnohú!
> S Bohom teda, putuj šťastne
> Na shľadanie naše krásne!
> Pán Bôh nás tam preca spojí.
> Kde nás nič viac nerozdvojí.
> Nebije už srdce bôľno,
> Ale je v ňom ticho, voľno!
>> Zuzína R. Lojková
>> *Orol* 3.6 (1872): 180–181.

Oľga Braxatorisová Mocková. (? –1918) "Olga Sládkovičová"
Rizner (3: 223–224) lists her as the wife of Ján Mocko (1843–1911), Lutheran pastor and well-known literary historian in western Slovakia (for him see *Ency. slov. spis.*, 1: 445–446). She was also the eldest daughter of the major poet Andrej Sládkovič (see Chapter 1) and sister of the minor poet Martin Braxatoris (1863–1934). Her obituary appeared in *Živena* (1918): 174.

95. Načo vravíš žes' Slovenka? (Why Do You Say You're a Slovak Woman?)

> Načo vravíš žes' Slovenka
> Slovenského rodu?
> Keď cudzia reč milšia ti je,
> A hľadíš na módu!
> Načo vravíš, že tam bývaš
> Kde len Slovák žije?
> Ale mrtvé ti je srdce,
> Za rod tvoj nebije!
> Načo vravíš, žes' Slovenka,
> V slovenskom Považí?
> Keď slovenský hlas z úst tvojích
> Slovákov neblaží!
> Zpýtajme sa rodu nášho.
> Či je s tým spokojný,
> Keď povieme: sme Slovenky,
> Je nás počeť hojný?
> Lež dôkaz žiadny nemáme,

Krem to prazdné slovo:
Som Slovenka, — i to len tam,
Kde to nič nie novô.
Slabí dôkaz, sestry moje,
S tým nezvíťazíme;
Len keď sa s telom i s dušou
Rodu posvätíme.
Keď nebudeme ohľad brať
Na zlých ľudí škreky,
Budeme si svoje brániť
S národom na veky.
Čo nás tam po cudzej reči,
Čo po cudzom speve?
Krem slovenskej reči, piesňí,
Srdce naše nevie.
    Olga Sládkovičová
    Sokol 7.5 (1868): 153.

96. Jarnia (Spring Is Coming)

Jaké krásné okamženie
Je to v jarňom čase,
Kde všetko, ako pospalé,
Prebúdza sa zase.
Jako milo je včeličkám,
Vonné lipy obletovať,
A z ních k ďalšiemu životu
Pokrm si zbieravať.
Jako milo je národu
V peknom hájku sa zabávať,
Medzi milým vtáctva spevom
Čas si príjemňovať.
Jako milo je mládeži
Kvietočky si hotoviti,
A národu, sebe k sláve,
Krásné vence viti.
Jak milo je stratenému,
Keď sa domov vrátil,
A tak svojích milých našiel
Jako jich bol stratil.
Tak mile milý mi ten čas,

Keď som národ znať začala,
K okrase mu, sebe k spase,
Slovenský spievať počala.
Dlho v mojom srdci tmavý
Mesiac svietil smutno;
Ale teraz nie len mesiac
Lež krásne slnko mi svitlo.
Ktoré večne svietiť musí
Vždy jasne a stále,
Náš národ lesknúť sa musí
Ako diamant, v Sláve.
   Olga Sládkovičová
    Sokol 7.6 (1868): 190.

97. Králiky (Daisies)

Po lúke peknej, zelenej, v tichom rozhovore
Prechodia sa dve priateľky hneď dole hneď hore.

Zpomedzi trávky zelej kvetinky kukajú,
Hneď ten, hneď ten tých dvoch očú na sebä pútajú.

Pozri, pozri sestra milá, jaká ti to krása —
A už idú bujnou trávou, čo jim je do pása.

Lež ktorý teraz odtrhnúť, Bože môj veliký?
Aha, já si tajdem tamto natrhať králiky.

Len dve a tri okamženia a už jich má za hrsť —
Teraz prelietla jej dušou jakási zvedavosť.

Posadí sa na sried lúky do zelenej trávy —
Králiky vloží do lona, tíško ku nim vraví:

Povedzte mi, ale pravdu, vy kvietočky biele,
Či môj milý miluje ma, *málo* a či *vrele*?

Jedon vraví, že *nevdojak*, druhý že zo *srdca*,
Tretí zase, že cele *nič*, štvrtý *trošku* predca.

Sprosté ste vy, kvietky milé, neverím žiadnemu:
Každý inak hovoríte — spýtam sa milému.

Ten mi povie iste pravdu, on je bohabojný,
Každý rídzy Slovák je i za pravdu bojovný.

V tom príde jej kamarátka, z myšlienok ju vzbudí:
Poď už domov, moja krásna, už večer prichodí.
    Olga Sládkovičová
        Orol 2.8 (1871): 251.

Ľudmila Kulišková   "Ľudmila Ku., Ludmilka K., Ludmila"
Rizner (2: 491) lists her work with no further information. She may have been the daughter (1845-1915) of Juraj Kulišek (1815–1898) and Anna Bóriková, and the wife of Pavol Beblavý

98. Všetko sa minie (All Things Pass Away)

    Na vršku kostolík stojí,
    Díva sa do doliny, —
    Dolu, sediac pri potôčku,
    Spieva pastier z dediny.
    Smutne zneje zvončok hore
    Prôvod ide s pohrabom,
    Pastuška spevy utíchly
    S zbožným na hor pohľadom.
    Hore nesená do hrobu,
    Tá čo kvitla v dedine,
    Oj ti chlapčok pri potôčku,
    Nenájdeš ju v doline.
    Preto slož ruky ku nebu
    Za zomretú sa modli,
    Ktorá nechajúc rodinu
    Medzi vami viac nedlí.
        Ľudmila
    Sokol 7.5 (1868): 153.

99. Na orla (About the Eagle)

    Orol náš bystrý, ty sa s víchricou
    Krúť do zatemnenej neba vyšiny,
    A z čiernavy blískavicou jasnou
    Osvecuj milé nám Tatier doliny.
    Orol náš milý, vsadni na oblaky
    A leť po nad šíre sveta končiny,
    Keď sa povzneseš nad syny vernými
    Daj jim hvezdy nádeje z výšiny.
    Nad krajinou zas letiac odrodenou

Roztrhni chmáru očmi ohnivými,
Skropiac slzami zboreniny Slávy
Des duše hriešne blesky hrmotnými.
    Ľudmila
        Sokol 7.6 (1868): 190.

100. Slovenka (Slovak Woman)

Ešte som len malá bola,
Mamička si žiadala:
Abych vernou slovenskému
Vždy národu zostala.
Slovenka som a Slovenkou
Vožďy vernou zostanem—
Kde mi možno všade svôj rod
I svoju reč zastanem.
Slovenkou buď! vravela mi
Moja dobrá mamička.
Slovenkou som a slováka
Rada mám čo bratrička.
Slovenkou buď dcerko moja,
Pre sláva ťa pestujem:
Slovenkou som, slovákovi
Rúčku svoju darujem.
    Ľudmila Ku
        Sokol 8.9 (1869): 283.

101–104. Piesne (Songs)

V jaseni (In Autumn)

Škoda ruže, krásnej ruže
V jaseň som si vzdychala,
Prečo že si má ružička
Prečo dolu spadala?
Škoda ruže, škoda veľka,
Vätšia škoda milého:
Bôh zná, v jaseň v ktorú stranu
Pošiel sveta šíreho?
Škoda ruže, krásnej ruže,
Že už viacej nekvete;
Škoda sa ti moj najmilší,

Škoda túlať po svete.
Prijde jaro — prijdeš milý?
Ruža sa zas rozvije,
A srdiečko moje smutné
Potom zase ožije.

Zima (Winter)

Prišla zima — ker ružový
Tu musíš ty samý stať,
Kým môj milý premilený
Bude zas k nám chodievať.
Zima, zima, keby sas' len
Dajakosi zkrátila,
Že by som ja na jar našla,
Čo som v jaseň stratila.

Na jaro (In the Spring)

Prešla zima — zima smutná.
Jaro sa už usmieva:
Teplý vetrík dolinkami
Lahunko si povieva
Jaro je tu, jaro milé
Pukajú sa kroviny:
Ale milý, srdco moje
Neprichodí z cudziny.
Ruža puká, ruža kvitne,
Ruže sa červeňajú,
Ale duša, srdco moje;
Po vždy v smútku stonajú.

Leto (Summer)

Lúky, pole, sady z kvitly:
Leto prepel už víta;
Ale ruža srdca mojho
Ešte po dnes nezkvitá.
Ruža kvitne — ale čo že
Keď ju nemám komu dať —
Ťažko je to, avšak predca
Musí srdco zabudzať.
Škoda ruže, krásnej ruže!

> V jaseň som si vzdychala,
> Škoda milý — teraz vzdychám,
> Že som ťa raz poznala.
>> Ludmilka K.
>> *Sokol* 8.11 (1869): 350–351.

Unknown Author   "Slovenka zpod Choča"

Rizner (5: 110) lists her with no further data. Conceivably she was Mária Pozdechová Bobulová, the wife of the editor of the two new publications in which these poems appeared, i.e. Ján Nepomuk Bobula (1844–1903). Bobulová was a translator from German in this same period. A note to the third poem says that the author's desire not to give her name brought an exception to the magazine's policy against anonymous works.

105–109 Moje svety (My Worlds)

1.

> Leťte piesne — leťte prudkým letom —
> Povzneste sa k nebies výšinám,
> Neste túžby všeslovanským svetom —
> Túžby devy — slavským krajinám!
> Tam kde junač mladá láskou horí
> K svojeti, a sbiera pre ňu kvety —
> Tam sa duchu jej i môj duch korí,
> Tam ja hľadám moje slasti — svety.

2.

> Pod Tatrami, kde žul strmé múry
> K oblakom sa pnú vždy vysokým;
> Kde za jäzdcom prach sa z zeme kúri
> Živôt hasne kozám divokým;
> Tam kde bystrý Váh sa kolom točí
> Pravda rastie — hyný klebety
> Kde sú perly — a útlych diev očí —
> Tam já hľadám moje slasti, svety.

3.

> Nábožné kde city srdcom vládnu,
> Nevoľa kde klesne — a klam padá;
> Lásku kde nevidí človek zradnú —
> Zlosť v svätinu ducha sa nevkráda;

Tam kde zpevy v hájoch, horách znejú,
V uši bijú milé sonnety:
Tam kde Tatier čerstvé vetry vejú —
Tam ja hľadám moje slasti, svety.

4.
A tu kráčam krajmi rozkošnými,
Duch môj vládne sveta prostorou;
Tu sa chlúbi mužmi údatnými
Ľud vždy schopný ducha výtvorou;
Tu kde nádej národa a vlasti —
Poráža vždy prázdny mysli vety:
Tu kde hynú márne ľudstva strasti:
Tam ja hľadám moje slasti, svety.

5.
Zavzni pieseň! hľadaj hrudu zeme
Človek z hrudy, z prachu stvorený!
Hľadaj družstvo, pobratimské plemä —
Duch nehodne svetom morený;
Tam kde matka svôj plod kolíbala,
Tam mám priateľkine C h o č a deti;
Tam kde ma vždy sláva objímala!
Tam ja hľadam moje slasti — svety.
    Slovenka zpod Choča
  Slovenské noviny, ed. J. N. Bobula, l.76 (1868).

110. Keď som ja malička bola (When I was a child)

Keď som ja malička bola
  Očká sa mi smialy
Lebo mä dobrí rodičia —
  Radi objímali;
Vek detinský som trávila
  V tichej samotnosti —
Hry a spevy mája rozkoš
  Boly len v mladosti.

Keď som ja malička bola
  Sbierala som kvety
Z ních si vila pestré vence
  V ních videla svety;

Hory, doly, nivy, háje
 Mä očarovaly
V rána trillery slávika
 Zo sna prebúdzaly.

Keď som ja malička bola
 Ľúbila som cele:
Pána Boha, otca, matku
 I priateľky vrele:
A v tejto ľúbosti čistej
 Hľadala som spásu —
V nej zočila som blaženstvo
 I života krásu.

Keď som ja malička bola
 Mala som i bábky,
Ktoré boly vždycky moje
 Verné kamarátky:
S ními smiala i plakala
 Som tajne, v skrytosti,
Jím som voždy rozprávala
 Bájek maličkosti.

Keď som ja malička bola
 A dostala v dare:
Perly, stužky, krásne šaty
 Perá, kalamáre:
Bola že to radosť v dome —
 Dušou to preniká,
Zvlášť keď zhliadla som na stole:
 Srdce z mädovníka!

Avšak uletely časy
 Dávnej minulosti
A v zapomenutie prišly
 Už tie hry mladosti;
Len tieň slabý značí priestor
 Môjho žitia rána,
A k novému pôsobeniu
 Brána sa otvára.

Skutočnému životu sa
 Chcem ja už zasvätiť,

Národ i vlasť skrze sebä
　　Rovnako zvelebiť;
Veď tak myslím — že je to nie
　　Žiadna veľká vina:
Keď k obveseleniu bratov
　　Zaspieva dievčina!

A vy bratia tiež spievajte
　　Piesne môjho rodu —
Veď to národu nebude
　　Verte mi — na škodu;
Pri tom venujte mi srdce
　　V ktorom láska vzniká,
Lebo ja už viac mať nechcem —
　　Srdce z mädovníka!
　　　　　　　Slovenka zpod Choča
Slovenské noviny, ed. J. N. Bobula, 1.86 (1868).

111. V matkinom lone   (In a Mother's Lap)

Bežká a skáče nevinné dieťa
Modré očičky jásavo svieta
　　Na rodinných sväzkov tone;
Otec objíma si neviniatko,
Matka pobozká útle dieťatko, —
　　Už snije v matkynom lone!

Život sa tratí a noc omdlieva,
Hodinu smrti tieseň ovieva
　　Pri zvonov, smutnom ozone!
Starec prežehná rodinné tváre —
Želá si pokoj — klesne na máre —
　　Je v hrobe, — v matkinom lone.
　　　　　　　Slovenka z pod Choča
　　Minerva Národní zábavník, (Pest, 1869) 280.

Anna Šipková Philadelphi (1843–1923)　　　　No pseudonym
　　Rizner (4: 56) lists her two poems with the fact that she was the wife of Móric Philadelphi (1834–1905), a Lutheran pastor and minor writer in Bohunice and Nemecká Ľupča in central Slovakia. No other information is available about her.

112. Try žitia hodiny

I.

Čo je ruža? Je krásny kvet,
Je nádejný útechy svet,
    Je zora žitia rána;
Ruža obraz nevinnosti
A panenskej stydlivosti
    Otvára city neba;
A zvlášť ruža v jarnom puku
Podáva mládeži ruku!

II.

Čo je ruža? Je krásny kvet
Tvorí nový života svet,
    Svet žitia v skutočnosti;
Nádeja sa v skutok mení
A v ľúbeznom život snení
    Najde v duši obľubu!
Keď ružička sa rozvila.
Túžba devy sa splnila.

III.

Čo je ruža? Je krásny kvet,
Lež zatvára života svet
    Keď lístočky jej vädnú.
Tak aj život hynie, hasne
Až človeku zrak vyhasne
    K poslednímu skonaniu.
Ruža keď už raz uspáva
Púť pustovník dokonáva.

* * *

To tie žitia sú hodiny
    V útlom kvete objasnené;
Len v čiastkach troch sú vidiny
    Žitia nášho znázornené.
Mládež, tá nádeji žije
    Mužský vek víťazstvo hľadá
Starcovi hodina bije
    K odchodu, keď ruža bľadá.
Try žitia nášho hodiny

Sú života try vidiny.
    Anna Philadelphy
    Minerva (Pest, 1869) 85-86.

113. K sestrám slovenským

Vy myslíte sestry drahé,
    Že sme osamelé?
Oj nie! máme popri sebe
    Srdcia mužov vrelé.

A junáci bodrí, bystrí
    Nám ruky dávajú,
A činon i úkolom svätým
    Nás povolávajú.

Preto sriaďme šíky svoje
    A k činom sa majme;
Milujme rod i reč našu —
    Padnuť jej nedajme!

* * *

Slovensko už viac nedrieme
    K životu sa budí,
A životom svojim z driemot
    Zbúdza množstvo ľudí;

Založila sa "Živena" —
    Kvitnúc v svojej kráse,
Rozložila blaha stány
    Len k národu spáse.

Preto zriaďme šíky svoje
    A k činom sa majme;
Milujme rod i reč našu —
    Padnuť jej nedajme!

* * *

V svetle krajšej budúcnosti
    Zkvitá "Omladina"
Púta k sebe nadšeného
    Slovenského syna;

A ku práci sa už chystá
    Mladistvá rodina,
"Živena" nám srdcom velie
    Umom "Omladina!"

Preto zriaďme šíky svoje,
    A k činom sa majme;
Milujme rod i reč našu:
    Padnuť jej nedajme!

* * *

A keď i "Matička" drahá
    Stán svoj upevnila
By synom i dcéram svojim
    Rozkvet dožičila:

Na zveľatku nášho rodu
    Vzájomne pracujme,
A národu čistú lásku
    I vernosť venujme!

Preto zriaďme šíky svoje,
    A k činom sa majme;
Milujme rod i reč našu
    Padnuť jej nedajme!
        Anna Philadelfi
            Orol, 2.1 (31 January 1871): 22.

Mária Praisingerová (? –)   No pseudonym

Rizner (4: 158) lists her and says she came from Moravia and was the ward of Martin Branislav Tamaškovič in Trnava. Tamaškovič (1803–1872), a minor nationalist poet and supporter of Slovak and Czech nationalists (*Ency. slov. spis.* 2: 184), married Mária Dobšová, but it is not known how he met Praisingerová. In 1869 she contributed to the Slovak gymnázium in Zniov (Biog. odd. MS). She was apparently Catholic, which makes her exceptional among Slovak women writers. The reference to Martin at the end of the poem refers to establishment of the women's organization Živena.

    114. Slovenkám (To Slovak Women)

    Hoj Slovenky, sestry! očujme "Hlásnika",

Keď nás volá k práci, k mužským za párnika.
Však nie skaly lámať a nie krovy stavať:
Len národ svoj ľúbiť, práva mu zastávať.
Slovenky, Slovenky, sestry drahé milé,
Buďteže mladuchy roda ušľachtilé!
Prečo nechcete mať národ za ženicha,
Ktorý tak za vašou láskou boľne vzdychá.
Ku nemu sa viňme s ochotou velikou
Tam najdeme bratov statných bojovníkov!
V ňom najdeme všetko, ale málo chlúby,
Ktorú u národov včulajší svet ľúbi.
Teda túto chlúbu dokážme my dcéry,
Že sme hodné jeho lásky i dôvery.
Že ho milujeme, že ho rady máme,
Že na jeho sláve pracovať hodláme.
Poďme teda všetky, kde nás "Hlásnik" volá;
Za ním do Martina, do ženského kola!
V Trnave, 20 junia. Mária Praisingerovie
Národní hlásnik 2.7 (1869): 206.

Klema Augustiny Ruppeldtová (1850–1926)   "Slovenka"
Rizner (1: 50, 4: 298) lists her separately under her maiden and married names, and does not include the letter she wrote to *Dom a škola* (Chapter 3, n.26). She was the wife of the nationalist teacher, writer, and musician Karol Ruppeldt (1840–1909), and her father Peter and brothers Gustáv and Bohdan were literarily active (*Slov. biog. slov.*, 1: 85–86). She became an official of Živena.

115. Za milým (To My Darling)

Zaleť vtáča zaleť
  Za tie hory doly,
Povedz tam milému
  Že ma láska morí.

Ani mi je z hora,
  Ani mi je z dola,
Len ako bez seba
  Chodím von do poľa.

Ani mi je večer

Ani mi je ráno
Pre teba milý môj
Stvorenie daromnô.

Ani mi je v chyži
Ani mi v zahrade,
Kde sa len obrátim
Vidím teba všade.

Len mi je tak bôlno
Koľ srdca mojeho,
Že som tak ďaleko
Od môjho milého.
      Klema Augustiny
Živena Národní almanach 1 (1872): 29.

116. Ej keby vedela (If My Mother Knew)

Ej keby vedela—
Tá moja mamička,
Prečo tak obľadly
Moje pekné líčka.

Ej keby vedela—
Tá moja mamička,
Prečo často plačú
Moje sivé očká.

Ej keby vedela—
Tá moja mamička,
Prečo mňa nechala
Tá moja vôlička.

Ej keby vedela—
Tá moja mamička,
Prečo mňa tak často
Bolieva hlavička.

Preto mňa hlavička
Tak často bolieva,
Že—chodil šuhaj k nám
A—už nechodieva.
      Klema Augustiny
Živena Národní almanach 1 (1872): 33–34.

117. Jedličkám (To Fir Trees)
Ej, horička jedlinová,
Však si štihlá, krásna!
V stredku tvojom lipka dumá —
Zdá sa, že je šťastná. —
Bo keď príde jaseň šutá,
Lipy listie zprchá;
Ty ho skryješ sťa hriešnika,
Čo pred nocou prchá.
Nepostihne lístok zletieť,
Ajhľa, padá iný,
Všetkým dajú dobrú nocľah
Tvoje baldachýny.
Ťahá, svádza, k sebe zove
Tôňa tvoja šerá,
Koho suďba dozrážala,
Lebo sovesť zžiera. —
Ach, a ten tvoj šelesť dumný,
Bájny, tajuplný,
Citné srdce rozčuluje,
Tklivú dušu zvlní.
A že nikdy nezablískaš
V plnom ruže-kvete,
Piesne, že si pozvädala,
Nenájdeš vo svete.
K tomu lúbiš samotenku
Ako orol skalný —
Hej, ako ten môj orlíčok
Falošný a dialny. —
   Klementina R.
Slovenské pohľady 6.1 (1886): 8.

Terézia Medvecká Vansová (1857–1942)   "Terézka M."
    Vansová is treated extensively in Chapters 3–4 on her organizational activities and her prose works. Her father, Samuel Medvecký, a lawyer in Zvolen, belonged to a gentry family with at least slightly literary women. He or his family preserved the verses in Nos.4–29, and "Sophia" (Nos.47–49) may have been Sophia Medvecká, who collected verses for Ján Kollár's songbook.

118–123. Moje piesne (My Songs)

I.

O samote smutne pejem
Sebe pieseň tichú,
O ktorej svet chladný, klamný
Nedočuje slýchu. —
Len tu i tu tón pieseňky
Temnejšie zazvučí —
Ach a to vzdych len hlboký
Žiaľu spievať učí.

II.

Piesne moje, piesne moje,
Tichunko mi z duše plynú:
Útlym citom, dumným znením
Len ku dobrým nech sa vinú.

III.

Útla fijalôčka
Hlávku si zklonila,
Sťa by na zem chladnú
Slzu vyronila; —
Slzu vyronila —
Tažkosťou zronená, —
Jako je neverným
Šuhajom zklamaná!

IV.

Padá lísťa po doline,
Leta krása mizne, hynie,
Hynie — — oj, ale sa vráti — —
Prijde — — čo sa teraz tratí.

Padajú i slzy moje
Srdce tratí lístky svoje —
Veselosť srdca sa tratí — — —
Hynie, čo sa viac nevráti.

V.

Prečo som vraj taká chladná,
Mnohí sa ma spýtali,
A ja som jim odvetila

Vzdychom, by ma nechali.
Radšej nech som vám ja chladná
Lež city svoje sverit' vám, —
Čo cítim nerozumiete,
Čože sa vám sdieľať mám?!

VI.

Piesne moje nie sú skvostne
Exotické byliny,
Ktoré ľudia obdivujúc
Donášajú z cudziny.
Moje piesne sú len skromné
Hôrne z úbočia kvietky,
Ktoré baviac si trhajú — —
Nevinné útle dietky.
Sú to plody rozochvenej
Mladistvej mysli mojej,
V nich zložil duch srdca city
K národu lásky svojej.
Venujem jich bratom svojim,
Ktorí za vlasť pracujú,
Venujem jich sestrám milým,
Ktoré národ milujú.
Piesňou kroťme žiale, boje
A tíšme túžby srdca, —
Láska všetkých nech nás spája
A Bôh budiž nám vodca!

    Terézka M.
    Orol 6.10 (1875): 263–264.

NOTES

1. Eugen Pauliny, *Dejiny spisovnej slovenčiny od začiatkov po súčasnosť* (Bratislava: Slovenské pedagogické nakladateľstvo, 1983) 198.

2. The following dictionaries of pseudonyms were consulted: Štefan Hanakovič et al., *Slovník slovenských pseudonymov* (Martin: Matica slovenská, 1961); Dezider Kormúth, *Slovník slovenských pseudonymov 1919–1944* (Martin: Matica slovenská, 1974); Ján V.

Ormis, *Slovník slovenských pseudonymov* (Martin: Slovenská národná knižnica, 1944); and Jaroslav Vopravil, *Slovník pseudonymů v české a slovenské literatuře* (Prague: Státní pedagogické nakladatelství, 1973).

3. A note in the original says Wepor is a peak near the southern town of Klenovec.

4. "Rymavská" is written in the margin by a different hand.

5. The word *ptáčj* is crossed out and the word *ptaci* is written in.

6. The word *swatý* is crossed out and given at the end of the line.

7. A note in the original says that *sirôtky* (little orphans) is a name for early violets in Gemer.

8. *Phar-hára* is a pejorative form of *farár* (pastor).

9. A note identifies him as Kornel Dobriansky, a candidate for the regional assembly.

(English text translated by Norma L. Rudinsky)

WORKS CITED

The following list covers most of the sources used here. However, the poems treated in Chapter 2 are given chronologically under their authors' names with full bibliographical data in the Appendix, and all of the poets in the Appendix are listed alphabetically in the Index. Therefore their works are not repeated here. Secondary references in the Appendix are included below.

Primary Sources:
Bachát, Daniel. "Ani to čert nevymyslí, Čo žena má v svojej mysli!" *Černokňažník* 2 (1862): 45–46, 60–62, 65–66, 74–75, and 81–83.
— . "Bohumil." *Národní hlásnik* 1.9 (30 September 1868): 208–212.
— . "Ľudmilka." *Národní hlásnik* 1.6 (30 June 1868): 138–142.
— . "Naša nová pieseň." *Sokol* 1.11 (15 August 1860): [85].
— . "Ozwena z Liptowa." *Národní hlásnik* 2.6 (June 1869): 173–175.
Banšell, Koloman. "Emancipovaná." *Živena: Národní Almanach* 1 (1872): 67–89.
Bílý, Jan Ev. "Osud ženy v pohanstvu a ve křesťanstvu." *Cyrill a Method* 3.5 (1854): 34–36.
Čajak, Janko. "Moderná Slovenka." *Sokol* 1.2 (15 May 1860): 9–10.
Chalupka, Ján. *Dobrovoľníci. Výber z diela v dvoch zväzkoch.* 2 vols. Bratislava: Slovenské vydavateľstvo krásnej literatúry, 1950. 2: 287–339.
Chrástek, Michal. "Nekoľko slov o vychovávaní vúbec, a zvlášte pohlavia ženského." *Cyrill a Method* 1.37 (18 September 1852): 299–300 and 1.38 (25 September 1852): 309–311.
Cykáni, anebo Nessťastný Ferdynand ... Amálie Westonská. Tábor: Aloizyus Jozef Landfras, 1835. 62 pp.
Drašković, Janko. *Staršt dějepis a nejnowější literarní obnowa národu ilirského.* Prague: Jar. Pospíšil, 1845. 72 pp.
Feldeková, Oľga. *Veverica.* Bratislava: Slovenský spisovateľ, 1985.
Figuli, Margita. *Tri gaštanové kone.* Martin: Matica slovenska, 1940.
Frič, Milan. "O ženskej otázke." *Dennica* 10.1 (January 1907): 22–25.
Gregorová, Hana. *Oživená nádej.* Ed. Karol Rosenbaum. Bratislava: Tatran, 1985.

Haľamová, Maša. *Červený mak.* Prague: Leopold Mazáč, 1932.
Hodžová, Marína. *Listy Maríny M. Hodžovej Viliamovi Paulinymu-Tóthovi.* Ed. Peter Liba. Martin: Matica slovenská, 1965.
Homola, Štefan. "Ústavi pre vichovávanja ďjevčat." *Slovenskje národňje novini* 70 (31 March 1846): 277–278.
Hurban, Jozef Miloslav. *Cesta Slováka k slovanským bratom na Moravu a v Čechách, 1839.* 1841. Bratislava: Slovenské vydavateľstvo krásnej literatúry, 1960.
— . "Opis Liptova." *Nitra* 4 (1847): 38–39.
— . "Slowenka." *Kwěty* 6.32 (5 May 1839): 181.
— . "Slowenka." *Nitra* 1 (1842): 168–169.
— , ed. *Nitra: Dar dcerám a synům Slovenska, Moravy, Čech a Slezska.* 1 (1842).
— , ed. *Nitra.* 2 (1844).
Kálal, Karel. "Dopisy." *Dennica* 1.1 (January 1898): 14–15.
— . "Ženská otázka." *Dom a škola* 12.10 (1896): 311–315.
Kello, Juraj. *Národní hlásnik* 2.9 (September 1869): 274–275.
— . "Reč." *Národní hlásnik* 2.11 (November 1869): 340–342.
Kollár, Ján. *Národnie zpievanky čili Písně swětské Slowákůw v Uhrách gak pospolitého lidu tak i Wyššjch stawů....* 2 vols. Budin, 1834–1835.
— . *Slávy dcera*, in *Na lutnu.* Ed. Cyril Kraus. Bratislava: Tatran, 1986. 142–245.
Krčméry, August H. "Hlas k dcerám Slovenska." *Sokol* 1.10 (1862): 390–392.
Križan, Štefan. "Milan a Milina." *Sokol* 1.4–9 (1862): 118+.
Lehocká, Johana. "Listy Johany Miloslavy Lehockej Bohuslave Rajskej a Samoslavovi Bohdanovi Hroboňovi." *Literárny archív* 7 (1970): 143–169.
— . "Z Liptova." *Slovenskje národňje novini* 83 (1846): 330–331.
Letter. *Národní hlásnik* 2.6 (June 1869): 176–177.
Lojková, Zuzína R. Zajac. *Dobré dieťa poklad rodičov.* Martin: J. Gašparík, 1924.
Mallý, Ján. "Vzdělanosť se zvláštním ohledem na ženské pohlaví." *Cyrill a Method* 2.18 (30 April 1853): 136–139.
Moštenanová, Hermína. "Opica čo zkúmatel lásky." *Živena: Národní almanach* 1 (1872): 90–95.
Nosák, Bohuslav. "Slowenka." *Nitra* 1 (1842): 162–165.
Obituary of Johana Lehocká. *Slovenské noviny* 1 (1 January 1850): 4.

Obituary of Karolina Pulíny. *Národnie noviny* 19.16 (7 February 1888): 3.
Pietor, Ambro. "Slovenkám." *Národní hlásnik* 2.5 (May 1869): 143–146.
— . "Slovenkám: Zakladajme miestne spolky ženské." *Národní hlásnik* 2.11 (November 1869): 337–339.
— . "Spolok slovenských žien." *Pešťbudínske vedomosti* 9 (June 2, 1869): [unpaged, 2].
Podjavorinská, Ľudmila Riznerová. *Dielo*. Bratislava: Tatran, 1987.
— . *Z vesny života*. Ružomberok: Karol Salva, 1895.
Pospíšilová, Maria. "Sen" and "Ginocha žel." *Kwěty* 5.9 (1 March 1838): 65, and 5.44 (1 November 1838): 351.
Rigellová, Luiza. "Slovenkám." *Dennica* 2.6 (June 1899): 18–19.
Rožnay, Samuel. "Plésání," in *Na lutnu*. Ed. Cyril Kraus. Bratislava: Tatran, 1986. 85–86.
Ruppeldtová, Klementina Augustiny. *Dom a škola*. 13.1 (January 1897): 20–21.
Rusnáková, M. "Vodná ľalia." *Dennica* 2.5 (May 1899): 73–76; "Neverník." *Dennica* 3.5/6 (May/June 1900): 97–100; and "Čajový večierok." *Dennica* 3.11 (November 1900): 198–203, 3.12 (December 1900): 211–212.
Šafárik, Pavol Jozef. *Basnické spisy*. Ed. Jan Vilikovský. Bratislava: Učené Společnosti Šafařikovy, 1930.
"Sestrám Slovenkám sestry Češky." *Národní hlásnik* 2.6 (June 1869): 175–177.
Selecký, Štefan Ferdinand. "Obraz panej krásnej, perem malovaný, která má v Trnave svoje prebývání." 1701. *Z klenotnice staršieho slovenského písomníctva. 3.Antológia barokových literárnych textov. 1.Poésia*. Ed. Jozef Minárik. Bratislava: Tatran, 1989. 265–275.
Sládkovič, Andrej. *Sobrané básne*. Martin: Matica slovenská, 1939.
Sokolová-Seidlová, Vilma. "Slovenky—naše nejbližší sestry." *Ženský svět* 1.2 (1897): 24–25; 1.6 (1897): 9–10; 1.10 (1897): 146–147.
— . "Z mých vzpomínek na Slovensko." *Slovenské pohľady* 45 (1929): 453–483.
Šoltésová, Elena Maróthy. "Načo sú tie ženské časopisy?" *Dennica* 1.2 (February 1898): 17–19.

—. *Pohľady na literatúre.* Ed. I. Kusý. Bratislava: Slovenské vydavateľstvo krásnej literatúry, 1958.
—. "Popolka." *Letopis Živeny* 2 (1898): 7–96.
—. "Potreba vzdelanosti pre ženu, zvlášť so stanoviska mravnosti." *Letopis Živeny* 2 (1898): 154–190.
—. "Prvé previnenie." *Letopis Živeny* 1 (1896): 38–81.
—. *Sobrané spisy.* 6 vols. Martin: Kníhtlačiarsky účastinársky spolok, 1921–1925.
—. *Začatá cesta.* Ed. Lea Mrázová. Martin: Živena, 1934.
Štěpánek, Hynek. "Ženská otázka a ženské hnutí." *Dennica* 5.1 (January 1902): 14–19 and 5.2 (February 1902): 35–38.
Štúr, Ľudovít. *Dielo.* Vol. 1. Bratislava: Slovenské vydavateľstvo krásnej literatúry, 1954.
Světlá, Karolina. *První Češka.* 1861. Prague: Jos. R. Vilímek, 1948.
Textorisová, Izabela. "Zásvit." *Dívčí svět.* Ed. Vilma Sokolová. Prague: F. Šimáček, 1893. 251–279.
—. Unpublished correspondence. Fond Vilma Sokolová-Seidlová 34/40. Památník národního písemnictví in Prague.
Tichá, Lidmila. "Zdálená." *Kwěty* 5.11 (15 March 1838): 81.
Timrava, Božena Slančíková. *Timrava.* 2 vols. Bratislava: Tatran, 1975.
—. *Zobrané spisy.* Ed. Ivan Kusy. 7 vols. Bratislava: Slovenské vydavateľstvo krásnej literatúry, 1955–1959.
Uram, Rehor, ed. "Zemianskí veršovníci slovenskí." *Slovenské pohľady* 14–15 (1894–1895): 624 + [See Appendix]
Vadkerti-Gavorníková, Lýdia. *Trvanie.* Bratislava: Slovenský spisovateľ, 1979.
—. *Vino.* Bratislava: Slovenský spisovateľ, 1982.
Vajanský, Svetozár Hurban. "Reč tajomníka." *Národnie noviny* 33 (7 August 1902): 2–3.
—. *Spisy.* 13 [projected] vols. Bratislava: Tatran, 1984– .
Vansová, Terézia. "Hojže Bože!" *Od Šumavy k Tatrám.* Ed. K. Salva and K. Kálal. Ružomberok, 1898. 102–125.
—. "Nový rok, nový krok." *Dennica* 1.1 (January 1898: 2–3.
—. "O nás." *Dennica* 1.1 (January 1898): 11–12.
—. "Pila v Gemeri. (Sestrám slovenským)." *Dom a škola* 13.4 (1897): 127.
—. "Prosba k našim dámam." *Dennica* 1.4 (April 1898): 52–55.

—. *Sirota Podhradských*. *Sobrané spisy*. Vol.8. Liptovský Mikuláš: Tranoscius, 1947.
—. "Stará pieseň." *Slovenské pohľady* 18.3 (1898): 154–161, and 10.4 (1898): 193–209.
—. "Supplikant." *Živena: Národní Almanach* 2 (1885): 17–67.
—. "Vlčia tma." *Sobrané spisy*. Vol. 1. Martin: Tatran, 1923. 61–131.
—. "Ženské hnutí. Poznámka redakcie." *Dennica* 5.2 (February 1902): 34–35.
Villani, Karel Ignac. "Wlastenkynym k Nowému Roku." *Kwěty* 5 (January 1838): 5.
Wagner, Ján A. "Umenie, veda a literatúra." *Národnie noviny* 26 (3 February 1898).
Zniovský, Jaroslav [pseud.?]. "Z Kláštor pod Zvievom." *Orol* 2.11 (30 November 1871): 349–353.
Zoch, Ivan Br. "Hostivít Gustáv Lojko." *Orol* 2.10 (30 October 1871): 292–295.

Secondary and General References:
Abel, Elizabeth, Marianne Hirsch, and Elizabeth Langland, eds. *The Voyage In*. Hannover, NH: University Press of New England, 1983.
Auty, Robert. "Dialect, Koiné, and Tradition in the Formation of Literary Slovak." *Slavonic and East European Review* 39 (1961): 339–345.
—. "Jan Kollár, 1793–1852." *Slavonic and East European Review* (December 1952): 74–91.
Bainton, Roland H. *Women of the Reformation in Germany and Italy*. Minneapolis: Augsberg Publishing House, 1971.
Ballová, Jozefína. "Chronológia autorkinho života a diela." *Dielo* by Ľudmila Podjavorinská. Bratislava: Tatran, 1987. 576–589.
Bartalská, Ľubica. "K začiatkom organizovania sa slovenských žien v Spojených Štátoch amerických." *Slováci v zahraniči* 11 (1985): 135–147.
Bodický, Michal. *Životopis Jána Kollára*. Ružomberok: Karol Salva, 1893.

Bosak, Edita. "Czech-Slovak Relations and the Student Organisation Detvan, 1882–1914." *Slovak Politics*. Cleveland: Slovak Institute, 1983. 6–36.
— . "The Slovak National Movement, 1848–1914." *Reflections on Slovak History*. Toronto: Slovak World Congress, 1987. 59–72.
Boxer, Marilyn J., and Jean H. Quataert, eds. *Socialist Women: European Socialist Feminism in the Nineteenth and Early Twentieth Centuries*. New York: Elsevier, 1978.
— , eds. *Connecting Spheres: Women in the Western World 1500 to the Present*. New York: Oxford U P, 1987.
Brock, Peter. *The Slovak National Awakening*. Toronto: U of Toronto P, 1976.
Brtáň, Rudo. "Torzo Hurbanovej Nitry 1843." *Slovenská literatúra* 12.5 (1965): 597–530.
— . "Z kultúrnej a literárnej činnosti Mikulášťanov a Liptákov v 16.–18. storočia." *Liptovský Mikuláš*. Liptovský Mikuláš, 1968.
Čapek, Jan B. *Československá literatura toleranční 1781–1861*. Vol. 1. Prague: Čin (Tiskové a nakladatelské družstvo československých legionářů), 1933.
Chovan, Juraj, ed. *Pamätnica z osláv dvojstého vyročia narodenia Jána Hollého*. Martin: Matica slovenská, 1985.
Cincura, Andrew, ed. *An Anthology of Slovak Literature*. Riverside: University Hardcovers, 1976.
Dějiny české literatury. Vol. 3. Prague: ČSAV, 1961.
Dejiny slovenskéj literatúry. 5 vols. Bratislava: Veda, 1958–1984.
Dejiny Slovenska. 6 vols. Bratislava: Veda, 1985–1989.
Deme, Laszlo. "Writers and Essayists and the Rise of Magyar Nationalism in the 1820s and 1830s." *Slavic Review* 43 (Winter 1984): 638–639.
Despalatovic, Elinor Murray. *Ljudevit Gaj and the Illyrian Movement*. Boulder: East European Monographs, 1975.
Ďurovič, Ľubomír. "Slovak." *The Slavic Literary Languages*. Eds. Alexander M. Schenker and Edward Stankiewicz. New Haven: Yale Concilium on International and Area Studies, 1980. 211–228.
Eliaš, Michal. "Problémy Kollárovej biografie." *Biografické štúdie* 6 (1976): 103–139.
Encyklopédia Slovenska. 6 vols. Bratislava: Veda, 1977–1982.

Encyklopédia slovenských spisovateľov. 2 vols. Bratislava: Obzor, 1984.
Engel, Barbara Alpern. *Mothers and Daughters: Women of the Intelligentsia in Nineteenth-Century Russia.* Cambridge: Cambridge U P, 1983.
Eterovich, Francis H., ed. *Croatia: Land, People, Culture.* 2 vols. Toronto: U of Toronto P, 1970.
Fáylné-Hentaller, Mariska. *A Magyar irónőkről.* Budapest, 1889.
Gáfrik, Michal. "Timrava a slovenská moderna." *Slovenská literatúra* 15 (1968): 174–179.
Gilbert, Sandra M., and Susan Gubar. *The Madwoman in the Attic.* New Haven: Yale U P, 1979.
Hanakovič, Štefan et al. *Slovník slovenských pseudonymov.* Martin: Matica slovenská, 1961.
Handzová, Želmíra, ed. *Múdrosť a skromnosť idú spolu: Elena Maróthy Šoltésová.* Martin: Osveta, 1989.
Harkins, William E. "Vajansky and Turgenev." *Slovakia* 30 (1982–1983): 92–99.
Heldt, Barbara. *Terrible Perfection.* Bloomington: Indiana U P, 1987.
Holotíková, Zdena. "Zástoj ženy v zápase pracujúceho človeka." *Zborník materiálov zo sympózia '100 rokov uvedomelého pohybu žien v dejinách slovenského národa,' 27–28 November 1968.* Bratislava: Živena, 1968. 23–33.
Horna, Jarmila L. A. "Current Literature on the Position and Roles of Women in Czechoslovakia." *Canadian Slavonic Papers* 20 (March 1978): 70–90.
Hučko, Ján. *Sociálne zloženie a pôvod slovenskej obrodenskej inteligencie.* Bratislava: Veda, 1974.
Hufton, Olwen, and Frank Tallett. "Communities of Women, the Religious Life, and Public Service in Eighteenth-Century France." *Connecting Spheres.* New York: Oxford U P, 1987. 75–85.
Jesenská, Zora. "O Maríne Hodžovej." *Živena* 31 (1941): 142–144.
Jílek, Václav. "R–a L–ová v Puchmajerových 'Nových básních' z r. 1798 je Rebeka Lešková." *Listy filologické* 54 (1927): 267–270.
Jozef Gregor Tajovský v kritike a spomienkach. Bratislava: Slovenské vydavateľstvo krásnej literatúry, 1956.

Kabelík, Jan. *Rodina pěvce Slávy dcera.* Prague: Pražské akciové tiskárny, 1928.
Kaššayová, Terézia, ed. "Personálna bibliografia Eleny Maróthy-Šoltésovej." *Elena Maróthy-Šoltésová.* Martin: Matica slovenská, 1987. 195–243.
Kimball, S. B. "The Austro-Slav Revival: A Study of Nineteenth-century Literary Foundations." *Trans. Amer. Phil. Soc.*, NS 63 (1973): 3–83.
Kirschbaum, J. M. *Slovak Language and Literature.* Winnipeg: U of Manitoba, 1975.
Kleinschnitzová, Flóra. "O Johane Miloslave Lehockej." *Živena* 23 (1933): 134–138.
— . *Z našej romantiky.* Bratislava: Slovenský spisovateľ, 1958.
Klementis, Eugen, ed. "Listy Johany Miloslavy Lehockej Bohuslave Rajskej a Samoslavovi Bohdanovi Hroboňovi." *Literárny archív* 7 (1970): 143–169.
Kochol, Victor. *Problémy a postavy slovenskej obrodeneckej literatúry.* Bratislava: SAV, 1965.
Kormúth, Dezider. *Slovník slovenských pseudonymov 1919–1944.* Martin: Matica slovenská, 1974.
Kovtun, George J. *Czech and Slovak Literature in English.* Washington, D.C.: Library of Congress, 1984.
Kraus, Cyril. "Kollár a štúrovci." *Biografické štúdie* 6 (1976): 61–72.
— , ed. *Na lutnu: Výber zo slovenskej klasicistickej poézie.* Bratislava: Tatran, 1986.
Krčméry, Štefan. Dejiny literatúry slovenskej. Ed. Ján Števček and Emília Nemsilová. 2 vols. Bratislava: Tatran, 1976.
Kusý, Ivan. "Timrava (K periodizácii jej diela)." *Timrava v kritike a spomienkach: Sborník.* Bratislava: Slovenské vydavateľstvo krásnej literatúry, 1958. 471–489.
— . "Timrava (Život a dielo)." *Timrava v kritike a spomienkach: Sborník.* Bratislava: Slovenské vydavateľstvo krásnej literatúry, 1958. 260–283.
Lauter, Estelle, and Carol Schreier Rupprecht, eds. *Feminist Archetypal Theory.* Knoxville: U of Tennessee P, 1985.
Liba, Peter, ed. *Listy Viliama Pauliny-Tótha Maríne Hodžovej.* Bratislava: Slovenské vydavateľstvo krásnej literatúry, 1961.
— , ed. *Listy Maríny M. Hodžovej Viliamovi Paulinymu-Tóthovi.* Martin: Matica slovenská, 1965.

The Linden Tree. Prague: Artia, 1962.
Makkai, Laszlo. "Istvan Bocskai's Insurrectionary Army." *From Hunyadi to Rakoczi.* Ed. Janos M. Bak and Bela K. Kiraly. New York: Brooklyn College P, 1982.
Matuška, Alexander. "Timrava." *Timrava v kritike a spomienkach: Sborník.* Bratislava: Slovenské vydavateľstvo krásnej literatúry, 1958. 490–431.
Mikušťáková, Anna. "Žena v slovenskej literatúre (Literárne a kultúrno-umelecké počiatky ženského hnutia na Slovensku)," Dissertation Education Faculty, Nitra, Czechoslovakia, 1987, 148 pp.
Miller, Nancy K. *The Heroine's Text.* New York: Columbia U P, 1980.
Minárik, Jozef. *Baroková literatúra.* Bratislava: Slovenské pedagogické nakladateľstvo, 1984.
— . *Renesančná a humanistická literatúra.* Bratislava: Slovenské pedagogické nakladateľstvo, 1985.
Mišianik, Ján. *Bibliografia slovenského písomníctva do konca XIX. stor. (Doplnky k Riznerovej bibliografii, sv I.–VI.)* 2nd ed. Martin: Matica slovenská, 1971.
Moers, Ellen. *Literary Women.* Garden City, NY: Doubleday, 1976.
Moon, S. Joan. "Feminism and Socialism: The Utopian Synthesis of Flora Tristan." *Socialist Women.* Ed. Marilyn J. Boxer and Jean H. Quataert. New York: Elsevier, 1978. 19–50.
Nagy, Iván. *Magyarország családai.* Vol. 6. Budapest, 1859.
Newton, Judith Lowder. *Power and Subversion: Social Strategies in British Fiction, 1778–1860.* Athens: U of Georgia P, 1981.
Noge, Július. *An Outline of Slovakian Literature.* Bratislava: Tatrapress, 1966.
Novák, Jozef. *Rodové erby na Slovensku II.* Bratislava: Osveta, 1986.
Ormis, Ján. *Doplnky a opravy k Riznerovej bibliografii.* Martin: Matica slovenská, 1972.
— . "Kto bola Rimavská Slovenka?" *Obzor Gemera* 7 (1976): 191–192.
— . "Novozistené pseudonymy z polstoročia 1842–1893." *Bibliografický sborník.* Martin: Matica slovenská, 1962. 203–210.

—. *Slovník slovenských pseudonymov.* Martin: Slovenská národná knižnica, 1944.
Pauliny, Eugen. "Štruktúra Timravinej poviedky Nemilí." *Timrava v kritike a spomienkach: Sborník.* Bratislava: Slovenské vydavateľstvo krásnej literatúry, 1958. 674–693.
—. *Dejiny spisovnej slovenčiny od začiatkov po súčasnosť.* Bratislava: Slovenské pedagogické nakladateľstvo, 1983.
Pišút, Milan. "Klasicizmus (roky dvadsiate a tridsiate)." *Dejiny slovenskej literatúry.* Ed. Milan Pišút et al. Bratislava: Obzor, 1984.
Pokrokové ženské hnutie na Slovensku 1918–1980. Bratislava: Ústredný výbor Slovenského zväzu žien, 1984.
Pope, Barbara Corrado. "The Influence of Rousseau's Ideology of Domesticity." *Connecting Spheres.* Ed. Marilyn J. Boxer and Jean H. Quataert. New York: Oxford U P, 1987. 136–145.
Pratt, Annis. *Archetypal Patterns in Women's Literature.* Bloomington: Indiana U P, 1961.
Rapant, Daniel. *K počiatkom maďarizácie.* 2 vols. Bratislava: Československé zemedelské muzeum, 1927, 1931.
Rizner, Ľudovít V. *Bibliografia písomníctva slovenského od najstarších čias do konca r. 1900.* 6 vols. Martin: Matica slovenská, 1929.
Rose, Mary Beth. "Introduction" and "Gender, Genre, and History: Seventeenth Century English Women and the Art of Autobiography." *Women in the Middle Ages and Renaissance.* Syracuse: Syracuse U P, 1986.
Rudinsky, Norma L. *The Context of the Marxist-Leninist View of Slovak Literature 1945–1969.* No. 505 Carl Beck Papers in Russian and East European Studies, University of Pittsburgh, 1986. 34 pp.
—. "Early Women Writers," in Panel 3-03 "Baroque Writing in Slovakia." AAASS Convention, Chicago, 2 November 1989.
—. "The Matica slovenská and Its Relation to the Development of Slovak Literature." *Slovakia* 31 (1984): 47–57.
—. "National Antiheroes: Symbolism and Narrative Voice as Coded National Identity in Oľga Feldeková's *Veverica*. *Modern Slovak Prose Fiction since 1954.* Ed. R. B. Pynsent. London: Macmillan, 1990. 205–214.

—. "Preliminary Notes on Martin Kukučín's Criticism of Americanized Slovaks and his Opposition to the Slovak Gentry." *Slovak Studies* 18 (1978): 153–165.
—. "Recent Prose of Hana Ponická and Oľga Feldeková." *Recent Developments in East European Literature.* Ed. Celia Hawkesworth. London: Macmillan, in press.
Ruppeldtová, Klema Augustiny. "Marína Hodžová." *Živena* 11.3 (1921): 57–58.
Sárdi, Margit S. *Petrőczy Kata Szidónia költészete.* Budapest: Akadémiai Kiadó, 1976
Seton-Watson, R. W. *A History of the Czechs and Slovaks.* London: Hutchinson and Co. Ltd., 1943.
Slovenský biografický slovník. 7 vols. [projected] Martin: Matica slovenská, 1986– . [Vols. 1–3 have appeared so far]
Srogoň, Tomáš. *Samuel Ormis: Život a dielo.* Bratislava: Slovenské pedagogické nakladateľstvo, 1976.
Stites, Richard. *The Women's Liberation Movement in Russia.* Princeton: Princeton U P, 1978.
Strmen, Karol. "Slovak Literature: A Brief History." *An Anthology of Slovak Literature.* Comp. Andrew Cincura. Riverside: University Hardcovers, 1976). xix–liv.
Svoreňová-Királyová, Blanka. "Emancipačné hnutie v druhej polovici 19. storočia a na začiatku 20. storočia: (Náčrt filozofického a ekonomického zázemie)." *Zborník materiálov zo sympózia '100 rokov uvedomelého pohybu žien v dejinách slovenského národa.'* Bratislava: Živena, 1968. 71–77.
Sziklay, Lászlo. "Maďarské vzťahy Jána Kollára v Pešti." *Dějiny a národy: Literárněhistorické studie o československo-maďarských vztazích.* Prague: ČSAV, 1965.
Szinnyei, József. *Magyar írók élete és munkái.* 16 vols. Budapest, 1891–1914.
Tibenský, Ján. "Úloha Jána Kollára v slovenskom národnom obrodení a hnutí." *Biografické štúdie* 6 (1976): 42–50.
Tkadlečková-Vantuchová, Jarmila. *Živena—spolok slovenskych žien.* Bratislava: Epocha, 1969.
Václaviková-Matulay, Margita. *Tvorba Ľudmily Podjavorinskej.* Bratislava: Nakladateľstvo Cas, [1942]. [This is the same author as Velehrachová below.]
—. *Život Terézie Vansovej.* Bratislava: Nakladateľstvo Slovenskej Ligy, 1937.

Varsik, Branislav. *Otázky vzniku a vývinu slovenského zemianstva.* Bratislava: Veda, 1988.
Velehrachová, Margita. *Izabela Textorisová: Zo života slovenskej botaničky.* Bratislava: Mladé leta, 1975.
Vongrej, Pavol. *Diamant v hrude.* Martin: Matica slovenská, 1970.
Vopravil, Jaroslav. *Slovník pseudonymů v české a slovenské literature.* Prague: Státní pedagogické nakladatelství, 1973.
Votrubová, Štefánia. *Živena: jej osudy a praca.* Martin: Živena, 1931.
Willard, Charity Cannon. "Christine de Pizan: The Franco-Italian Professional Writer." *Medieval Women Writers.* Ed. Katharina M. Wilson. Athens: U of Georgia P, 1984. 222–363.
Wilson, Katharina M., ed. Introduction. *Medieval Women Writers.* Athens: U of Georgia P, 1984.
— , ed. "Žofia Kubini, Ľudmila Podjavorinská, Božena Slančíková Timrava, Elena Maróthy Šoltésová." *Dictionary of Continental Women Writers.* New York: Garland, in press.
Zborník materiálov zo sympózia '100 rokov uvedomelého pohybu žien v dejinách slovenského národa,' 27–28 novembra 1968. Bratislava: Živena, 1968.

INDEX

Amerling, Karel Slavoj: 32, 37, 64
"Angel in the house": See Woman's place
"Anička": 53, 227–228
Apotheosis of woman: as muse 11, 17, 21, 114; as nation by Kollár 17–19, 23, 27, 55, by Sládkovič 22–24, 27, 55, by Vajanský 112–113. See also Overidealization of women
Archetypal criticism: useful with Timrava 169–170, 175
Astell, Mary: 167
Augustiny, Klema: See Ruppeldtová
Austen, Jane: 170–171, 174
Bachát, Daniel: 50, 53, 56, 64 n.29, 67 n.52, 79, 223
Banšell, Koloman: 176
Barrett Browning, Elizabeth: 52
Beblavý, Pavol: 251
Bernolák, Anton: 29, 85–86, 184
Bílý, Jan: 40
Blok, Liubov': See Overidealization of women
Bobula, Ján Nepomuk: 54, 58, 254
Bobulová, Mária Pozdechová: 254–257
Bóriková Kulišková, Anna: 251
Botto, Ján: 21, 64 n.29, 185
Braxatoris, Martin: 248
Brigand heroes: Ján Botto, Samo Chalupka, Janko Kráľ, 21
Brontë, Charlotte: 106, 174
Byronism: 21

Capko, Ján: 40
Carbortrany, Catherine: 17
Celibacy: among Štúrists 60; as sacrifice for nation 59–60, 168–170. See also Heroines, spinster type
Chaloupecká, Ľudmila Groeblová: 162, 166 n.12
Chaloupecký, Václav: 166 n.12
Chalupka Ján: 50
Chalupka, Samo: 21, 185
Chrástek, Michal: 39
Christian doctrine: language of, in nationalism 73, 77, 128–129; on education of women 39–40, 42, 128; on equality of sexes 40, 92–93, 96, 100, 131–132, 138, 157–158, 160; Saint Paul to the Galatians 100, 128, 158, 160
Czarist Russia as "salvation": See Pan-slavism
Czech: cultural influence 8, 95, 97; disagreement over Slovak language 29, 32–33, 83–89; nationalism 29, 32–33, 37, 99, 101 n.5
Czobor, Anna: 11, 42, 50
Čajak, Janko: 52–53
Čulen, Martin: 76
Descartes, René: 167
Dobriansky, Kornel: 266
Dobšová Tamaškovičová, Mária: 260
Double standard of sexual morality: 99, 128–129, 143–148, 164, 176–177
Draškovič, Count Janko: 28–29, 39

Education of women: example of Czech schools 37–38, 63 n.20; for morality 39–40, 74–75, 95, 98, 128, 141–150, 162–163; for nationalism 34–40, 69–78, 80, 82–83, 89, 156, 164; self-study 40–41, 42, 89, 184–185. See also Language, Slovak

Eliot, George: 106, 122, 174

Emancipation movement: 11, 13, 15 n.6, 38–39, 77–78, 94–95, 100, 101 n.5, 111, 116, 128–133, 148, 159–160, 176–177

Empowerment of women: by celibacy 59–60, 167; by education 35–39, 77–78, 83, 90, 98, 127, 129, 133, 138–139, 150; by nationalism 10–13, 28–29, 34, 77–78, 107–108, 127, 129, 168–170; in historically flux situations 106; in reform movements and "epic age" phenomenon 10, 106–107

Enlightenment period: 20, 28, 42

"Eva z pod Baby": 54, 235–239

Feldeková, Oľga: 181

Feminization of virtue: See Overidealization of women

Ferienčik, Mikuláš Štefan: 69, 75

Figuli, Margita: 181

Francisci-Rimavský, Ján: 32

French revolution: 9–10, 27, 160–161

Frič, Milan: 158–164

Gaskell, Elizabeth: 106

Germanization: 8, 17, 23, 33–34, 83, 98, 185

Gerzso, Georg: 24

Goddess, agricultural: mother earth 17–18, 21; Sláva 18–21, 27, 48–49, 54, 107; Vesna 49, 79–80; Živena 21, 68, 79–80

Goldman, Emma: 128

Goldpergerová, Ema: 168

Gorky, Maxim: 172–173

Great Moravian Kingdom: 7, 21

Gregor Tajovský, Jozef: 175, 177

Gregorová, Hana: 175–177

"Haff, Tomónia": 53, 231–232

Haľamová, Maša: 182

Herder, Johann Gottfried: 9–11, 18, 21

Heroine: Gothic, 115; incipient feminist 122, 167–172, 177–178; nationalist by male authors Bachát 50, 56, 109, Ján Chalupka 50, Križan 109, Vajanský, 109–113, by women writers Czech 108, Slovak 101, 115–121, 167–170, Russian 107; reform types in English and American novels 106–107; relation to literary realism 60, 108; spinster type 60, 106–107, 116, 167–170

Heyduk, Adolf: 88

Hlasist movement: conflict with nationalists in Martin 97–98, 177; Frič's essay 158–164; Masaryk's influence 104 n.33, 159

Hodža, Michal Miloslav: 41

Hodžová, Marína: poetry 41,

53, 102 n.7, 109, 223, 228–230, 239; school 40–41
Hollý, Ján: 21, 29, 185
Homola, Štefan: 34–36, 39, 50, 216
Horváthová, Marína Oľga: 122
Hrebendová, Jana Bóriková: 50
"Hronka": 54, 233–234
Huľuk, Ján: 222
Hungary: multicultural 7–12, 68, 81; multilingual 8–9; *natio hungarica* 9–12, 15 n.4, 44
Hurban, Jozef Miloslav: authenticity of women poets questioned 49–50; poetry 31, 46, 49; supporter of women's poetry 30–32, 46, 48, 111, 186, 195, 197, 204, 210; Štúrist editor 31, 46, 48–49
Hymn writing: by early women 11–12; by later women 50–51, 186
Ivanková, Elena: 122
Kálal, Karel: 90, 92, 127
Kello, Juraj: 79–80
Kisely, Katarína: 45, 185, 195
Koléni family: Daniel, Ľudmila 210
Kollár, Ján: collector of folk songs 43–45, 190–191, 212, 263; creator of *Slávy dcera* 17–24, 38, 55–56, 96, 113, 181, 235; daughter Ľudmila 23; use of Czech language 29, 85.
Kollontai, Alexandra: 128
Kováč, Mína: 53, 230–231
Kráľ, Janko: 21, 185

Krasnohorská, Eliška: 77, 126 n.30
Kristeva, Julia: 182
Križan, Štefan: See Heroine, nationalist
"K. š.": 56, 240
Kubini family: Anna and Žofia 11, 42, 45, 50; Lorinc 45; Mária 44, 185, 190–191
Kukučín, Martin: 125 n.20
Kulišek, Ján: 251
Kulišková, Ľudmila: 56–57, 251–254
Kusá Vyšná, Eva: 204
Kuzmány, Superintendent Karol: 39, 68
Language, Slovak: codification of 29, 184; dependence upon politics and geography 7; Slovak use of Czech language 8, 10, 11, 18, 29–30, 43, 46, 50, 83–89, 184–187; women's defense of standard Slovak 29–30, 32–33, 84–89; women's need for school in own language 34–41, 83–89, 185
Lániová Lehocká, Žofia: 102 n.11
Lauček, Martin: 42, 188
Laučeková, Zuzana: 65 n.36
Launer Huľuková, Amália: 53, 222–223
Lehocká, Johana: correspondence with Rajská 32–33; interest in women's education 35–39, 77, 84, 102 n.11, 127; poetry 47–48, 55, 109, 186, 204–210; praise by Štúrists 31–33

Lehocký, Ján: 32, 102 n.11, 204
Leška, Štefan: 42–43, 188
Lešková, Rebeka: 42–44, 61 n.2, 185, 187–190
Locke, John: 167
Lohinská, Milina: 54, 186, 233
Lojko, G. Hostivít: 57, 60, 216, 241
Lojková, Zuzína Ružena Zajac: 57–58, 60, 216, 240–248
"Ľudmila K" [Koléni?]: 49, 210–211
Luther, Martin: 42
Lutheran pastors and teachers: family education for women writers 42, 114, 184; numerous in Slovak intelligentsia 41–42, 184; reflected in fictional partnership marriage 118–119, 129
Magazines for women: Czech 85, 91, 93–95, German and Magyar 28, 98, 120, Slovak 90–100; male opposition to 93–98; male support of *Dennica* 90–93
Magyar: as term for ethnic Hungarians 6; cultural influence 8, 28; early women writers 11–12; nationalism 28
Magyarization: against Slovak language and culture 33, 40, 51–52, 60, 74, 81–82, 86, 90, 102 n.13, 106, 115, 177, 185–186; for assimilation of Slovak gentry 113–114, 117-118, 122; liberalized 68, 81; related to Magyar language lack 7–9

Maliaková, Marína Ormisová: 122
Mallý, Ján: 64 n.26
Marčeková, Zuzanna: 57
"Marína z pod Kohúta": 54–56, 60, 239–240
Markovičová, Ľudmila Boorová: 162, 166 n.12
Maróthy, Daniel: 82
Marxist historiography: neglect of women's studies 12–13; proving nationhood 8; rediscovery of Timrava 172–174
Masaryk, Tomaš G.: 104 n.33, 159. See also Hlasist movement
Matica slovenská: 59, 68, 75, 81–82, 106 and passim
Mayer, Judita Ruttkay: 45, 185, 194
Medvecká, Sophia: 212, 263
Medvecký, Samuel: 192, 263
"Milina": See Rumanová
Mill, J. S.: 122, 158
Mína (Frederika Wilhelmina Schmidt): 19, 23–24, 55, 113–114
Mocko, Ján: 56, 248
Mocková, Oľga Braxatorisová: 56, 248–251
Moravčík, Ján: 197
Moravčíková, Zuzana Reguli: 46–47, 48, 186, 196–199
Moštenanová, Hermína: 121
Moyses, Bishop Štefan: 39, 68
Náprstek, Josef: 101 n.5
Nationalism: cultural and linguistic 7–12, 84, 86–87; fostering sisterhood 54, 60, 90–93; German influence

upon 8–10, 17–18; ideology and language 8–12, 73; opportunity for women in Slovak movement 10–12, 61, 69, in other movements 10, 15 n.6, 106–108; opposition to aristocratic *natio hungarica* 9–10

Němcová, Božena: 123 n.5

Nosák, Bohuslav: 49–50

Nováková, Tereza: 85

"Opustená": 53, 232–233

Organizations for women: cooperation with Czech women, 77–79, 81, 91; effort to found girls' school 32, 34–40, 82–89; local branch Vesna 79–81; publications 82, 89–90; sister Živena in U. S. 81; Živena 30, 54, 59, 68–82, 89, 92, 98, 111, 117, 260–261 and passim

Ormis, Samuel: 41

Orphanides, Hermína: 121

Overidealization of women: effect on Liubov' Blok 23; feminization of virtue 80–81, 107; negative effects 23, 107, 167, 170–172

Palkovič, Juraj: 18, 27–28

Pan–slavism: Czarist Russia as "salvation" 17, 104 n.33; effect of *Slávy dcera* 20; Slovaks central in Slavdom 88–89

Patmore, Coventry: See Woman's place

Pauliny–Tóth, Viliam: 41, 53, 76, 222, 230

Petrőczy, Kata–Szidónia: 11–12

Phelps, Elizabeth Stuart: 106

Philadelphi, Anna: 58–59, 257–260.

Philadelphi, Móric: 59, 257

Pietor, Ambro: founder of Živena 69, 73, 76–77, 79–80, 90; increasingly conservative 89, 94; officer and editor 82, 89, 93–94, 102 n.9; support for women 69, 74–75, 77, 80, 127, 158

Pischl, Mária: 22, 24

Pivková, Anna: 82, 89

de Pizan, Christine: 158

Platthy, Juliana: 45

Podjavorinská, Ľudmila Riznerová: 60, 119–121, 162

Poetry, women's: "bride of the nation" 41, 59–60, 108, 167; doubts about authorship 49–50; female personae by male poets 49–50; fugitive and pseudonymous nature 12–13, 30, 41, 47, 186–187 and passim; nationalistic 30, 42, 45–49, 54, 56–60, 107, 109, 114, 118, 185 and passim; romantic 42, 45–46, 54–58, 60, 67 n.56, 185 and passim

Polish women nationalists: 31, 37

Pospíšil, Jaroslav: 31, 49

Pospíšilová, Maria: 31, 46, 55

Praisinger, Mária: 59–60, 260–261

Puchmajer, Antonín Jaromír: 43, 185

Pulíny family: Nathanael, Samuel 215

Pulíny, Karolina: 50–52, 60, 186, 215–222
Pushkin, Alexander: 22
Rajská, Bohuslava (Antonia Reisová): 32–33, 37, 84
Reguli, Emília: 197
Rigellová, Luiza: 67 n.56
"Rosália" and "Amália": 46, 186, 195–196
Rousseau, Jean–Jacques: contrast of nature to city 21; women's domestic nature 11, 27, 107, 110. See also Woman's place
Rožnay, Samuel: 27–28
Rumanová Bachátová, A. Emília: 53, 186, 223–227
Ruppeldt family: Bohdan, Gustáv, Karol, Peter 261
Ruppeldtová, Klema Augustiny: 60, 64 n.30, 90–92, 261–263
Rusnáková, M.: 121
Ruttkay family: Daniel, Ezechiel 192, 194
Ruttkay, Judita Kisely: 45, 185, 192–194
Ryba, Jan Jakob: 43, 188
Sand, George: 108
Satire on women: 45, 52, 119, 195
Selecký, Štefan Ferdinand: 17
Sládkovič, Andrej Braxatoris: creator of *Marína* 22–24, 27, 55, 113, 181; daughter as poet 56, 248; influence of Alexander Pushkin 22; language used 29, 46; poetry 46, 64 n.29, 121, 185
"Slovenka Sitňjanska": 49, 186, 211–212

"Slovenka zpod Choča": 58, 254–257
"Sofia z Oravi" and "Žofia": 49, 186, 212–215, 263
Sokolová–Seidlová, Vilma: 84-85, 93, 102 n.14, 122
de Staël, Madame Anne Louise Germaine: 116
Světlá, Karolina: 77, 101 n.5, 108
Šafárik, Ján: 65 n.36
Šafárik, Pavol Jozef: 17–18, 43
Škultéty, A. H.: 41
Škultéty, Jozef: 93
Šoltésová, Elena Maróthy: editor and official of Živena 82–83, 89–90, 92–94, 98; effort to reclaim the Magyarized Slovak gentry 117–118; on language 83, 85–89; on sexual equality 127–157, 162, 177; nationalist heroines 117–119, 121, 175
Šoltýs, Michal: 200
Šoltýsová, Anna Zusana: 47, 186, 200–204
Štěpánek, Hynek: 99–100
Štúr, Ľudovít: codifier of Slovak 29, 32, 85–86, 184, 186, 210 and passim; editor 31, 33–35, 49; on celibacy 60; support of women 34–35, 39
Štúrist movement: codification of Slovak language 29, 32 –33, 48, 83, 89, 186 and passim; interest in folklore 27, 45, 47, 49, 89; on celibacy 60
Šulek family: Gašpar, Ján, Ľudovít, Matej, Viliam 44–45, 191

Šuleková, Ester: 44–45, 185, 191–192
Tablic, Bohuslav: 188
Tamaškovič, Martin Branislav: 260
Textorisová, Izabela: 84–85, 122
Textorisová, Oľga: 122
Tichá, Lidmila: 31, 46
Timrava, Božena Slančíková: archetypal criticism useful 170, 175; incipient feminists 170–175; Marxist critics' rediscovery of her 172–173; rebellious heroines 168, 170–175, 177; spinster nationalists 5, 168–170
Tristan, Flora: 158
Uram, Rehor: 45, 185, 192, 194–195
Vadásfy, Emília: 54, 234–235
Vadkerti–Gavorniková, Lýdia: 182
Vajanský, Svetozár Hurban: chauvinism 93–94, 109–114, 165 n.5; effort to attract Magyarized Slovak gentry 113–114, 117; heroines 110–113; official of Živena and editor 82, 89–90, 93–95, 111 112; opposition to Hlasist movement 104 n.33, 177; view of women as sacrificial 110–111, 175–176, as national guardians 111–113
Vansová, Terézia Medvecká: first novel by woman in Slovak 115; Christian fatalism 96; editor of *Dennica* 89, 92–96, 99–100; nationalist heroine 115–116, 121, 175; poetry 60, 114, 162, 263–265
Vesna: See Goddess, agricultural or see Organizations for women
Villani, Karel Ignac: 29, 31
Vitališ, Gregor: 195
Vitališová, Terézia: 45, 185, 195
Votruba, František: 100, 177
Vyšný, Matej: 204
Wagner, Ján A.: 96–98
Ward, Mary: 39
"Wlastimila": See Moravčíková
Wollstonecraft, Mary: 27, 158
Woman's place: domestic role exalted 11, 27, 68, 97, 107, 112, 134; internalization and empowerment of nationalist women Czech 78, 108, Russian 107, and Slovak 10, 77, 107, 167–170; symbolized as "angel in the house" by Coventry Patmore 11; three patterns of, in Slovak nationalism 10–11, 27, 79, 122, 127
Yonge, Charlotte: 106
"Zlatina": 53, 227
Živena: See Goddess, agricultural or see Organizations for women
Zmeškal family: Job, Juliana, Václav 45
Zochová, Milina Laciaková: 121

Other Books From Slavica

Ronelle Alexander: *The Structure of Vasko Popa's Poetry*.
American Contributions to the Tenth, Ninth, and Eighth International Congress of Slavists.
A. Barker: *The Mother Syndrome in the Russian Folk Imagination*.
R. P. Bartlett, A. G. Cross, and Karen Rasmussen, eds.: *Russia and the World of the Eighteenth Century*.
H. Birnbaum & T. Eekman, eds.: *Fiction and Drama in Eastern and Southeastern Europe*.
M. D. Birnbaum: *Humanists in a Shattered World: Croatian and Hungarian Latinity in the Sixteenth Century*.
K. Black, ed.: *A Biobibliographical Handbook of Bulgarian Authors*.
R. L. Busch: *Humor in the Major Novels of Dostoevsky*.
Jozef Cíger-Hronský: *Jozef Mak* (a novel), translated from Slovak.
J. Douglas Clayton, ed.: *Issues in Russian Literature before 1917*.
Gary Cox: *Tyrant and Victim in Dostoevsky*.
Carolina De Maegd-Soëp: *Chekhov and Women*.
Thomas Eekman and Dean S. Worth, eds.: *Russian Poetics*.
John M. Foley, ed.: *Oral Traditional Literature*.
Morris Halle, ed.: *Roman Jakobson: What He Taught Us*.
L. A. Johnson: *The Experience of Time in* <u>Crime and Punishment</u>.
Robert Mann: *Lances Sing: A Study of the Igor Tale*.
Vasa D. Mihailovich and Mateja Matejic: *A Comprehensive Bibliography of Yugoslav Literature in English, 1593-1980*.
E. Možejko, ed.: *V. P.Aksënov: A Writer in Quest of Himself*.
T. Pachmuss: *Russian Literature in the Baltic between the World Wars*.
Gerald J. Sabo, S.J., ed.: *Valaská Škola, by Hugolin Gavlovič*, with a linguistic sketch by **Ľubomír Ďurovič**.
Barry P. Scherr and Dean S. Worth, eds.: *Russian Verse Theory*.
P. Seyffert: *Soviet Literary Structuralism: Background Debate Issues*.
J. Thomas Shaw: *Pushkin A Concordance to the Poetry*.
Efraim Sicher: *Style and Structure in the Prose of Isaak Babel'*.
David A. Sloane: *Aleksandr Blok and the Dynamics of the Lyric Cycle*.
G. Slobin, ed.: *Aleksej Remizov: Approaches to a Protean Writer*.
Oscar E. Swan and Sylvia Gálová-Lorinc: *Beginning Slovak*.
J. Taubman: *A Life Through Poetry Marina Tsvetaeva's Lyric Diary*.
Janet G. Tucker: *Innokentij Annenskij and the Acmeist Doctrine*.
Vickery, ed.: *Aleksandr Blok Centennial Conference*.
J. Woodward: *The Symbolic Art of Gogol: Essays on His Short Fiction*.